NARCISSO-FASCISM
The psychopathology of right-wing extremism.

Niall McLaren

Modern History Press

Ann Arbor, MI

2nd Printing – September 2023

ISBN 978-1-61599-754-1 paperback
ISBN 978-1-61599-755-8 hardcover
ISBN 978-1-61599-756-5 eBook

Modern History Press   www.ModernHistoryPress.com
5145 Pontiac Trail   info@ModernHistoryPress.com
Ann Arbor, MI   Tollfree 888-761-6268

Distributed by Ingram Media Group (USA, CAN, EU, AU, UK)

Library of Congress Cataloging-in-Publication Data

Names: McLaren, Niall, 1947- author.
Title: Narcisso-fascism : the psychopathology of right-wing extremism /
  Niall McLaren.
Description: First edition. | Ann Arbor, MI : Modern History Press, [2023]
  | Includes bibliographical references and index. | Summary: "Examines
  the biological, social and psychological influences driving one of the
  most important, and frightening, trends in modern international
  politics, right-wing extremism. Historically analyzes parallels between
  past Fascist leaders such Hitler, Mussolini, and Mao Zedong versus
  contemporary would-be Fascists including Donald J. Trump, Narendra
  Modi, Benjamin Netanyahu, and others"-- Provided by publisher.
Identifiers: LCCN 2023034628 (print) | LCCN 2023034629 (ebook) |
ISBN
  9781615997541 (paperback) | ISBN 9781615997558 (hardcover) |
ISBN
  9781615997565 (eBook)
Subjects: LCSH: Fascism. | Fascists. | Radicalism. | Right-wing extremists.
  | Psychology, Pathological.
Classification: LCC JC481 .M15 2023 (print) | LCC JC481 (ebook) |
DDC
  320.53/3--dc23/eng/20230906
LC record available at https://lccn.loc.gov/2023034628
LC ebook record available at https://lccn.loc.gov/2023034629

The interconnexion between sadism, masochism, success-worship, power-worship, nationalism and totalitarianism is a huge subject whose edges have barely been scratched ... All of them are worshipping power and successful cruelty. It is important to notice that the cult of power tends to be mixed up with a love of cruelty and wickedness *for their own sakes.*

George Orwell.
Raffles and Miss Blandish (1944),
in *The Decline of the English Murder and other essays.*
(Emphasis in original)

Also by Niall McLaren

Anxiety—The Inside Story: How Biological Psychiatry Got it Wrong

Title Available

The Mind-Body Problem Explained: The Biocognitive Model for Psychiatry

A (Somewhat Irreverent) Introduction to Philosophy for Medical Students and Other Busy People

Humanizing Psychiatrists: Toward a Humane Psychiatry

Humanizing Psychiatry: The Biocognitive Model

Humanizing Madness: Psychiatry and the Cognitive Neurosciences

Humanizing Madness: Psychiatry and the Cognitive Neurosciences

Contents

Preface

Since about 1980, across a very large part of the world, the political spectrum has undergone a major shift to the right. In the early post-war period, most developed nations were committed to centrist or mildly left-of-centre domestic and international policies, including state-sponsored industrial policies, major public infrastructure projects, and creating welfare states to reduce inequality. Today, however, we see country after country embracing harsh "neo-liberal" policies. The ultimate goal here is restricting state-provided services for those who don't pay much tax, meaning the poor, in order to reduce the taxes paid by those who feel they pay too much, meaning the rich. At the same time, country after country has been adopting aggressive "anti-immigrant" policies, designed to make life difficult for outsiders, often to the point where they can't enter the country or are driven to leave.

In theory, neoliberalism would consist of limiting the welfare state and privatising national services but, in practice, we see state assets sold cheap to the best-connected bidders, accelerating militarism of foreign policies, militarisation of police and custodial forces, and the ever-widening reach of internal and external spying agencies. Hand in hand, there is relentlessly rising corruption and increasing destruction of the natural environment, while the drive to reduce inequality has gone into reverse. Between 1978 and 2021, real (inflation-adjusted) pay for US workers increased by 18%; the income of their CEOs, by contrast, increased by an astounding 1,460%. The irony is that, in most cases, this has been done by governments elected for the express purpose of restricting state benefits and generally making life more difficult for the very people who voted for them.

Is this apparent burst of mass irrationality an accident of history? I don't believe so. The purpose of this book is to show how the contemporary "stampede to the right" is the predictable result of unscrupulous politicians exploiting particular, poorly understood biological, psychological and socio-political themes or drives. We need to understand these drives, to tell when we are being manipulated so we can control them before they destroy us.

This work is offered as an exploration of some ideas, the intention being to start a debate by clarifying the forces that drive apparently sensible citizens to embrace extremist and self-destructive politics, and to vote against their own interests. It is based in the theoretical framework developed in author's model of mental disorder, the Biocognitive Model for Psychiatry [1]. The purpose is first, to demonstrate the broad applicability of that model and second, to explain disturbing political trends in the modern world.

Readers may ask: Do we need another book on fascism? The short answer is yes, because fascism hasn't gone away. Various writers have offered their views on how and why fascism arises. Looking at all the information available, they have tried to assemble a coherent account of the causes of extremism by "joining the dots." This is like people looking at the starry sky and seeing particular images. One person looks up and says he can see an image of a mighty warrior smiting his enemies' heads off, another sees a sleeping elephant while a third just sees stars. This very human tendency, of seeing patterns in what are essentially random, nebulous or neutral fields, is known as pareidolia. So one author looks at the recent history of fascism and sees compulsive German perfidy, at which a lot of people settle back with a relieved sigh, secure in the belief that "It can't happen here." [1] Another looks at the same evidence and sees corruption and incompetence among the elite, quite forgetting that massed storm troopers don't come from the elite. A third person sees the clearest picture of the work of supernatural forces of evil which can only be countered by everybody falling on their knees and praying.

This book's intention is to look at much the same evidence and draw an entirely different picture, one which goes beyond description, to explanation and thence, if all goes well, to prediction. As a psychiatrist, I see things from a particular point of view, but most definitely not the way modern psychiatry locates the cause of mental disorder as a genetic defect in the individual. Thus, people looking at, say, the life of Adolph Hitler, will often say "He was sick, he was schizophrenic," as though that explains it all. No, he wasn't but, even if he were, it wouldn't explain why his followers acted as they did. That sort of "explanation" tries to shift the locus of responsibility to one

---

[1]   This is the title of a novel by Sinclair Lewis, which shows that it can.

person and is little more than pseudoscience. Instead, I will look at contributing factors on three levels of explanation, the biological, the psychological and the level of society itself.

First, I should point to a problem for anybody researching this field, that the very words themselves have been so misused over the years that they now mean more or less whatever anybody wants them to mean. The first step, therefore, is to clarify just what all these terms mean and to explain how they will be used. This will occupy the first three chapters. Chapter 1 looks at the psychology of certain personality types, particularly that known as the narcissistic personality disorder and its relation to psychopathy, and concludes by considering the role of fear in human behaviour. Chapter 2 will look at the political phenomenon known as fascism. In Chapter 3, we will approach the features described in Chapter 2 via a biological framework. The rest of the book brings these themes together, with the intention of building a coherent theoretical program by which we can start to reverse our lemming-like rush to the far right.

Nobody should think change will be easy. As will become apparent, anybody who wishes to change the direction of society will be declaring war on the darkest forces in the human mind. This way could be dangerous, but doing nothing will surely be more dangerous.

References:

1. McLaren N (2021) *Natural Dualism and Mental Disorder: The biocognitive model for psychiatry.* London: Routledge.

Chapter 1: The idea of narcissism.

I am the only person in the world I should like to know thoroughly.
Oscar Wilde

1.1: Why narcissism?

Several years into my training in psychiatry, when a psychologist told me that all psychiatrists are narcissistic, I had to make a quick trip to the library to understand what he meant. According to Google Trends, mentions of narcissism have been rising steadily since 2004 with, interestingly, a peak in 2013-14. Very often, it isn't clear what people mean by it, except that it isn't complimentary. However, whenever we use the word, it is essential to remember that it refers to a personality type. It does *not* mean mental disorder/illness/disease etc.

The word originates with the Greek myth of the beautiful youth who caught sight of his reflection in a pool and was so smitten with his image that he sat staring into the water until he wasted away. In psychology, it has come to mean excessive self-interest to the point where it dominates and controls the individual's life. Naturally enough, as part of the normal personality, we all need to have some concern for ourselves, some level of self-regard, but normality is a broad range, not a point. There is no cut-off point separating normal from pathological; at its edges, normal self-interest merges imperceptibly with excessive self-involvement.

What we class as "normal" varies tremendously, from one culture to the next, the age of the individual, the gender, occupation, intelligence, and so on. Another point is that self-interest varies over time. The bridal couple at a wedding reception will be much more self-aware (and entitled to be on their big day) than an elderly relative seated at a distant table. Sick people, especially people in pain, tend to be more self-aware because they know how easily they can be hurt or how reliant they are on other people to satisfy their needs. At the same time, there is a huge variety of ways people can indulge their hobby of losing themselves in themselves. All this means there is no firm definition of "normal self-involvement," and no fixed rules on what is or is not acceptable behaviour. For somebody of my generation, the modern habit of putting hundreds of photos of yourself on the internet is appalling. To us old folks, posing for an unnecessary photograph, even the word "selfie" itself, is just cheap showing off.

Why would anybody show off? Clearly, we are talking about two different things, the observable behaviour, and the underlying personality that generates the behaviour. Personality precedes the behaviour, and we can define it as:

> ... the *total set* of explicit and implicit mental rules (including attitudes, beliefs, etc) that *generates* the uniquely distinguishing habitual patterns of interaction between the healthy, sober individual and her environment, in the stable adult mode of behaviour.

That is, personality amounts to the set of rules you have acquired over your lifetime that govern what you do, how you do it and how you react to the world. As such, personality is essentially no different from any other set of rules in your life, such as the rules governing your accent, your likes and dislikes or, indeed, a sporting game, except you don't "learn" your personality the way you learn football or tennis. Starting very early in life, we acquire these rules through daily experience, some of it good, some bad. There certainly isn't a single place in your head where all these rules reside although most of them seem to be clustered in the frontal regions. Thus, frontal brain damage typically produces "personality change."

Depending on their content, rules tend to cluster in groups so that people who are fussy about cleanliness and tidiness also tend to be fussy about punctuality and order. Those who don't trust their neighbours are also likely to be suspicious of authority or will see innocent mistakes as evidence of plots and conspiracies. These clusters are known as traits, and while psychology once thought personality traits were determined by genetics, there is very little evidence for it. Overwhelmingly, we are the products of our upbringing, including home, school, playground and workplace. Personality is more or less fixed by about age eighteen to twenty but change is still possible. People can improve if life goes well and they set their minds to it but, all too often, following bad life experiences in adulthood, things can get worse.

Very often, the most important rules are not fully conscious, perhaps because they were learned early in life, even preverbally, or they are what we call implicit learning rather than explicit. This allows us to see the difference between normal and abnormal personality:

> An *ordered* or *normal personality* is said to exist when the individual's set of rules is *both* internally coherent, thus generating a euthymic (pleasant) state, *and* consistent with the larger society's set of rules, thus leading to harmonious and productive interactions.
>
> *Personality disorder* exists when *either* the individual's set of rules is internally incoherent, causing inner distress (episodic or persistent), *or* when it repeatedly brings him into conflict with his social environment, resulting in distress in the individual and/or society, *or* all of the above.

Full-blown narcissism is a personality disorder, as in "Oh, don't don't take any notice of him, that's just how he always is," rather than a recent change, as in "She's always been such a happy and caring person, I don't know what's come over her."

> A narcissistic personality disorder is a lifelong pattern of abnormally self-involved behaviour which causes inner conflict and personal distress, and leads to friction with the social environment.

Unfortunately, modern society notices the self-involved and tends to reward them while neglecting the quiet workers who actually keep the business of life turning over.

One of the earliest authors to promote the concept of narcissism was Sigmund Freud, the Viennese neurologist who developed the psychological theory known as psychoanalysis. While over the past forty years or so, Freud's work has largely faded from view, it was immensely influential in the middle part of the last century. It dominated not just psychiatry and psychology, but also the public idea of what the well-educated person should be able to talk about. Many psychoanalytic terms crept into everyday language, mostly wrongly. To Freud, excessive preoccupation with self was a sign of arrested psychological development resulting from poor relationships with the parents and significant others.

As a primary psychological disorder, the narcissistic personality could be treated by psychological methods, meaning talk therapy. Freud's method consisted of one-hour sessions each day, during which the patient was encouraged to talk about himself, week after week, for years. Was it successful? That depends on who you ask but the notion that insatiable involvement in self can be cured by encouraging the "sufferer" to become more self-involved is counterintuitive. Be that as it may, only the wealthy and self-indulgent could afford the time and money for Freudian psychoanalysis, so analysts probably didn't do much damage, either.

Since the decline of Freud's theories, psychiatry has adopted a biological approach to mental disorder. The standard view is that mental disorder is just a special case of brain disorder in which mental symptoms predominate. That is, the final explanation for mental problems consists of a statement about the patient's physical brain. Psychology doesn't get a mention. As part of the biological push, modern psychiatry has adopted the categorical concept of mental disorder, meaning that each and every mental disorder is a separate category of illness. While they may be similar in clinical presentation, it is claimed that the different diagnostic categories are fundamentally different at the level that counts, the level of brain function. Mostly, this is taken to mean at the level of neurotransmitters, the chemicals that transfer messages from one neuron to the next through the brain's indescribably complex neural pathways. In this biological view, since the cause of mental disorder is physical, it follows that treatment should also be physical. Thus, people who see a psychiatrist about feeling worried or depressed will be told "You've got a genetic chemical imbalance of the brain, take these tablets and come back in a month. They will make you feel better but they won't change your genes. You have to learn to live with your disease."

By the same view, a person who suffers severe anxiety, which causes him to lose his job, which leads to depression, will be told he has two separate chemical imbalances of the brain so he needs more drugs. If he starts to worry about making mistakes because of feeling drugged, that's another disorder which needs its own drugs; if he gets irritable and needs a drink, that's two more to be treated, and so on. It is not uncommon to see people with a dozen or more distinct diagnoses, taking up to ten different psychiatric drugs, usually in what are politely called "heroic dosages."

Why would anybody bother with such a complex system? Surely it is clear that mental problems can have causes in life, that depression, for example, is a reaction to life events? The answer is that each distinct diagnosis is assumed to have a separate biological cause, for which there should be a separate and specific drug treatment. The categorical approach to mental disorder justifies vast expenditure on drug research and treatment.

Personality disorder is a little different. Firstly, modern psychiatry only accepts a limited number of distinct personality disorders – currently ten – so one person can easily meet the criteria for half a dozen separate personality diagnoses. Second, there is no scientific evidence to say that any of this is true. Personality factors do not fit a categorical model as all personality traits are dimensional, meaning they range in a continuous line from normal to the wildest extremes. Third, there is no reason to believe personality is a biological phenomenon and every reason to believe it is wholly a matter of psychology. Finally, mainstream psychiatry has no treatment to offer. Psychiatrists no longer offer psychotherapy, and their drugs don't work on personality; if they did, we would put them in the water supply.

My view is that the whole concept of personality disorder in modern psychiatry is a complete mess [1]. It is an artefact of psychiatry's desperate need to squeeze all mental disorder into a biological model, a house of cards built on sand and held up by the skyhook of artful manipulation of the concept of personality traits. Personality disorder is both common and troublesome but psychiatrists have no approved method of treating it. However, since psychiatrists make their living from treating people (prescribing drugs), not by telling them to go away and live with it, mainstream psychiatry is now engaged in a long-term program of reclassifying people with personality disorders as mentally ill and putting them on drugs [2]. This quietens the worst of their complaining and difficult behaviour, because that's what psychiatric drugs do, and it means the newly-minted mental patients have to keep coming back for treatment in the very long term. Problem solved.

But back to narcissistic personality disorder: who are these people and why should we bother with them? The answer is that while there is no such *thing* as a narcissist, and no such *thing* as narcissism, the behaviour which constitutes the narcissistic *trait* is universal. *We all show behaviour of the self-regarding type, the only question is the extent.* However, the trouble with self-regard is that it readily links forces with other, more destructive personality characteristics and the combination quickly spirals out of control. Abnormal personality traits amplify each other so that, in one person, behaviour which is a bit of a nuisance or even amusing can, in another individual, suddenly explode to produce major disturbance. And that is the central theme of this essay: while narcissistic behaviour in isolation varies from amusing to a nuisance to self-damaging (i.e. at its worst, it is a problem for the individual and his "significant others"), when combined with other, destructive human characteristics, it becomes exceedingly dangerous. We need to understand this point and deal with it as a matter of urgency.

1.2: Lights. Cameras. Bring on the narcissists.

In talking about human behaviour, we need to avoid stereotypes, but... as shown by the opening quote from Oscar Wilde, one of history's most famous narcissists, it's hard to avoid stereotyping people who want to be seen as stereotypes. Or, as George Orwell said of the surrealist artist, Salvador Dali, "His autobiography was simply a strip-tease act conducted in pink limelight." So while I would prefer not to mention "those narcissists" or talk about "their narcissism," I will sometimes do so but remember, it's just a figure of speech.

The key to understanding narcissistic behaviour is to remember that the subject is living life as an act in which he is writer, producer, director, lead actor *and* adoring audience, all at once. We will talk about the essential features of the narcissistic personality disorder, then look at some examples.

The central point or core of the personality type is *self-absorption*: everything else flows from this. Oscar Wilde again: "I am always astonishing myself. It is the only thing that makes life worth living" (remember that half of what he said wasn't serious but nobody, least of all himself, knew which half to ignore). Narcissism means believing that my feelings are always more interesting and more important than yours, that my opinions trump yours or my needs take priority over yours. All of this has to be seen in its context: for example, the professor's opinion is more likely to be right than yours; or the experienced gardener who says your choice of plant isn't suitable for the soil is more likely to be right but, since you're paying, you can have what you want. However, if you say you're unhappy with something that I want to do, it's not enough for me to tell you to stop being a spoilsport. You may actually be right but, for the committed narcissist, that possibility doesn't arise: "I'm an interesting person but you're boring. Nobody wants to hear your dumb opinions so keep quiet and listen to me."

Very often, via the lust to be the undisputed centre of attention, self-absorption comes across as a need to *dominate and control*. It's just not possible to have two centres of attention in the same room, it interferes with the endlessly fascinating drama of self-glorification. The narcissistic personality (aka narcissist) wants to take control to make sure nobody else gets a foot into the limelight, that he gets the best and most interesting of whatever is going as he deserves it because he is the best and most interesting person at the party. He wants to be president of the local sports club, not the secretary and certainly not treasurer because that's dull and involves too much work. He wants the best clothes, the biggest car, the fastest motorbike or the flashiest house. He should have the corner office, he should meet the visiting bigwigs or have the lead role in the play. Partly this is his sense of superiority – he firmly believes he is the best – and partly it's a need to nobble the competition. As the writer and supremely-polished narcissist, Gore Vidal, said: "Success is not enough. One's friends must also fail."

However, in tandem with the drive to take control is a total lack of interest in the hard work of actually running something. Narcissists quickly lose interest in a job as it distracts from the most important thing in life, I, me, myself. They will undertake all sorts of machinations to get the position that brings the most attention but they don't actually want to do the work. They're a bit like a dog chasing a bus: if he catches it, he wouldn't know what to do with it. It's not that they can't attend to detail, it's just that they only attend to details they find interesting, meaning detail that relates to them, such as clothes, makeup, who sits where, who stays in the best hotel, on and on. When the detail involves them, they micromanage to the point of driving everybody mad but, when it doesn't, they brush it off and leave it to somebody else. If something goes wrong, they blame somebody else. All too often, this leads them to deception and even outright crime as they try to cover up their failings. One offence leads to another, and another, until one day the whole thing falls in a heap. Then everybody says:

"Who would have expected that? He's the last person I would have suspected." That's because he has been so successful in distracting people from his real self.

The darker side of the need to take control is suspicion: "Uneasy lies the head that wears the crown." The true narcissist is always worried that somebody will come through the door wearing something more dramatic, or arrive in a bigger car, or have a prettier girlfriend on his arm or a more muscular arm to support her. He is never sure that people are being genuine or that they aren't planning to rush off to meet somebody else. He is constantly on the lookout for something better or for signs of competition, and he assumes that everybody else is the same. Mistrust is typical of the personality disorder but it can blur across to frankly paranoid thinking, especially under pressure, such as facing arrest or through alcohol and drug abuse.

This is important: mainstream psychiatry says that true paranoid thinking is only seen in paranoid personality disorder but, again, this is false. We are all suspicious to some extent, we have to be otherwise we would be robbed blind in a few hours. I always lock my house and my car, my passport is kept in a safe unless it's in my hand, I don't write down passwords of any sort, and so on. But we don't call that suspicion, we call it prudent care except nobody knows where normal caution stops and suspicion takes over [2]. The more abnormal a person is on one personality factor, the more likely it is that he will be abnormal on others. In general, however, narcissistic people don't show the sustained, poisonous hatred of the true paranoid, or the icy, calculated vengefulness seen in psychopathic personalities. Narcissists are too easily distracted to maintain a vendetta; the show must go on. They forget it, brush it off until, months or years later, something happens and it all comes back, as fresh as if it were yesterday.

Many narcissistic people radiate an air of superiority or grandiosity, the sense that they firmly believe they are better than everybody else. This often takes the form of spiteful comments, aimed at humiliating people they see as competition, but also just putting people down generally for laughs. Often, they will lead the laughter, which is cruel and deliberately hurtful, then turn it off suddenly and change the subject. Underneath the show, however, life is very different. Almost always, these people have poor or fragile self-esteem; their surface

---

[2]   Yes, we do. I'm prudent, you're suspicious and he's paranoid.

behaviour is designed to lead people away from this truth. When things go wrong, such as losing a job, a car accident, or being arrested, they crumple into pathetic caricatures of themselves. The exceptions are people who are born to wealth and privilege, who firmly believe they deserve and are entitled to worshipful attention and who exclude from the entourage anybody who doesn't show a suitably servile attitude. If their favourite project goes wrong or they are arrested for something, they fly into towering rages and threaten eternal retribution for everybody who has let them down. The narcissist is never wrong.

Narcissistic people believe that ordinary rules don't apply to them. Everything exists for them but, if it doesn't, it's too boring to think about. Their emotions are shallow and showy, often mercurial; they love to meet new people and can be charming and entertaining but they quickly work out whom they should cultivate and forget everybody else's names. They will say whatever they think people want to hear, especially if it makes them look good, but it's insincere, a flood of empty words designed to charm people and make them feel good. As every narcissist learns very early, happy people are more likely to give you what you want. Confidence tricksters often show strongly narcissistic behaviour. They like to appear clever, witty, sophisticated and experienced when, very often, they are not. Sexually, they like to play seduction games but their sexual identity is often poorly formed and they rarely have the experience they claim, although they manage to blame the partner before moving on.

This is more or less the stereotype of the narcissistic personality but we should mention a couple of variants. People now use the expression "malignant narcissism." Here, the emphasis is on the individual's cruel or destructive behaviour so it is more or less synonymous with the older term "creative psychopath." The central features of the psychopathic syndrome were remorselessness, failure to learn from experience, failure to form caring relationships, and dishonesty. There were three types. The aggressive psychopath was exactly what you would expect, unpredictably violent, destructive, cruel, callous, dishonest, and contemptuous of others' feelings and of society and its laws. If he wanted something, he got it and anybody who got in the way was smashed down. He moved from one violent relationship to another, leaving a trail of damaged partners and children for others to tend. The inadequate psychopath was similar but tended to drink heavily or use a lot of drugs, and constantly got into trouble for petty dishonesty, unpaid bills, drunken fights he started but quickly lost, and other stupid things. Aggressive when he thought he could win, he quickly dissolved into snivelling and weeping when anybody called him out. He was well-known to the police, who knew they could lean on him for information when they wanted it but he was too unreliable to be a successful criminal. He tended to be more dependent on partners and more manipulative but also more likely to try to suicide when they got sick of his nonsense and kicked him out.

The third flavour was called the creative psychopath. These men (the stereotypes were all male, but there are many psychopathic women as well), these men were charming, urbane, considerate and seductive in equal measure but there was always a goal, an ulterior motive. Again, the central feature was their utter lack of empathy for other humans. Quite often, they would openly say that they saw people as objects to be manipulated and won over, then discarded when they were no longer useful. Generally, they were quite tall, good looking and looked after themselves. Not for them the drugs and alcohol and all night parties; they were on a mission and nothing would stop them. If you would like examples, read the story of the New York financier, Bernard Madoff, but remember: regardless of what anybody said of him after his arrest, Madoff didn't suddenly become a psychopath just because he was caught. He was one all along, right from his teenage years, because that's what personality means. However, even if anybody suspected him (the forensic accountant and fraud investigator, Harry Markopoulos, certainly did but nobody believed him because Madoff was rich and good-looking and well-connected), even if anybody had thought he was a psychopath, nobody would have dared breathe it because you couldn't say that sort of thing about that sort of man. This was also true of the arch-manipulator, Jeffrey Epstein, who had managed to wriggle out of a criminal conviction that should have sunk him. However, because there were so many rich, good-looking and well-connected men who stole, cheated and lied, the diagnosis became an embarrassment to psychiatry and it had to go.

Years ago, when the American Psychiatric Association was revising its Diagnostic and Statistical Manual (DSM), somebody realised that if they applied the diagnostic criteria for creative psychopath fairly, then it was clear that it applied to a large proportion of the American political, financial, industrial, military, academic, sporting, religious, entertainment, and any other establishment you care to mention. And not just American, it was equally true of all other countries as well. So they did the only honourable thing open to them, they changed the name and rejigged the criteria so that the wealthy would never meet them – well, until they went to prison, which wealthy law-breakers almost never do. The term "psychopath" was dropped and replaced by "sociopath' (now known as "antisocial personality disorder") of which the essential feature is constant law-breaking due to physical and sexual aggression. High-flying businessmen and politicians could avoid the label although, as Jeffrey Epstein and Ghislaine Maxwell showed, only because the rich can conceal their crimes whereas the poor can't.

As for examples, who do you want? Maxwell's father, Robert? A classic creative psychopath, friend of the uber-wealthy and over-powerful. What about the chairman of Lehman Bros, the Wall St investment bank that collapsed in 2008, who, because of his aggressive and ultimately destructive behaviour, was known as "the gorilla of Wall St"? That was not a title freely handed out: he earned it against some very stiff competition but he wasn't a sociopath because he has never been convicted. More recently, the Silicon Valley venture capitalist, Peter Thiel, was quoted as saying "I'd rather be seen as evil than incompetent" [3]. Needless to say, I've never met Mr Thiel so I don't know anything about his personality but, whether he said it or not and regardless of context, that statement is the very essence of narcissism and psychopathy. It is narcissistic in that it implies the person's image is more important than anything else, including morality, and it is psychopathic in that it licences evil. If everybody followed that principle, the world would descend into anarchy. Or further than it already has.

In short, the concept of malignant narcissism is more or less the same as the creative psychopath. It would be a brave psychiatrist who would call a powerful politician or the son of a fabulously wealthy businessman a psychopath. So they get the fashionable but artfully misleading diagnosis of "malignant narcissism" that gets them off the hook for their various escapades.

Now just as there were "inadequate psychopaths," however we define those terms, it is the case that there are plenty of people who will meet the criteria for narcissistic personality disorder who also warrant the unflattering label "inadequate." In fact, we're not supposed to use terms like "inadequate" these days, on the basis that they are demeaning and pejorative. That's fine, but it is still the case that many people with strongly narcissistic traits are also fearful, miserable, irritable, withdrawn, prickly, defensive, unreliable, inclined to gamble, drink or use drugs, and are promiscuous and dishonest. That is, they are inadequate to the social demands of functioning as independent adults. My view is that a careful psychiatric history and examination will show that most of them are seriously anxious [4], their lives complicated by secondary depression, but they tend to conceal this. At the same time, most psychiatrists, who don't take anxiety seriously, don't enquire too hard. As soon as they find the criteria for personality disorder, they either push the patient out the door or, if he can afford to come back, adroitly relabel him as bipolar, ADHD, ASD, ODD, substance abuse, major depression and so on, and put him on drugs.

The final point to make is to answer the very obvious question: Why would anybody bother with the drama? Who cares whether she is the centre of attention? Who cares who is president of the local fishing club, why would anybody waste money on having the biggest car, newest outfit, flashiest hair style and so on? The answer is clear: people with no inner sense of self-worth who have to generate a sense of worth on the outside. They are hoping to fool others and, in the process, to fool themselves but, inside, things are never as good as they make out. Mostly, they are unhappy with everything about themselves and their lives; the concept of "Be satisfied with what you've got, it could always be worse," as your old granny told you, bounces off them. They're never satisfied with what they've got because they're not satisfied with who they are. At base, narcissism is a self-esteem issue. They try to construct an illusion of self-assurance but it's brittle and easily shatters.

That, as Freud pointed out, goes back to childhood but, as a general rule, people who show a desperate need to be at the centre of attention, to be in control at all times, either have very little sense of self-worth or, rarely, a bloated sense of self-worth as in the pampered offspring of absolute monarchs or the obscenely wealthy. People who inherit power and money believe they should be the centre of attention because they deserve it, they want people to believe they're wonderful because they firmly believe that, by birth, they are indeed wonderful and everybody should bow down as they pass or risk losing their heads. But we won't be talking about them as the problems of the wealthy are rather small (as distinct from the problems they cause the rest of us).

1.3: Narcissism is as narcissism does.

What does all this mean in practice? People don't walk around with a scarlet N stitched to their sleeves, so how is the ordinary citizen to recognise "one of them"? Is there any need to? To a large extent, that depends on what you want. If you're a talent scout looking for extras in a TV show, you will want somebody who, as they say, "projects" herself. You don't want a shy, self-effacing little thing who hangs around at the back of the crowd and bursts into nervous giggling when anybody tries to talk to her. Your director wants somebody who can make an impression, who stands out boldly, somebody a bit larger than life whose very presence demands "Look at me, everybody." This is the hallmark of the narcissist, the sense that this person lives on a stage, that she is supremely aware of all eyes being on her, drinking her in, which, in turn, she drinks in. Yes, you can almost hear her saying to herself, this I like, their attention is better than any drug, their applause is so exciting, better even than sex, so give it to me, give it to me. The clothes, the hair, teeth, makeup and jewellery, the cars and travel and restaurants are all part of the endless act called life. After all, who would look at a narcissist in cast-off clothes waiting in the rain for the bus?

And she gives it back. Her laughter makes the day brighter, even her smiles seem loud; the room feels busier and more exciting when she comes in and rather flat when, with but a single, breathy goodbye, she takes heartfelt, individual leave of every person in the room – or so it feels. And that's important: she charms everybody. She radiates a buoyant confidence and security that make people feel they are important to her, that her approval counts, that they want to be in her life even if only by cleaning up after the party. Who does she charm? Certainly not other narcissists, as the history of catfights among film stars shows (of Tallulah Bankhead's passing, Bette Davis said: "It's bad to speak ill of the dead. She's dead. Good"). No, they charm their polar opposites: the sad and lonely, the insecure and easily intimidated, the vague and uncertain, but also the stern and humourless and, above all, the powerful, wealthy and influential, meaning about 50% of the population in total. The closer unhappy people are to one of nature's inspiringly bright souls, the better they feel and the more they want to do to help. Of course, there will always be the odd curmudgeon who can't abide her but criticism of the sainted one provokes her followers to immediate and fierce defence. Thus we chance upon a peculiar dyad:

while the narcissist demands undying devotion, her loyal followers are eager, even desperate, to give it just because being part of her entourage makes their drab lives better. But devotion is nothing more than iron control dressed in a velvet glove. Have we heard this before? We have, many times, and we'll return to it.

One of the defining features of narcissism is that they are attracted to power and wealth. Wherever the spotlight is, that's where they want to be. Most narcissists, however, are not so lucky; while washing the dishes, they may dream of bestriding Tinseltown but most will need to be satisfied with dominating the office or workshop, the school play, the church or sports club committee or local political branch meetings. That's the fun side of suburban narcissism but if that's all they did, nobody would bother writing books about them. A happy narcissist who is getting the attention he feels he deserves can be entertaining but, when things go wrong and he's unhappy or angry, it's a different story. Suddenly, the glamorous mask comes off and the suspicious and resentful bits show through. He becomes irritable and demanding; nothing is good enough; people are letting him down; he can't rely on anybody; nobody cares; people are all the same; nobody understands; nobody wants to listen; don't they realise he's a person with feelings? But even the tantrums are scripted for an audience: not for him the grim withdrawal and silent self-denial. Even the sulking bouts are theatrically dramatic. Always there is that impression that he is watching himself perform, scanning his every effusive word. Even in the sulks, his dramatic gestures are planned to a T, his entrances are grand, his compliments over the top, hair and clothes too elaborate, his laughter a bit too loud, his hints are actually demands, on and on. But to see the real person, all you need to do is look away while he's talking, or compliment somebody else, or change the subject, and then the drama starts.

The trouble for the audience caught up in a tantrum is that nobody ever really knows what's gone wrong or, if they have worked it out, it seems blown out of all proportion. However, everybody knows better than to say so, it can turn a minor storm in a teacup into world war three. And so he controls people, moves them around like pawns on a board or supporting actors in a huge drama in which he is *prima donna assoluta*. The true narcissist uses people as props in his lifelong drama. If he wants something, including a person, he drops everything and goes for it. When he gets whatever it is, it must play its role in his never-ending soap. If he can't get it, he throws a tantrum then declares he didn't want it anyway. Typically for female narcissists, children have to play the roles mummy decides for them. One will be a famous dancer or actor, one has already decided to be a doctor "Haven't you, darling," one has the makings of a poet, and heaven help them if they don't slot into their appointed roles. They will be dragged off to a psychiatrist who, under the deluge of troubles recounted by the mother, will have little choice but to declare the child does indeed have the diagnosis mother has decided and needs to be put on drugs. Then she is able to play the role of the long-suffering mother, which has endless subthemes and never runs out.

The narcissistic personality disorder is disordered personality first and egotist second. The trait of self-centredness is universal; all that differs is the degree. The only problem with all that has been said so far is that most people assume narcissists are either women or effeminate. In one of the most remarkable feats of manipulating public sentiment in humanity's long and dispiriting history, heterosexual men have managed to convince the world that narcissism afflicts only women and gays. Look at all the money they spend on clothes, the real men say; look at their jewellery, their cosmetics, hair, nails, and all the time they spend in front of mirrors, primping and preening to "look their best." Women can't walk past a mirror without checking to see their seams are straight, their hair fluffed, their tattoos showing to their best... Men, as they will eagerly tell you, are far too rational and sensible to fall for nonsense such as self-involvement, self-interest and all that. Men they just get on with the job and do it without a fuss, with no drama and no shrieks of "But what will people think of me?" Men don't care what people think, they decide what to wear by checking the weather forecast; they have their hair cut according to the calendar; they change their socks only when necessary; and they don't lose sleep over a few holes in the undies. Men are sensible, grounded, pragmatic... or so their story goes.

This, of course, is utter rubbish but the amazing part of this inestimable duplicity is that men actually believe it too. The example par excellence is, of course, one Donald J Trump, sometime president of the USA. Some psychiatrists are on record as saying Trump was delusional, a paranoid psychotic, but that's incorrect. He showed all the features of a personality disorder; his claims that he was the greatest, or his crowds were the biggest, or he won in 2020, were not delusional as he didn't believe them. He said them just for effect and he knew that if he kept repeating a bit of self-serving nonsense, eventually everyone would believe it and he could go from there. But he never believed anything he said.[3] He wasn't interested in the job, he just resented being treated as a bit of New York low-life outsider by the insiders, so he showed them. He snatched their golden fleece from under their noses and then didn't know what to do with it. So he simply carried on in Trumpian manner, wheeling and dealing, scheming, manipulating, threatening people or charming them, wheedling and cajoling but with most of his limited attention fixed firmly on his ratings.

Other people said he was a political genius. No, he wasn't. He simply had the immeasurable luck to stumble into the public eye at a time when people were increasingly tired of the corruption, contempt and incompetence of the mainstream political, financial, industrial, military, academic, sporting, religious, entertainment, and any other establishment you care to mention. By shouting out that the establishment were corrupt and incompetent which, as an outsider, he believed and which they are, he fooled enough voters into thinking that he would do something about their enemies and that their miserable lives would thereby get better. He didn't, and they haven't. He simply fed voters what they wanted to hear, meaning their prejudices, over and over again because their prejudices were also his prejudices and he had nothing else to offer. He had no policies and no plans beyond throwing dirt at his enemies (who happened to be his voters' enemies) and watching them squirm. He didn't know anything at all about government and he cared even less. All he wanted was the TV cameras and the satisfaction of sitting at the Big Desk, tossing off insults to the people who despised him while the suits and uniforms stood silently by, in awe of his majesty. That is pure personality disorder.

Others said he was just a crook. Probably, but he was certainly not alone. During his term, Trump is recorded as telling 30,573 lies, in addition to the ten thousand a month since he left office. That is quite a lot, even for a politician, but his were silly little lies, as distinct from the

---

[3] As an example, consider the debacle of the "insurrection" at the Capitol Building on January 6th 2021. In his speech to the ecstatic rabble of "deplorables," he said: "You walk on down to the Capitol, I'll be there with you." He then got in his limousine and was driven to the White House to watch his handiwork unfold. They should have known that Trump never walked anywhere. Even his golf cart is driven to him.

Big Lies that are the stock in trade of the denizens of parliaments the world over. He claimed his inauguration crowd was the biggest when everybody could see it wasn't. Boris Johnston slithered his way to power by promising that Brexit would deliver the country to sunny uplands. By any estimation, it has been an abject failure and could well result in the country fracturing but nobody is holding him to account because, as they say, he told only one lie.

If Trump had had any sense, he would not have come down the golden escalator. He should have stayed where he was, amusing the masses, irritating the liberal and corporate elite and making lots of money to hide overseas. He had spent his entire life effortlessly fooling people to get what he wanted and he didn't see why the presidency should be different. He couldn't stand the idea of the wealthy, educated classes sneering at him so he gambled on the election. To his astonishment, he won, and panicked as he realised he didn't know what to do. But that didn't long trouble him. He quickly realised that he could continue fooling people by feeding them more of the same old promises. Again, common sense would dictate that he should have been satisfied with just one term but of course, he couldn't. For Trump, the thought of another Obama, sitting at the same desk in the Oval Office signing bills to reverse his orders, drove him far beyond the limits of his very limited common sense. Now, because of his role in the January 6th insurrection, in interfering with the Georgia elections, for alleged tax fraud over decades, and many other follies that he could have kept hidden if he'd not over-reached himself, he faces the very real prospect of imprisonment.

But that's narcissists: they don't stop because they can't. They have to keep going, pushing the crowds to cheer louder, spending more time, more of other people's money, to get more adulation … always more and more, because there's nothing underneath it. Any approval they get vanishes into the inner black hole where other people have their self-esteem. There is no substance to the personality, there is no policy behind the show business of politics, there was no money behind Madoff, it's all show: WYSIATI [4]. They have to keep running to stay upright because, stripped of the drama and the makeup, narcissists feel they have as much substance as a balloon stripped of its rubber. At

---

[4] WYSIATI: What you see is all there is. A very important point in psychology.

base, they are sad, posturing buffoons trying to keep the crowds excited because being ignored is living death. Oscar Wilde again:

> There's only one thing worse than being talked about, and that's not being talked about.

1.4: Fear: the intolerable spur.

Before leaving the field of individual psychology, we need to mention another immensely powerful and widely underrated emotion, fear. Apprehension, trepidation, anxiety, fear, terror, panic, these are all degrees of the same universal avoidance drive, the drive to survive. All animals on earth show some sort of fear response, the flight part of 'flight or fight,' meaning the need to take evasive action to avoid a threat. In fact, that is part of the circular definition of anxiety: it is the response to the perception of a threat. So what is a threat? A signal indicating imminent danger. How do we know danger? Because it is scary. I have written about anxiety, describing it as one of the most powerful of all human emotions because, of all emotions, it alone works back to intensify itself [4]. To borrow a mathematical term, anxiety acts recursively. The role of anxiety is to force you to get away from a danger. It has no upper limit; it simply keeps intensifying until you do whatever is necessary to escape. It cannot be controlled by willpower; once you see a threat, you must deal with it otherwise the anxiety will become unbearable. Anxiety is a terrible feeling; it has to be otherwise we would ignore it and fail to respond to what it is telling us to do.

Unfortunately, it is true that a lot of people who have never experienced real anxiety are happy to tell sufferers they're over-reacting, there's nothing to be scared of, it's all in the mind so get a grip and stop being weak. In particular, this is true of people who are successful. They all believe they are successful because they're clever, industrious, diligent, honest and all round solid chaps. What they don't realise is that, yes, brains do play a part in success but let's not forget that intelligence is largely genetic. You can thank mummy and daddy but there's no credit for you there. Second, while as Thomas Edison said, genius is 1% inspiration and 99% perspiration, success itself is 1% inspiration, 49% perspiration and 50% luck.

In particular, the wealthy and successful like to take personal credit for their success. However, even putting aside the benefits of being born into the right family in the right place at the right time, of being able to sleep safely in your own bed and go to school next morning with clean clothes and breakfast warm in your stomach, they have had the immeasurable luck of being born into a middle class family or better, in a safe country where education is both valued and available. Moreover, they have got through life without being disabled by rheumatic fever or asthma, run over by the school bus, abducted, molested by drunken relatives, or blown up by a car bomb leaving them with epilepsy and chronic headaches, on and on. Generals and other senior military officers are particularly prone to believe that being promoted was just a matter of guts, grit, brains and balls. This, of course, is nonsense on stilts. The fact that they are able to walk around covered with medals and fancy ribbons says only this: "Nothing has ever gone wrong in my entire life. I have had a charmed life." Being blown up early in your military career has nothing to do with your brilliance as a soldier and everything to do with where the enemy decides to lob a shell. As has been said: "I have no concerns about the bullet with my name on it. What worries me is the shell with *To Whom It May Concern* written on it." Success is 50% luck.

To return to fear, it is important to remember that successful people rarely know what the word means so anything they have to say about it can be ignored. The problem of anxiety is far more complex than mere willpower. In animals, the fear response is provoked by a direct sign of a threat: the sight, sound, touch or smell of something that is looking for breakfast. Immediately, the animal responds in a stereotyped way, freezing, running to shelter or releasing nasty chemicals, or all of these prior to the last ditch effort to survive, attacking the danger. Humans are a little different in that, alone of all animals, we can be scared by the *idea* of a threat. That is, if we believe something bad is going to happen tomorrow, we will become increasingly anxious as the hours tick past. The problem of anxiety lies in the fact that anxiety itself is very unpleasant, so if we expect to be anxious tomorrow, i.e. that we will feel very bad tomorrow, that thought alone will produce anxiety today. This recursive loop or vicious circle is the basis of all anticipatory anxiety states, commonly known as phobias: If I go near that frog, I will feel very scared, and the thought of feeling scared terrifies me so I'll keep right away. Nobody is scared of frogs, they are among the most harmless creatures on earth, but plenty of people are scared of *how they will feel* if a frog jumps on them.

The picture is further complicated by people becoming scared of the individual symptoms of fear. For example, fear causes the heart to beat faster. If a person is scared of a heart attack, say because all his relatives have died of heart trouble, then the fact of his heart beating faster will be enough to make him anxious. And what does anxiety do? It makes his heart beat faster, which convinces him he is on the verge of a cardiac disaster, so he falls in a chair and begs his relatives to call the ambulance.

These are the obvious fear states but they are individual. It becomes dangerous when a group of people who share the same fears get together and convince themselves there's nothing wrong with them, it's those damned frogs so we'd better wipe them out. Fear, of course, is the most communicable of emotions. We have this problem with snakes in Australia. Yes, we have three of the five most dangerous snakes in the world in this country, and people certainly do die of snake bite, but that is not justification for trying to wipe them out. Most people who are bitten are doing something they shouldn't be, like attacking the snake. It is pointless asking people: "Why do you want to kill that snake?" as they will answer: "Because it's dangerous." "Yes," you say, "but if it's dangerous, shouldn't you just keep right away from it?" That goes nowhere. The solution is: Never attack a snake. A snake will only strike through fear and it can strike faster than you can pull your hand away.

The problem is, we do this to humans as well. Our politicians get together and agree that yes, those Ruritanians over the border are a menace so we need to do something to make sure they can't attack us. Meanwhile, the Ruritanians, who are simply going about their business and aren't interested in attacking anybody, see what is happening over their border and decide they need to do something to defend themselves in case the clowns next door get big ideas. None of this is based in reality; it is all based in fear but, because we are so used to it, we don't see its inherent irrationality.

We can see a perfect example of fear running riot and taking control of politicians' idle minds here in Australia over the past few years. A certain sector of the right wing Liberal-National alliance, associated with their friends in the right wing media and in the military industries, have decided that we need to label China as a threat and start buying very expensive weapons, including nuclear submarines, to stop them in their tracks. This is all based in fear, grandiosity and the chance to make a quick buck; it has no firm basis in reality. We will return to this point but the principle is universal: half of what we do, the destructive half, is based in irrational fears that amplify between people whose grasp of reality is tenuous at best, who automatically take their own and others' exaggerated fears as fact, who never question themselves, and who shape our national policies accordingly. Such paranoid fantasists should not be allowed anywhere near the levers of government but, by communicating their own fears to the electorate, they can build political momentum which becomes difficult to resist.

What has this to do with narcissists? A lot, because most politicians are seriously narcissistic, and narcissists almost never admit they are anxious. That would make people laugh at them which, for the committed narcissist, is social death.

1.5: Conclusion: Le narcissique, c'est moi.

The message is that narcissism is a *universal* personality trait ranging from valid self-respect, to amusing and entertaining, all the way to destructive. We all need to have regard for ourselves but it must be kept firmly anchored in reality, or grounded as they now say. We need to have a realistic assessment of our abilities and our importance and be satisfied with who we are. In other words, we need to have adequate self-esteem. Now this is a problem, because self-esteem is largely the result of early life experiences. School teachers have told me that by the end of the first day for a class entering school for the first time, they can sort the children into a line, with those with the highest self-esteem at this end and the poor little mites with the worst at the other end. By the end of their school careers, twelve years later, they will be in more or less the same order, the only difference being that they will be further apart. Children with strong self-esteem will feel better about themselves while those with poor esteem, if they have survived their schooling at all, will be worse off.

All too often, people with poor self-esteem feel that if they can just convince everybody they're fantastic, all with be well. People who lack self-approval are attracted to whatever they think will impress people and get them more attention in the hope that will mean more approval. It never does, of course, it just leads to the treadmill of endlessly lusting for more. They are attracted to any field that seems to guarantee attention, the most alluring being entertainment and politics. It is not for nothing that politics has been described as Hollywood for ugly people but anything that will get your face on TV will do. Sport is a good one for people with the talent to kick a ball or throw a tennis racket but it doesn't last. One day, every world champion becomes yesterday's news but what will replace the ecstasy of a roaring stadium? Too many of them turn to alcohol and drugs and life unravels. Lately, cooking has come from nowhere although it still requires talent but for those with vast ambition, little talent and fewer scruples, nothing beats religion.

Of course, not all celebrities are fake all the time but the problem for the rest of us is working out who can be trusted, sorting the genuine from the charlatans. With entertainers, it doesn't matter; the drama is all part of the show, so let the show go on. A lot of them crash and burn but that's show business and the funeral video guarantees more sales.

For politicians, however, it does matter. These days, politicians are quite literally dicing with the future of the planet so we have a very real need to know who of them are genuine, and who are simply in it for themselves. With worryingly few exceptions, narcissists are in it for themselves.

Caveat suffragator. Let the voter beware.

References

1. McLaren N (2007) The categorical system of diagnosis: personality disorder. Chapter 8 in *Humanizing Madness: Psychiatry and the Cognitive Neurosciences.*; Ann Arbor, Mi.: Future Psychiatry Press.

2. McLaren N (2012) Testing the Biocognitive Model: Clinical Syndromes. Chapters 14-16 in *The Mind-Body Problem Explained: The Biocognitive Model for Psychiatry.* Ann Arbor, MI: Future Psychiatry Press.

3. Schumpeter, in *The Economist*, September 25th 2021, last line on page 56.

4. McLaren N (2018). *Anxiety: The Inside Story.* Ann Arbor, MI: Future Psychiatry Press.

Chapter 2: The idea of fascism.

When fascism comes to America it will be wrapped in the flag and carrying a cross.

Sinclair Lewis.

2.1. Whence fascism?

At some of Donald Trump's election rallies in 2016, supporters were filmed giving straight arm salutes while shouting "Heil Trump." After he assumed the presidency, pranksters posted on the internet photos of him giving speeches, along with quotes from *Mein Kampf*, as though they were his. Unfortunately, the joke backfired: his supporters took them as actual quotes from the Dear Leader and went into raptures. This adds new and ominous depths of meaning to what is now known as Poe's Law, which originally said:

> Without a winking smiley or other blatant display of humor, it is impossible to parody Creationism in such a way that *someone* won't mistake for the genuine article [5].

What this says is that it is impossible to put a picture of Trump on the same page as a quote from the very font of fascism, and not have somebody take it as a genuine utterance from The Donald. This means that the expectations of his "base" were so extreme that they saw nothing wrong with identifying him with one of modern history's most appalling regimes. Because their views, and what they wanted from him, fitted snugly into the Nazi template, people applauded tweeted quotes like these:

---

[5] The converse is that people often put smiley faces on statements to indicate they are joking when, in fact, they are deadly serious.

> Any alliance whose purpose is not to wage war is senseless and
> useless (of NATO).
> The great masses of the people will more easily fall victim to a
> big lie than a small one[6].

This points to the message in the usually rather delphic writer,
Theodor Adorno:

> I consider the survival of [fascism] within democracy to be
> potentially more menacing than the survival of fascist
> tendencies against democracy.

That is, the danger of fascism lies within the nation, not outside. But
Trump wasn't alone: all around the world, country after country seems
to be moving rapidly toward the hard right wing of politics. Brazil's
Jair Bolsonaro clearly idolised Trump and has himself been called the
"Trump of the tropics." In the UK, nativists pushed the country to sign
itself out of the European Union, even though none of them appear to
have considered the consequences. India's Narendra Modi has ridden
the twin tigers of nationalism and religious intolerance to power, and
looks set to stay for some time to come. In the Philippines, Rodrigo
Duterte has turned death squads on anybody who offends him. Nearby
Thailand (which means Land of the Free in Thai) languishes under yet
another military junta. Meanwhile, neighbouring Myanmar's army has
bludgeoned its way back into power and has unleashed the army and
bands of religious fanatics on defenceless villagers.

In Europe, Poland and Hungary are pushing a nativist and socially
reactionary program while throughout the continent, ultra-right wing
parties are gaining ever-larger shares of the votes. In the Middle East,
Saudi Arabia is an unabashed clericalist-fascist dictatorship but nobody
bothers about this. Instead, the West directs its hostility at the marginally less malign Iranian theocracy. Across the Red Sea, Egypt's brief
experiment with democracy resulted in a military takeover, financed by
Saudi Wahhabists who loathed the blundering but freely elected
president in Cairo. In Africa, dictatorships are once again the norm, as
in Ruanda and Uganda where the current autocrats came to power by
deposing appalling regimes but, decades later, show no signs of wanting

---

[6] With this statement, Hitler was actually identifying what he saw as characteristic
of the Jewish-controlled press; he was not formulating Nazi policy, which will be
mentioned in Chap. 6.2.

to go. This is in addition to the usual crop of intolerant and repressive regimes, such as Cuba, Venezuela, Byelarus, Cambodia, Uzbekistan and those hardy perennials, Russia, China and North Korea.

What does this mean? Are we reprising 1933, when Hitler was appointed Reichskanzler, opening the way for the Nazi dictatorship and all it brought? Is this a fascist revival? Before we can answer that question, we need to be clear that we know what fascism is, and whether we can recognise its early stages.

Very briefly, the Latin word *fasce* originally meant bundle or group. Its modern use derives from the insignia of office of the magistrates of Ancient Rome, an axe wrapped in a bundle of sticks. As the magistrate made his way through the throngs, a man preceded him carrying a fasce, just so the plebeians would know their fate if they offended the great man, the rod or the chopping block. This was adopted by the *Fasci d'Azione Rivoluzionaria,* the group of ardent nationalists and populists formed by Benito Mussolini in 1914, after he was expelled from the Socialist Party for supporting what became the Great War. It means *Group for Revolutionary Action*, they called themselves *Fascisti*, Fascists, and they adopted the ancient insignia so there was no mistaking them for socialists. In 1917, the British security service MI5 began paying Mussolini's party £100 a week, in modern terms about £7,500, to publish prowar propaganda, which saved his motley collection of *Fascisti* from failure. The strident mix of nationalism, populism and conservatism was potent and, in 1922 (100 years ago this month), after considerable agitation and disturbance, the Fascists took control of the incompetent national government and began implementing their program.

Despite efforts to portray Mussolini as a comic opera dictator, he was anything but that. He was intelligent, capable, very hard-working, widely read and a man of the people (and, as everybody knew and accepted as his right, a man of the ladies as well). To neutralise the appeal of the Marxists who dominated the Italian Socialist Party, he and his colleagues formulated a set of principles collectively known as fascist doctrine. In various combinations, these have since served a considerable number of right wing governments, even though most of them resent anyone calling them fascists.

At about the same time in Germany, the post-war chaos was threatening the integrity of the state. Following the abortive French occupation of the Rhineland in early 1923, the German economy was in free fall. There was a real danger that, under French urgings, Bavaria and perhaps other states would separate from the Reich, allying with Catholic Austria or perhaps merging to form a new central European German-speaking state hostile to Protestant northern Germany. In November of that year, a small and essentially unknown group called the National Socialist German Workers' Party, led by an Austrian who had served as a corporal in a Bavarian regiment, tried to block what they saw as an attempt by the Bavarian government to declare independence. Their putsch failed and the leaders were imprisoned for their troubles but the corporal made the best of his months in jail, dictating to his faithful assistant his thoughts on politics, society and the future directions of the Reich.

Adolf Hitler would come close to the top of the list of Most Reviled Humans of All Time but again, a lot of what is said about him is not true. He was not schizophrenic. He was paranoid in the sense of believing he was surrounded by enemies but he certainly was and it never reached psychotic intensity. He was not homosexual, repressed or otherwise. He believed that politics was violent and if they wanted to win, his party had to play it better but he was not personally violent. He was intelligent and again, widely-read; and he had an astounding memory for facts. Educationally, he left school by about age fifteen, after his father died, which he later regretted, but he also had no time for academics who did not have his life experience. He read voraciously, including Marx's *Das Kapital*, which he found interesting. Socially, he was quite a misfit as he preferred to read history and politics rather than stand around drinking (he didn't drink and later became vegetarian). He was not sociable in the ordinary sense of the word but he had considerable sympathy for the working classes and the down-trodden although not much for the wealthy and privileged. Ordinary Germans saw him as disciplined and ascetic, single-minded and selflessly devoted to the nation and the people, which amplified his appeal.

It seems unlikely that he knew of Mussolini's work while dictating his political treatise, known as *Mein Kampf* [1], but he echoed many of the same cluster of ideas and showed how they could be applied to bring about a German recovery. Otherwise, he argued, the country would collapse in the chaos of a new dark age that would last for a very long time, and humanity itself would be so much the worse off. Since he took power in 1933, there have been numerous governments who either openly adhered to the principles of fascism, such as Franco's Phalangist government in Spain, or followed the model in spirit, if not in name. Out of the many varieties, we can distil some essential features.

2.2: Essence of fascism.

Wikipedia's entry on *Definitions of Fascism* is not encouraging, gloomily opining:

> (This) is a highly disputed subject that has proved complicated and contentious. Historians, political scientists, and other scholars have engaged in long and furious debates concerning the exact nature of fascism and its core tenets.

It then lists definitions from some eighteen authors, starting with the Bulgarian communist, Georgi Dmitrov, from 1935:

> Fascism is an open terrorist dictatorship of the most reactionary, the most chauvinistic, the most imperialistic elements of the financial capital... Fascism is neither the government beyond classes nor the government of the petty bourgeois or the lumpen-proletariat over the financial capital. Fascism is the government of the financial capital itself. It is an organised massacre of the working class and the revolutionary slice of peasantry and intelligentsia. Fascism in its foreign policy is the most brutal kind of chauvinism, which cultivates zoological hatred against other peoples.

Dmitrov identified half a dozen features: it is authoritarian, capitalist, chauvinist, expansionist, reactionary and xenophobic.

Other writers found a different half dozen points, while others extended his list to nine, a dozen and even fourteen features that characterise a fascist movement. These include the myth of national superiority coupled with the notion that the nation is under existential threat from enemies without and within. To survive, it must undergo a cathartic moral purification before it can achieve its predestined greatness, a process which only the fascist government has the courage and determination to implement. Roger Griffin, for example, said:

> [F]ascism is best defined as a revolutionary form of nationalism, one that sets out to be a political, social and ethical revolution, welding the 'people' into a dynamic national

community under new elites infused with heroic values. The core myth that inspires this project is that only a populist, trans-class movement of purifying, cathartic national rebirth (palingenesis) can stem the tide of decadence (1991).

Half a century before, Franklin D Roosevelt had added another notion to the growing list:

The first truth is that the liberty of a democracy is not safe if the people tolerate the growth of private power to a point where it becomes stronger than their democratic state itself. That, in its essence, is fascism — ownership of government by an individual, by a group, or by any other controlling private power (Message to Congress, April 29, 1938).

Later that year, he voiced a more urgent fear:

I venture the challenging statement that if American democracy ceases to move forward as a living force, seeking day and night by peaceful means to better the lot of our citizens, fascism will grow in strength in our land.

The English anti-totalitarian writer, George Orwell, emphasised fascism's aggressive, expansionist militarism:

Fascism, at any rate the German version, is a form of capitalism that borrows from Socialism just such features as will make it efficient for war purposes ... It is a planned system geared to a definite purpose, world-conquest, and not allowing any private interest, either of capitalist or worker, to stand in its way.

In 1944, he wrote that the word had been applied to and used against so many different types of people that it was little more than an insult, roughly synonymous with 'bully.' With respect to Orwell, this seriously understates the matter and conveys entirely the wrong impression about the doctrines behind the resurgent push by the political right we are now seeing.

To summarise, fascism incorporates an array of sociopolitical tropes from which its followers are free to pick and choose. No two movements will be exactly alike (Mussolini did not agree with Nazi hostility toward Jews) but their similarities outweigh their differences. From a range of sources, we can cobble together a list of essential elements:

Fascism is ...

(1)   a *hyper-nationalist* movement directed at taking ...

(2)   *exclusive control* of government to effect a ...

(3)   *populist program* of *radical national and social renewal,* aimed at ...

(4)   *eradicating the internal and external enemies* who have caused an ...

(5)   *existential crisis of sociopolitical decline.*

Fascism arises from and appeals to ...

(6)   *frightened and disempowered* common people who feel ...

(7)   *betrayed by the traditional elite,* but is normally ...

(8)   *supported and ultimately captured* by established capital. It is ...

(9)   *regressively conservative,* with rigidly defined sexual roles. It elevates physical activity above intellectual and is thus ...

(10) *anti-elitist, anti-intellectual* and *anti-modernist.*

Fascist movements see the world as a Darwinian struggle for survival. All citizens must be totally committed to permanent warfare otherwise they become internal enemies who must be eliminated. To this end, it is ...

(11) *authoritarian, rigidly hierarchical* and *ultracompetitive,* in every aspect of life. It is therefore ...

(12) *flamboyantly and aggressively militarist,* using a malleable mix of ...

(13) *mythical, historical or religious themes* to gain and justify its hold on power. It sees the warrior as the heroic peak of human achievement, and is thus ...

(14) *aggressively hyper-masculine, patriarchal/misogynist,* and worshipful of physical beauty, especially in males, who are seen as the true inheritors of the national tradition. Fascism exists by and through men and male pursuits, as thinking and intellectual pursuits are effeminate, betraying the masculine ethos and thence the national spirit.

As an ...

(15) *extreme reaction to intense political insecurity*, and, despite its traditionalist themes, it claims to be ...

(16) *free of traditional morality*, justifying itself in terms of the supposed crisis facing the nation. Displacing the traditional elites (of breeding, church, capitalists, intelligentsia, public service and officer class), it proposes a new sainthood of ...

(17) *heroic and self-sacrificing commoners* such as workers, farmers, soldiers, mothers and students. By ...

(18) *incorporating and promoting the dispossessed*, it broadens its appeal, entraps its converts and isolates the traditional elites.

In order to maintain power, it ...

(19) *politicises and militarises daily life* to a minute degree. To gain and maintain power, its public pronouncements comprise a ceaseless turmoil of ...

(20) *threats* (from the internal and external enemies), *self-glorification* and *promises* (of social, national and military glories to come) backed by a ...

(21) *brutal amorality* in which the public are invited to participate, thereby ...

(22) *justifying* and *institutionalising their most violent urges* by appeals to the crusade for the salvation of the nation.[7]

Essentially, fascism is a radical nationalist attempt to save the nation from crisis by unleashing the repressed violence of the masses, vanquishing its enemies and leading it to a golden future based in its mythical past. Only the fascists have the political insight to recognise the danger, as well as the discipline and courage to lead the people to safety. It has powerful appeal to frightened, insecure or unhappy

---

[7] Note that each of these factors is scalar, that is, they range from mild to severe. We could give individuals or parties or countries a score ranging from 0 = not present, 1 = mild, 2 = moderate, 3 = intense. It's a bit like, say, the corruption index compiled by Transparency International. Countries are rated on a number of factors to give a final score, which determines their place on the index, but no two countries are corrupt in the same way. Similarly, no two countries are fascist in the same way.

people, offering them a valued place in a vibrant community of like-minded people committed to the sacred task of destroying the nation's enemies. Clad in the fascist uniform, marching behind brave standards to the thump of soul-stirring music, even the most mournful fellow can start to feel a sense of pride that, yes, he is worthwhile after all: "Behold my new Self, cast anew as a heroic Defender of the Nation and of our Holy Womanhood against the evil Other."

Fascism should not be seen as a political program, as Marxism was, but as a flexible set of tools to be used in resolving the crucial issue for all aspiring politicians (including religious leaders): how to gain and maintain power. By replacing the word "nation" in this list with "religion," we create a new political class, the religious or clericalist fascist. Despite the apparent contradiction, this is a very real entity and, in fact, the two strains of nationalist and religious fascism often blur and merge. Thus, we can have a fascist political movement with religious overtones, and a religious movement (such as revivalism) with fascist overtones, or what is called Christian nationalism in the US. This points to a bigger question: Why fascism?

Given all the political possibilities in human society, why has this particular constellation arisen so often and in such diverse cultures? What is its appeal? Looking at its ghastly record, why are apparently intelligent people still attracted to it? There is a single answer to these questions but it doesn't come from political theory. In fact, it has nothing to do with politics, so answering it will require a diversion into some quite different fields. This will also show why, despite the wild excitement it generates, fascism inevitably has only one outcome, failure. Before we do that, we should look at the extent and impact of fascism in the modern world.

2.3: The fascist society.

The first point to note is that fascism is not a coherent political entity or doctrine: there has never been a Fascist International. There was no seminal writer, as with Karl Marx's theories on the left, nor an academic industry developing a body of work, such as with neoliberalism. There was no single centre as the fount of all wisdom, as in the Roman Church, and no preeminent living authority such as Lenin, Mao, FIFA or the Pope. Similarly, just as there is no such *thing* as narcissism, only people showing narcissistic behaviour, there is also no such *thing* as fascism, only political parties showing fascist themes.

It is therefore a simple matter of grading governments and political parties on the checklist above. However, it soon becomes clear that those features don't have much to do with which end of the political spectrum the party occupies. Government is about power; fascism is just one approach among many to taking and maintaining power, very successful one but it certainly doesn't have a patent on any political tactics. A tactic that is successful on the right will soon be copied on the left, and vice versa. Extremists feed off each other until they become hostile mirror images of each other.

The prime difference between left and right wings lies in the goals of each movement, not the tactics. If politics is discourse in the service of power, right wing politics is essentially tribalism writ large, with the goal that my tribe should overcome yours before yours does mine in. The right wing sees the entire socio-political landscape as a merciless battle for survival. Fascism is about dominance of and superiority over The Other, with the goal of enslaving or even eradicating the appointed enemy. The Other is always hostile: in the dog-eat-dog world of fascist politics, there are no friends, only mortal enemies or vassals. Fascism is therefore and inevitably ultra-nationalist, racist, sexist and aggressive. In this central sense, it is devoid of a social or economic content. Unlike socialism, it is not a coherent political entity as it doesn't exist to implement a common social program. Its goal is to become bigger and ever more powerful in order to save the tribe from annihilation. Taking power is its entire *raison d'être*, as Orwell wrote:

> ...no one ever seizes power with the intention of relinquishing it. Power is not a means; it is an end. One does not establish a dictatorship in order to safeguard a revolution; one makes the revolution in order to establish the dictatorship. The object of persecution is persecution. The object of torture is torture. The object of power is power [2].

That is to say, the sole objective of fascist politics is domination. It has no other end. In contrast, the left has a specific goal of social reconstruction which could broadly be described as opposing or reversing the effects of the right wing. In its pure form, the left wing of politics is egalitarian, internationalist, pacifist, altruist, cooperative, and tolerant of deviation and experiment. Tell it to Mao or Stalin, you may say, but that is the point: each of them started his political life in an egalitarian, internationalist, pacifist, altruist, etc. movement. However, faced with the limitless hostility of their right wing opponents, the revolutionaries soon adopted whatever political tactics they felt would safeguard their revolution. As Mao realised, "Power grows out of the barrel of a gun." Since that meant using political and thence military power to maintain control, both socialist dictators quickly adopted many of the measures used by the right wing.

The mere fact of starting one's political life opposing a rapaciously unequal, brutally repressive and corrupt hierarchy, as Stalin and Mao both did, doesn't make one a leftist for life. In order to fight the fascists, they had to become fascists themselves, although there is little to suggest either of them suffered any great mental anguish in the process. Dictatorship came easily to them; it is not surprising that they had no time for each other.

Right wing politics sees the world through competitive eyes, which extends to all aspects of life. While the name of the Nazi party in Germany was National *Socialist* German Workers' Party, fascism's dominant theme of social Darwinism extends to the economy. Such socialism as there is (not much) extends mainly to building the military machine in its many facets. Everybody has to be totally committed to the endless battle of surviving in a hostile world, meaning people who get to the top obviously deserved to do so, while those who were left behind didn't try hard enough and deserve no pity. Unlike Marxism, fascism is comfortable with private property and private enterprise, so people who build fortunes are to be commended for their industry.

On the other hand, shirkers such as the unemployed and the mentally disturbed are not just lazy or unfortunate people, they are betraying the sacred trust of building the tribe and must be punished accordingly. This extends to strikers, who are seen as the very worst sorts of saboteurs. Hitler himself made this clear in *Mein Kampf*, where he castigated the strikers in German munitions plants in early 1918 as betraying the troops while sending the clearest signal to the Allies that they only needed to hang on a bit longer as Germany was about to fall apart. Thus arose the myth of the German military being "stabbed in the back" by venal politicians and financiers, and by treacherous internationalists, meaning socialists, which was so powerful in Germany's resurgent militarism.

At its extreme, the social Darwinism of "routine" fascism and the concept of a neoliberal or unregulated economy become indistinguishable. For a fascist government, the economy is the means to the end of building a powerful nation; how that is achieved isn't of much concern. Some authors take the view, as Orwell did, that fascism is a form of capitalism. However, this narrow view completely misses the point that fascism is driven by much deeper and more primitive forces than mere money. If it were only an extreme version of capitalism, then we could solve the problem just by moving to a socialist economy but socialism hasn't had a good press over the past century. The essential point is that Stalinist communism and German fascism had much more in common than they had differences. We need to account for those common features, not gloss over them as historical accidents.

In a fascist society, the fact that a few well-placed people get very rich while the lower grades of workers, who aren't directly important to industry, go without is neither contradictory nor of any real consequence. As long as the unemployed get enough to survive and they have plenty of parades and spectacles to amuse them, then the secret police and their informers will deal with the few malcontents. However, there will never be mass unemployment under fascism as the military will soak up excess workers and make them feel important. All this points to an inevitable conclusion: the right wing economy must ultimately fail.

Talking of failing economies, it is apposite to start with a prominent example of the rush to the right in politics, the United Kingdom. After leading the world in planning and instituting a social net in the 1940s to 50s, the UK drifted before falling under the sway of right wing ideologues, who attempted to make a virtue out of greed, as Galbraith warned:

> The modern conservative is engaged in one of man's oldest exercises in moral philosophy; that is, the search for a superior moral justification for selfishness.

In 1979, Margaret Thatcher became prime minister, with the clear intent of forcing a radical and painful readjustment on the nation, to counter the efforts of enemies without and within who, she believed, were intent on its destruction. The enemy without was that old favourite, the USSR, while the enemies within were the fifth column of ultra-left trade unionists who were intent on destroying the economy. Why would they do that? She never explained this point but it was perfectly clear she did not accept they could be reasonable people who simply had a different point of view. In classic fashion, she firmly believed she was right in everything she did ("I can only do what is right"), meaning anybody who opposed her was wrong and needed to be contained, if not destroyed outright. She believed the country was facing an existential threat of terminal decline, that it needed to regain its fighting ("Dunkirk") spirit in order to regain its rightful position as a major actor on the world scene. This could only be done by a radical program of national and social renewal, sweeping away the old elite who were standing greedily or incompetently by while the enemy within hollowed out all that was Great about Britain.

Thatcher was lucky in that, by invading the Falkland Islands, one of Britain's remnant colonial possessions, the even more incompetent, US-sponsored military regime in Argentina handed her the perfect excuse to bang the nationalist-cum-militarist drum, thereby diverting attention from the devastation her policies were wreaking on the industrial heartlands of the country. For a time, she feted herself as even more central to the nation's soul than the monarchy but she proved incapable of dealing with major social problems in a democratic state. The daughter of a shopkeeper in the suburbs, with an education gifted to her by the Labour reforms, she was the classic outsider: shrill [8], pretentious, self-centred and fanatically self-opinionated, domineering but equally resentful of and thrilled by her proximity to power (in his early days, Hitler was also an ardent monarchist); an eager tradition-alist but also contemptuous of the conventional morality which dictated that the nation must take care of its underdogs; and deeply resentful of mere Europeans telling the UK what to do. She was an example of the petty bourgeois Little-England fascist but the country eventually tired of her and, uncomprehending, she was ejected by her own party in favour of the less doctrinaire John Major.

The former incumbent, Alexander Boris de Pfeffel Johnson, has far too many contradictions and far too little substance to be a successful fascist. Born into privilege, with an elitist education, he markets himself as a blatantly amoral man of the people with an Oxford accent. By dint of flagrant dishonesty and diligent manipulation of his privileged connections, he has managed to claw his way into the nation's top job as the man who would "Do Brexit." That apart, he appears to have no policy of any kind apart from keeping himself in power by blaming the European Union for everything the resentful burghers of Little England

---

[8] One of her many nicknames was Attila the Hen.

dislike. As such, he leads but has no real following, as in "I'm their leader, which way did they go?" A crucial feature of fascists is that they are servants of a much bigger cause, the individual submerges himself in the numberless infantry fighting the Good Battle. While a lot of British voters wish Johnson would submerge himself in something very deep and wet, honest and ascetic anonymity is not his style. The danger he represents, however, is that, believing he can use them to get ahead, he facilitates people with much more extremist political opinions. That was also true of the politicians in the late Weimar Republic who believed they could use Hitler to advance their personal ambitions. He repaid them on June 30th 1934, the Night of the Long Knives.

History is replete with examples of unscrupulous politicians fostering extremist groups for their personal gain, only to have the group turn on them later. The Germans sent Lenin back to Russia in 1915; in 1945, the USSR he created smashed the Reichswehr and split Germany in two for nearly half a century. Britain encouraged the rise of Mussolini's tiny group of fascists; Indira Ghandi sponsored the Akali Dal, who later assassinated her; and the US poured money into a little-known group of religious fanatics so they would bog down the atheist Soviet forces in Afghanistan. Their leader, a Saudi heir named Osama bin-Laden, later gave the US an object lesson in what fanaticism means.

Apropos the USSR, was Stalin a fascist? In 1946, writing in the *New York Times*, Herbert Matthews asked: "Should we now place Stalinist Russia in the same category as Hitlerite Germany? Should we say that she is Fascist?" In 1946, J. Edgar Hoover, longtime FBI director, ferocious anti-communist and alleged cross-dresser, published an article on "Red Fascism" although it may have been ghost-written by an FBI employee. Stalin certainly played the nationalist card when it suited him (World War II is still known to Russians as the Great Patriotic War); he believed, with very good reason, that the nation was under attack (five invasions in under thirty years); he forced through a radical program of social, national and industrial renewal, even at ruinous cost to the citizens; he played a major part in destroying the old Czarist elite; he militarised his country to the limit, essentially turning it into a giant military prison camp; his version of Marxism had clear religious and salvationist overtones, on and on.

In brief, Stalin's USSR met all criteria for a genuine fascist state superimposed on the Marxist program of delivering the downtrodden masses into a new, egalitarian society. This emphasises the point that fascism is not itself a doctrine but is an assembly of socio-political elements that anybody can adopt, in any order and for any purpose. Take the massive parades that were such a feature of Nazi Germany; the USSR had the same and, in its annual Victory Parade through Moscow's Red Square, Russia still does. North Korea, a nation perpetually on the brink of starvation, puts on astounding shows of massed choreography and militarism. However, this is also true of the US where, of all the options, militarism is joyously celebrated at sports events. Against a backdrop of flags and accompanied by thunderous renditions of the national anthem and military tunes, a recent football match involving the Minnesota Vikings had the spectators displaying the giant words *Thank You Military* on flash cards. Norman Mailer recognised this in 2003, just prior to the Iraq invasion:

> The dire prospect that opens, therefore, is that America is going to become a mega-banana republic where the army will have more and more importance in Americans' lives... [D]emocracy is the special condition—a condition we will be called upon to defend in the coming years. That will be enormously difficult because the combination of the corporation, the military, and the complete investiture of the flag with mass spectator sports has set up a pre-fascistic atmosphere in America already.

While we would normally think of a fascist state as the policy or product of a single, enduring government, such as North Korea or Saudi Arabia, it happens that apparently opposed political parties can endorse the central elements of fascism (albeit different elements), such that governments come and go but fascism is forever. We will look at several examples, starting with the USSR and its successor state, the Russian Federation. As described above, Stalin's USSR relied on many fascist features which, despite Nikita Khruschev's efforts from 1953-1964, continued throughout the "Years of Stagnation" of Leonid Brezhnev's rule (1964-1982). Due to the perceived threat from the US and its Nato allies, the country was constantly on a war footing with all that it entails: a rigidly hierarchical and regimented society, secret police, internal conscription of labour, closed borders, conservative and anti-modernist trends, etc.

There was, however, an opportunity for change after the USSR broke up in 1991 but this was lost when, with Western help, the country was taken over by the KGB fronting organised crime [3].

Russia has been called a *kataskopocracy*, a rule of spies – a spy is κατάσκοπος, kataskopos, because eighty percent of Russia's current high officials served in the Soviet KGB or its successors. Superficially, Russia is a modern liberal economy but the populace is kept in line by the same methods Hitler used in 1933-38: selective use of laws drawn up with the intention of protecting the powerful and wealthy, and diverting the rest of the country with militarist shows and foreign adventures while keeping them in a state of low grade fear. Opponents of Vladimir Putin's kleptocracy, be they in Russia or overseas, are regularly murdered; others are thrown into prisons described as hellholes.

For the rest, Putin's clique closely follows the fascist playbook above, albeit rather less obtrusively than in the days of the USSR. Undoubtedly, Putin is clever and reads political trends very well. His foreign policy is committed to rebuilding Russia's prestige; domestically, he is breathtakingly corrupt. From 2007-14, the Estonian branch of Denmark's prestigious Danske Bank processed some €200 billion, flowing mainly from Russia to the West. That money was stolen from the Russian people but is thought to be only a proportion of the capital that has been illegally removed from the country. Putin knew all about it because a large part of it went into his and his friends' accounts.

Since he assumed power in 1999, Putin has built a mafia state modelled along czarist lines but, for himself, he is now caught in the mafia don's dilemma: how does he guarantee his ill-gotten gains and protect his family when he is no longer in power? For centuries, the czars had everybody convinced that their wealth was God's will until, one day in 1917, the people got sick of it. Putin surrounds himself with czarist trappings but as his coterie of mercilessly corrupt, former KGB operatives ages, and the rising generation comes to despise all they stand for, what will stop another revolution? As they say, in life, two things are certain, death and taxes. Putin has solved the tax problem by diverting all Russian taxes to himself and his cronies but death is more problematic. In politics, only one thing is certain: fascist regimes never last. Eventually, the common people get sick of being told what to think.

2.4: Fascism: A case study.

Having said that, we should look at another country where governments come and go, but nothing much seems to change. The

United States of America has all the trappings of a democratic society: regular rule-based elections involving opposing political parties; separate branches of state (executive, legislature, judiciary) with no concentration of power; an elaborate system of legalised checks and balances, and so on. At first glance, it would seem that it could not be a fascist state, not least because the parties take turns in governing and there is currently no registered fascist party in the country. But that misses the point: opposing football teams may loathe each other 9 but they are still going to play football together and will link arms to fight anybody who tries to stop them. So it is in the US: Republicans and Democrats may detest each other and be sure the other party will consign the country to damnation but, on the basics, like which is the greatest country and greatest political and military and financial and cultural system on earth, which country deserves to be the world leader, and how to distribute the nation's wealth, they stand shoulder to shoulder. What are the basics? Let's go back to the list above:

(1)   *Hyper-nationalism*: Yes, the US is fanatically, even bizarrely, patriotic. Both parties firmly believe in its exceptionalism and manifest destiny.

(2)   *Exclusive control of government*: True, the two major parties are united in their agreement to keep third parties out of office, and practically all elected officials are chosen from the same elite.

(3)   *Populist program* of *radical national and social renewal*: This is problematic; the people in the US who are in greatest need of radical reform, the poor and minority communities, have least control over government, essentially none. All renewal consists of reforms directed at benefiting the rich, such as the Trump tax reforms, but since Big Money appoints the governments, politicians must direct their pitches to the wealthy, who want root-and-branch change—in their favour—which satisfies the condition. This calls to mind the acerbic comment of Aneurin Bevan, architect of Britain's National Health Service: "The whole art of Conservative (party) politics in the 20th century is being deployed to

---

9   For example, Glasgow's Rangers and Celts.

enable wealth to persuade poverty to use its political freedom to keep wealth in power."

(4) *Eradicating the internal and external enemies*: Despite its overwhelming military, industrial and financial might, the US firmly believes it is perennially surrounded by external enemies intent on dismembering it, who are kept at bay only by dint of regular displays of brute power. Of the enemies, only their names and politics change regularly. For decades, it was international socialism/communism (nobody in the US knows the difference); then Muslims, and now back to Russia and China with a side of Latino interlopers. To a very large extent, the US defines itself as a nation forced into permanent warfare by an ever-changing cast of dastardly enemies. The cynic could say that without the external threats, the country may fall apart. Its internal enemies are also legion: as Edward Snowden showed [4], since long before McCarthyism, the FBI and the rest of the "national security state" has illegally spied on everybody it doesn't like.

(5) *Existential crisis of sociopolitical decline.* That's what *Make America Great Again* means.

(6) Appeals to *frightened and disempowered* common people. All political parties play on the fears of the electorate, that's what they do (Henry Mencken: "The whole aim of practical politics is to keep the populace alarmed—and hence clamorous to be led to safety—by menacing it with an endless series of hobgoblins, all of them imaginary"). When the populace is frightened and disempowered, say following a global financial crisis or during a pandemic, then the politician's role is easier as criticising him becomes an act of bad faith.

(7) People feel *betrayed by the traditional elite*. This is most definitely true and was the major factor in the election of Donald Trump. He appealed to the common people over the heads of the corrupt elite, promising that only he understood them and would lead them back to the greatness they deserved. He betrayed them, of course, he knew nothing about government and cared even less, handing the reins of

administrative power to a group of corrupt ideologues who certainly knew all about dismantling government regulations for their own benefit.

(8) The new populist government is *ultimately captured* by established capital. In the US, established capital has never lost control, it merely changes its grip.

(9) Fascism is *regressively conservative*. It is important to distinguish between American pop culture, which moves quickly to take advantage of commercial trends, and the moral culture, which is deeply conservative, particularly in matters of religion and sexuality. Over the past 200 years, practically all Christian heresies, such as "prosperity gospel," have emerged from the US. These are backward looking and bitterly antagonistic to liberalisation of the social creed [5].

(10) It is *anti-elitist, anti-intellectual* and *anti-modernist*. It is just over fifty years since the term "pointy-headed intellectuals" was thrown into the arena. American politicians of both parties tout themselves as men of action, firmly based in the hurley-burley of real life, unlike the effete denizens of the ivory towers of academia. This helps explain why, unlike every other Western nation, retired generals are liberally sprinkled throughout the political-bureaucratic-industrial-academic complex.

(11) *Authoritarian, rigidly hierarchical* and *ultracompetitive,* in every aspect of life. That is true of the US, particularly in the sense that vertical social mobility has declined to the point where the boy from the log cabin or the slums who makes good is a freak.

(12) *Flamboyantly and aggressively militarist*. This is most definitely true, as the example of the football game noted above shows, as well as its record of invading smaller countries.

(13) *Mythical, historical or religious themes*. US politicians constantly play on the country's mythological origins as a bastion of freedom (although not for the natives, the black slaves, and all the other marginalised groups such as poor workers and immigrants). Public displays of religion are a

constant but hypocrisy is rampant, e.g. the numbers of televangelists, priests and God-fearing politicians who are convicted of sexual, financial and other crimes. We should also not forget the excrutiating display by former President Trump when he had a demonstration cleared by force so he could walk across the road to wave a Bible in front of a church.

(14) *Aggressively masculine, patriarchal/misogynist.* That's why *#MeToo* was born.

(15) *Extreme reaction to intense political insecurity.* The US is not and never has been in danger from external enemies but this theme has been a constant since 1776. The population has to be kept in a state of high agitation over the notion that the red hordes (or yellow, or brown) are sneaking through their suburbs right now, intent on slitting their throats, otherwise the militarised police would look ridiculous instead of menacing. The police armoured cars, drones and all the other military gear which is passed to them are not intended to keep people safe in their beds; their role is to prevent uprisings by minorities and assorted "leftists." Note that the "well-armed militias" mentioned in the Second Amendment were intended to put down slave rebellions, while the right/duty of citizens to bear arms was explicitly denied to the black *non*-citizens.

(16) *Free of traditional morality.* This would appear to be a contradiction as we have already said the US political system is intensely traditionalist. However, once across their borders, the kindly masks are ripped off, revealing the true, amoral character. Internationally, the US does not recognise any constraints on its actions, anywhere, at any time, against any person or nation, for any reason whatsoever. As the "Exceptional Nation," the US firmly believes it can do what it likes, even while loudly declaiming that everybody else has to follow a "rules-based international order" that it has written and amends or discards without notice. Thus, it has illegally invaded or effected coups in dozens of countries, with no repercussions whatsoever. Politicians of both sides condemned the trivial interference in the 2016 presidential

election by some unnamed Russian operators, completely overlooking the fact that the US maintains entire government departments whose role is to interfere in foreign elections. So the answer is Yes, both political parties most definitely believe the US is free of traditional international morality. Domestically, the US establishment is almost entirely devoid of moral constraints but they don't broadcast this.

(17) *Heroic and self-sacrificing commoners.* That is normal American fare. Having dispensed with an hereditary nobility, and having put the church in its place, its heroes come from sport, industry, entertainment, business, etc., as well as the fictional frontier mythology of Daniel Boone, Davey Crockett and General Custer.

(18) *Incorporating and promoting the dispossessed.* Again, this is not true of the country internally, where the dispossessed are kept poor and underfoot by ploys such as low wages, high costs of education and health, brutally repressive policing and penal systems, and so on, but it is true overseas: the US routinely isolates the traditional elites and promotes outsiders in order to interfere with elections, destabilise the establishment, etc.

(19) *Politicises and militarises daily life.* To foreigners, the notion that people can be elected to, say, judicial positions just because they belong to a particular political party or that anybody would know a bureaucrat's party affiliation is both outrageous and ridiculous.

(20) A ceaseless turmoil of *threats* (from the internal and external enemies), *self-glorification* and *promises* (of social, national and military glories to come). All true but Americans are so inured to self-involvement that they don't even notice it.

(21) *Brutal amorality in which the public are invited to partici-pate.* Beside lynchings, this ranges from dropping nuclear weapons on undefended cities, to lying about weapons of mass destruction, to flagrant corruption at every level of the society, or separating immigrant children from their parents, all the way down to "Stand your ground" legislation, which

encourages citizens to shoot unarmed people with impunity (as long as the shooter is white and the victim is black).

(22) *Justifying and institutionalising their most violent urges.* See above, Second Amendment and "Stand your ground." With about 45,000 gun-related deaths each year, Americans simply do not recognise the extent to which violence pervades their society. To a foreigner, the idea that students at a university should be allowed to carry concealed firearms is a travesty. Each year, about 1,300 people are killed by police but, tellingly, no official figures are recorded. Nobody in government, meaning both parties, cares enough about police violence or thinks it is so exceptional as to require attention. It was one thing that, just on suspicion of passing a counterfeit $20 note and over a period of nine minutes, George Floyd was murdered on a street in full view of the passers-by; it was something else again that the other four police involved didn't think it was so remarkable that they needed to stop it.

For a country that so fulsomely satisfies the panoply of criteria, fascism is not just creeping through the back door, "wrapped in the flag and carrying a cross," but has taken up residence in the living room. Despite apparent changes of government, a state can become and remain covertly fascist if the parties involved agree on the major points. However, due to its inherent contradictions, it will not survive in the long term.

2.5: Conclusion: Fascism *Prêt-à-Porter*.

To summarise, fascism has been around in one form or another since the dawn of history. Its persistence stems from the fact that it is not the sort of thing that can go out of date. It is a collection of *tools* that can be used to turbocharge any socio-political movement in its drive to gain power, but it is not a political movement in its own right. As will be explained in the next chapter, the elements of fascism appeal to and amplify some of humanity's most basic urges and drives. It's like sex, in that each generation will eventually discover it and think it's the first. Thus, the same tools can be successfully applied to more or less any socio-political movement, anywhere, at any time:

Marxism + fascism = Stalinism, Maoism.

Religion + fascism = Extremist fundamentalism.

Neoliberal economics + fascism = Thatcherist/Trumpist corporatism.

Kleptocracy + fascism = Putinist autocracy.

Racism + fascism = Nazism/Jim Crow (note that fascism is not itself frankly racist).

Militarism + corporatism + fascism = Imperialism.

Religion + corporatism + fascism = Medieval popery.

It just takes a bit of imagination. Fascism is like an elaborate costume waiting for an actor to climb inside to make it seem real and alive. It is a *façade*, an assemblage of flourishes, flags and beating drums designed to excite the audience and make them clamour to join in. It is smoke and mirrors, all colour and movement, noise and spectacle but it has no substance of its own:

> Yes sir, you have a political movement that lacks something, that *élan vitale* to turn it into the raging success you believe it ought to be? That's not a problem sir, we have just what you need. Follow this program and you'll soon have them beating down the doors to join...

> What happens at the end? Oh don't worry, there's no end, all you need is bigger and better spectacles, more diabolical and threatening enemies and you can string it out indefinitely...

> No, don't be silly, nobody will ever ask to see your doctrine, they'll be too excited chasing the enemies you're pointing out. You can trust us sir, we've been in this business a long time. Thousands of years, you could say...

> That's correct sir, you nailed it. There's always another sucker.

References:

1. Hitler A (1925) *Mein Kampf*. Tr. J Murphy 1939. Publisher not stated.

2. Orwell, G (1948) *1984*. London: Secker and Warburg; Middlesex: Penguin (1954 etc)

3. Belton C (2020) *Putin's People: How the KGB Took Back Russia and Then Took on the West.* London: Farrar, Strauss, Giroux

4. Snowden E (2019) *Permanent Record.* New York: McMillan.

5. Hedges C (2007) *American Fascists: The Christian Right and the War on America.* London: Jonathon Cape/Random House – Vintage (2008).

Chapter 3: The idea of dominance.

The right wing politician has less of a distance to go to exploit our tribal fears and hatreds than his opponent, who would engage our better selves.

Edgar L Doctorow (1994)

3.1: Testosterone and birds.

In the first chapter, we considered the psychological phenomenon of the narcissistic personality type. In the second, we turned to the sociology of fascist regimes. In this chapter, we will look at the biology of dominance, how it relates to the first two phenomena, and what it means for human behaviour. Of necessity, it is a little technical but I will reduce it to the basics. But before we talk about humans, we need to talk about birds for a while.

For longer than recorded history, farmers have known that the male gonads are essential for normal masculine behaviour in their animals. They have castrated excess male stock to pacify and fatten them, otherwise they became too aggressive to manage. Similarly, for hundreds of years, until as late as 1870 in Italy, boy sopranos were emasculated to preserve their ethereal voices. The hormone involved in developing masculine qualities was isolated in Chicago in 1927, using material from the vast abattoirs in that city. It was synthesised in Europe in 1935, and given the name testosterone, meaning the steroid hormone from the testicles. Its discoverers were awarded the Nobel Prize in 1939, just as World War II erupted. Postwar, it was studied in much greater detail as ease of manufacture and assay led to all sorts of applications.

As a chemical, testosterone is widespread in nature, which implies that it appeared early in evolution. It is of major importance in biology, with similar substances having almost identical effects in reptiles, birds and mammals. In all species studied, testosterone is essential for normal prenatal development of the male brain. Male foetuses have high levels which persist until birth, when it drops to what are called latency levels, more or less the same as prepubertal girls. At puberty, the hormone is triggered, after which it begins to exert a wide range of effects. These include the primary sexual changes, meaning enlargement of the genitalia and onset of spermatogenesis, as well as the familiar secondary sexual characteristics. In mammals, these consist of rapid growth of muscle bulk, enlargement of the larynx, and hair growth. However, testosterone does more than produce large, bulky males who sit around gossiping in bass voices while grooming their beards. It also has profound effects on behaviour: the sexually mature male is active, exploratory, and aggressively competitive.

For decades, psychiatrists and others tried to tie testosterone to mental disorders, with no luck. In the 1950s, when cheap assay techniques became available, it was hoped that unusually aggressive behaviour associated with the psychopathic (now sociopathic) personality disorder could be explained as the result of excessive testosterone; if so, an almost miraculous line of treatment would open. It didn't happen: there is practically no relationship between male aggression, either sexual or otherwise, and resting testosterone levels. Part of the problem is that testosterone production varies so much, not just between individuals, but from hour to hour within the same subject. However, that led to another observation, which is how we manage to bring birds into the story of fascism (a more detailed treatment of this topic is available at [1], which contains full citations for this chapter).

In the early 1970s, researchers studying testosterone levels in birds found some interesting results. For adult male birds in the non-breeding season, testosterone levels are low, not much different from mature females. Their plumage is dull, their behaviour quiet and they are content to spend their time foraging for food, preening and sleeping. With the onset of the breeding season, due to whatever environmental triggers are specific to the species studied, testosterone levels rise sharply and the bird's physiology and appearance change. The gonads enlarge, spermatogenesis begins and the typical breeding plumage appears. As the season progresses, and in birds this is usually days or a few weeks at most, the hormone levels rise again and he starts to show the typical behaviour of a cock bird seeking a mate. He stakes out a territory and actively guards it against interlopers, as well as singing or other displays to attract a mate. This may involve building a nest or bower but this is all part of the same stage. His behaviour now is very different from the dull, retiring bird of the non-breeding season. He is active, highly visible, protective of his territory and his mate, and responds aggressively to competition from other males.

This led to the interesting finding that, even though he was sexually capable and fully prepared to breed, males in this stage can show a further increase in testosterone, but only if they are exposed to a challenge from another male. This has given the phenomenon its name, the *Challenge Hypothesis*, [2] which says that a male who sees a challenge or threat in his environment will require extra testosterone to deal with it. The perception of a threat produces a sudden surge of the hormone, whose widespread physiological effects get him ready to fight and also provide the energy and mental determination to do it.

Assuming he has impregnated his little mate and is successful in seeing off the competition, the male will stay at the second level of hormone production until the eggs hatch and he takes up parenting. After that, it slowly drops toward the resting level with occasional peaks due to threats of various kinds. Challenges, of course, are not limited to the same species. A cock bird defending his nest against a predator needs a spurt of testosterone to induce the aggressive behaviour he needs to display. In polygamous species, the male's testosterone level does not decline but remains high as he continues searching for other mates.

There are thus four distinct levels of testosterone production recognised. First is the basal, non-breeding level which is just enough to keep the male healthy and ready to respond to the breeding season. Second, there is the level required to get him physically ready to breed. Third, there is the level required to attract a mate, build a nest and to defend her and his territory. Finally, there is an additional brief surge of the hormone to allow him to respond to challenges in the environment. Once the challenge passes, he reverts to whatever level he needs in the breeding cycle. This is true of a wide range of animals, including fish and reptiles and, bearing in mind that we don't have a distinct breeding season, it is also true of *Homo sapiens*.

In all species, testosterone is a powerful anabolic hormone. It builds and strengthens skin, muscle bulk, tendons and ligaments, affecting cardiac function and many other organs. In humans, in both males and females, it is a "feel good" hormone. With testosterone, people feel better, more confident, more capable and better able to handle pain, hunger, cold, exertion etc. In men, it produces higher levels of activity, with more assertive and exploratory behaviour, sexually and otherwise. Their testosterone secretion changes a lot during the day, with a surge in the early morning followed by a slow decline but, as in birds and other animals, it is also dramatically affected by challenges. For non-human species, a threat response is triggered by the sight, sound or smell of a competitor. As long as there are no other males around, the subject animal gets on with whatever he has to do; if he senses a challenge, he shows a spurt of the hormone followed by immediate changes in his behaviour. He becomes more active and assertive, rushing around until he finds the threat and then confronting it. That is, testosterone is needed to deal with the threat but ... in his excited state, he is more likely to perceive neutral events as threats, and more likely to respond aggressively to them. Events which ordinarily wouldn't bother him much now provoke further aggression.

So testosterone is not just a feel-good hormone, it is also intensely destabilising. It produces the means of reacting to a threat (i.e. physical strength and assertive behaviour) but also increases the likelihood that he will see further threats where there are none, which will provoke more hormone, leading to more aggression with less chance of him backing down, in a spiral of aggression. This phenomenon, *an integral part of human male behaviour*, has been seriously underestimated, if it has been given any recognition at all.

As a matter of physiology, relying on testosterone is not just essential for success but, depending on the breeding strategy used by the species, it can carry significant risks. In some species, such as elephant seals, the male gathers as many females as he can and tries to impregnate them all, but he must then remain at the highest level of physical strength and aggression to defend his harem, meaning at the highest level of testosterone secretion. Of course, he can't take any part in parenting and, after the breeding season, he is too tired even if he survives. This is a high risk breeding strategy, for both the dominant harem boss and for the other males who have to fight him for the chance to breed. The males of a tiny Australian marsupial, *Antechinus argentus*, rarely survive beyond a year because they enter a state of hypersecretion of testosterone due to enormously enlarged testes. Over a period of two or three weeks, they search frantically for females to mate. They fight and don't have time to eat but this affects cortisol production. Their fur falls out, they go blind and soon die of steroid toxicity.

Other species do it differently. Albatrosses and penguins, for example, are devoted fathers, putting all their energy into raising one or perhaps two chicks, but those chicks are likely to survive, whereas the offspring of promiscuous avian fathers, who may have four or more chicks in each clutch with several partners, are much less likely to reach adulthood. In albatrosses, testosterone levels drop as soon as the female lays her egg but it does not go back to non-breeding levels until the young has fledged and left the nest.

3.2: Testosterone and humans.

In humans, levels of testosterone vary widely depending on a range of factors. Physical exercise increases it, pain, inactivity and anxiety reduce it, but the most powerful effects are related to challenges, sexual or otherwise. Studies of single men in western countries show that testosterone levels rise on Friday, in preparation for the weekend. In a couple who want to have a child, the male's levels generally rise on days 10-14 of his partner's menstrual cycle. In daily life, a man who sees an attractive woman is likely to experience a significant surge of hormone, with predictable effects on his behaviour. He becomes louder and more assertive, to her and to others around him, especially males who may be competitors. He will be sexually suggestive, perhaps frivolous but there is always an edge to it and it can quickly slide into aggression. This is also true if there are no women around but a man feels he has to assert himself or dominate others, which leads to an important finding relating to testosterone metabolism.

Humans are social animals. Scatter a group of humans around the landscape and, in no time, they will find each other and form a group which is likely to stay together. We can imagine there were powerful evolutionary pressures at work early in our history: the little protohuman who was content to wander away by himself and lose sight of the group was unlikely to survive to leave his wandering genes to posterity. Those who stuck together bred together. We feel anxious if we are separated from familiar humans, but that anxiety quickly settles with company. This isn't absolute, it is a strong general trend but the second most obvious feature of humans is close to absolute: our urge to form dominance hierarchies. As soon as we have formed a little society or tribe, the next thing we do is establish a dominance hierarchy inside the group. Very quickly, we sort ourselves into the top dog and the bottom dogs, the alpha male and all the rest.

Now this is not just a matter of aesthetics, or ease of communication or management, or anything sensible like that: it is wholly related to hormones. Entirely as a matter of biology, testosterone levels are higher in high status males and lower in low status. While the mechanism of this phenomenon is entirely unconscious, its effects are fully conscious. The problem is that high levels of hormone feel good, while low levels produce dull, apathetic and disinterested behaviour. Men at the top of the hierarchy feel cheerful, confident, energetic, social and ready to go. They will see more challenges, and respond quickly and assertively to them. For men at the bottom, testosterone levels are low and they couldn't care less. They are bored, flat, insecure and will avoid challenges if possible. If a man is promoted to the top of the hierarchy, he quickly shows behaviour consistent with higher levels of hormone; if he is then demoted, his hormone levels drop and his behaviour reverts to the norm for people at that level.

Testosterone levels are very responsive to changes in social status. Everybody knows that being at the top feels better than being at the bottom, and now we know why. This hormonal response is the physiological basis of the great bulk of human competitive behaviour. Granted, many people are anxious about assuming the responsibilities of being boss or scared of being assailed, so they will avoid it if they can. However, if they can be encouraged to make the change, or if they are compelled and have no choice, they often find it isn't so bad after all and they soon start to enjoy bossing everybody around. Not long after that, they start to see being in charge as their right, and resent competition.

For humans, the nature of the impending challenge doesn't matter. It can be a sporting event, an important exam or difficult job at work, an election, a court case, knowing you have to deal with an aggressive person at work, hunting, fishing: anything that requires you to rise to a challenge and assert yourself. Before a sporting match, all contestants (individuals or teams) show rising levels of

testosterone. After the match, the winner's level stays high or may even rise further. He struts around, highly aroused and cheerful and will stay that way for hours. The chances of him seeking sexual activity that night are very high. On the other hand, the loser's levels will drop precipitously at the end of the match. He mopes around, avoiding conflict of any kind and will usually go home if he can. His interest in sex is low and will stay low for some days.

The same surge is seen when driving a powerful car or driving a big truck, especially if it makes a lot of noise; riding a big horse is stimulating, motorcycles, catching a big fish, and, above all, handling weapons. Merely holding and stroking a gun produces a surge in testosterone. That is the reason people like guns; all talk of "second amendment rights" is mere window-dressing. The real answer is that playing with guns gives a sense of power and importance – and better erections. And herein lies the risk in so-called "Stand your ground" laws. A person who is walking around with a pistol shoved in his belt is experiencing – and enjoying – a surge of testosterone. This is having a number of effects, some physical (sexual arousal, blood flow to muscles, etc) but more important are the psychological effects. An armed man feels better, stronger and more assertive but, simply by virtue of being armed, he is also more likely to perceive a neutral event as a threat, less likely to ignore it and more likely to respond aggressively. The same man, walking unarmed down the same street, will not feel this way and will react differently njust because he feels he has less to lose. Anybody at the top of a dominance hierarchy automatically worries that he will lose status; a man in the middle is less concerned, so less likely to see neutral events as a threat. Armed men are *ipso facto* more aggressive, it is the fact of having the gun that produces the urge to use it. Of course, this also applies to knives, clubs and other weapons. People who carry knives have plans to use them; they do not carry a knife with the intention of running from a threat. And once they have knives in their pockets, they want to use them. The knife becomes an itch that can only be resolved one way.

There are many other factors that produce the "testosterone rush," including being in a group of men with a single purpose (as distinct from standing in a queue at the bus stop). It is amplified if they are all wearing the same uniform; by marching as a group; by thumping bands, flags and pennants, loud noises, flashing lights, and by weapons, weapons, weapons. A big truck produces it, so a big vehicle with a big gun (known as a tank) produces a lot more. A big boat produces a rush; having a big boat with lots of guns is even more exciting and leads to more aggressive behaviour. The same goes for aircraft; flying a jet produces bigger thrills than wafting around in a glider; a fighter or bomber produces more fun for the crew than flying an airliner. And, second only to direct sexual arousal, violence itself produces a powerful and thrilling surge of testosterone. Hunting is innately exciting; shooting living creatures causes a hormone-mediated rush of excitement and delight. Top of the list is killing another human being. These are all part of the domination urge, the teststerone-driven urge to get to the top and stay there by beating back competitors.

This is so characteristic of human behaviour that, to a large extent, people don't even notice it. Wherever there are humans, there will be hierarchies, there will be people on top and people underfoot. People urgently want to win, they want to have the most, the biggest, the best, the most powerful or most valuable, not because these things have any inherent advantage (a Mini will get you to your destination just as fast as a Rolls; a $50 Citizen watch is just as accurate as a Rolex) but because they signal that the owner is higher up the ladder, that he can look down on everybody else, and looking down feels so very much better than being looked down upon. This led the American economist, Thorsten Veblen, to the idea of conspicuous consumption, where people spend more time and money on goods, services and leisure than necessary, simply to signal their status to the rest of the community. People are pointedly wasteful as a form of display of their wealth and to intimidate their social inferiors. But, once ensconced in a Lamborghini, a driver, any driver, will start to act in an uncharacter-istically assertive manner, taking risks to push his way to the front or overtaking dangerously. Studies in women are much less clear-cut but the evidence points in the same direction. Daily life shows that women can be quite as competitive as men, there are entire industries built around it, but the psychology and physiology are different.

Why are we like this? Because we are the products of hundreds of millions of years of evolution which rewarded the winner and eliminated the loser. But the reward has to be in the here and now. It isn't enough to know that your genes will still be around in three generations, the winner wants to feel good now. Anyway, birds don't know anything about genes, but they know all about driving other males away from their territory, because watching the other bird scuttle away gives a rush. As in birds, so in humans.

3.3: Testosterone and social dominance.

Physiologically, walking around with high levels of testosterone is very demanding, as rutting bull elephant seals know. It burns energy and leads to fights, so humans have devised a range of measures to broadcast their status in the hierarchy without having to prove it every day. We have mentioned expensive cars and watches but consider corner offices; reserved parking; wearing a suit versus overalls; leather shoes vs. work boots; monogrammed luggage compared with a mismatched collection of battered cases; big houses and elaborate gardens; sipping champagne or scotch vs slugging down a beer; on and on. But for men, the most potent status indicators are seen in the group which is most concerned with domination, the military. Military uniforms are specifically designed, not just to make the wearer look more powerful and more intimidating than he actually is, but also to make him feel more powerful. Military uniforms are about testosterone: they are about producing a hormonal surge in the wearer, and either a sympathetic surge in the audience, if they are on the same side, or to block the hormone in the enemy, forcing him to yield in despair. Of course, none of this was known when uniforms were first devised; all the emperors and generals knew, and all their troops knew, was that helmets with waving scarlet plumes felt better than being bare-headed.

Everything about the military has the same dual impact: on the soldiers, by making them feel so much more powerful, and on others, meaning either the enemy or supporters. The uniform makes soldiers feel "I am part of something powerful, and that feels very exciting." It makes them feel good about themselves and drives them to want to dominate further. That is the essential point of testosterone: it is immensely self-reinforcing. Men like dressing in uniforms and marching along in formation, their rifles over their shoulders; women like watching them, and the men like being watched. It's all about "Look at me, am I not a magnificent specimen? I sure am, I feel ten foot tall and bullet proof."

Once a man is firmly entrenched in a military hierarchy, regardless of its nature, the social drive re-exerts itself. He identifies with the group as the source of his feeling good, so the fear of being expelled from the group and losing that feeling becomes a real thing. The need to conform is driven by the urge to get up the ladder and also by the twin fear of being kicked out. Without his group, without his uniform, he is nothing, a shell of a man who mopes around miserably, unable to establish a new life that could match the thrill of the military. Secretly, all soldiers know this so the two drives synergise to produce ever more conformist behaviour. A soldier told to bash enemy prisoners will most likely do it, partly because it is inherently exciting, but also because he fears what will happen if he refuses. Everybody else is doing it and laughing about it, so the idea of telling the officer it is forbidden by the Geneva convention frightens him. He cannot live with the thought of his comrades scorning him for being weak, mocking him, maybe even bashing him, so he does as he is told. Later, he says to himself: "Well, that wasn't so bad after all. I don't know what I was so worried about." From there, it is but a small step to bashing and raping civilians, then to shooting prisoners of war, then to shooting civilians. By the inexorable calculus of hormonally-driven aggression, step-by-inexorable-step, the mild-mannered conscript becomes a murderer in order to feel stronger and to avoid his secret fears.

Quite apart from the whole of human history and of current events, there is strong evidence from psychological experiments to confirm that ordinary men will alter their behaviour to conform with illegal or immoral orders or expectations if they feel pressured or encouraged to do so (I am not aware if these types of experiments have been performed with female subjects). Starting in the early 1960s, psychologist Stanley Milgram investigated the idea that people have remarkably little difficulty following orders, even when they know they are wrong. His work showed that it is not just the "evil Other" (Germans, Japanese, Russians etc) who will cheerfully inflict suffering on an innocent person, it is us. For humans, the most dangerous animal of all is other humans which, so soon after World War II, should have come as no great surprise, but it did. His results were considered so shocking that he was denied tenure at Harvard. However, events since then have proven beyond doubt that, for many people, dominating others by inflicting pain and humiliation causes little or no concern. All animals try to dominate each other but, for all species on earth bar ours, it has survival and reproductive value. We try to dominate for reasons which have nothing to do with survival: we do it because we like it. Milgram concluded:

> Ordinary people, simply doing their jobs, and without any particular hostility on their part, can become agents in a terrible destructive process. Moreover, even when the destructive effects of their work become patently clear, and they

are asked to carry out actions incompatible with fundamental standards of morality, relatively few people have the resources needed to resist authority [3].

In 1971, psychologist Phillip Zimbardo conducted a similar experiment over a period of a week. Eighteen students were split in two groups of nine, one given police and warden uniforms, the other treated as prisoners. The settings were realistic. Very quickly, the "police" started to act in an authoritarian and demeaning manner toward the defenceless "prisoners" and the experiment was abandoned after six days. He emphasised how, in the process of "dehumanising" their charges, the guards used devices such as the sort of obscene and disparaging slang seen in prisons the world over. He attributed this to their role and the experimental situation, in that the guards began to act in a stereotyped manner independently of their personalities. But that was also true of the "prisoners." Denied control over their lives, they also began to display the type of passive and apathetic behaviour seen in inmates of institutions the world over, regardless of their purpose.

The real problem arises when people who are so aroused by dominating others realise they don't need a superior telling them to break the fundamental laws of human society, they will do it because they enjoy it. We now know why they enjoy it, the testosterone rush, but we haven't worked out how to stop it. That's assuming, of course, that the people who have the authority to stop it actually want to do so. Mostly, they are so swollen with pleasure at being at the top of the hierarchy, so deeply entrenched in "the system," that the thought of doing something to limit it wouldn't occur to them. But if it did, they would likely be so frightened of disapproval that they would simply sit on their hands and pretend there was nothing to worry about.

3.4: When dominance becomes dysfunction.

Hierarchies are such a quintessentially human feature that, all too often, we don't even think about them. For us, it is absolutely normal to have a boss standing over workers, officers and NCOs standing over privates, parents and teachers over children, wealthy over poor, big over small, strong over weak ... The concept of dominance hierarchies is so deeply entrenched in human society that we can scarcely envisage equality. Only recently have we started to realise that perhaps it isn't written in the stars that men should dominate women the way they dominate children and dogs, or that domination, which is what hierarchies are all about, isn't necessarily the only way to organise human societies. It goes further: do we have the right to inflict pain and suffering on animals for fun, as in hunting, horse-racing and bullfighting; for profit, as in factory farming of cattle, pigs and chickens; or for decoration, as in shooting elephants for tusks, leopards for skins or clubbing baby seals for their fur?

Slowly, at glacial pace, we humans are starting to see that there is some deep-seated flaw in the very concept of domination. Far from producing a stable, ordered society, domination necessarily produces instabilty. The more goods and power people have, the more their sense of entitlement grows. People at the top soon start to want more, while those at the bottom will inevitably start to resent their lot. Our insatiable, hormone-driven need to dominate impels people at the top to want more, bigger, more powerful and more luxurious, just to show those underlings or those upstarts who's boss, just to hold power: *The object of power is power.* If also fuels the underlings' resentment and drives them to demand their rights, which leads the rulers to get more troops, more weapons, more repression. But once we have weapons, in and of themselves they produce both the urge to use them and the justification, as Madeline Albright believed:

> If we have to use force it is because we are America. We are the indispensable nation. We stand tall. We see further into the future.

There is no arguing with this type of attitude. It oozes self-justification, self-entitlement and self-aggrandisement. It shows an unwavering contempt for others' rights and needs dressed in the self-righteous talk of a person who is so deeply entrenched in the concept of dominance that alternatives simply don't present themselves (despite upheavals, Albright, who was born in Prague and arrived in the US aged eleven, had a life of considerable privilege). This is the attitude that produced the villainous inequality of Rome, of Czarist Russia and of much of the modern world, but she was only echoing the views of the man who appointed her, one WJ Clinton. In an address to the UN General Assembly, Sept. 27th 1993, Mr Clinton stated:

> ...the United States is entitled to resort to the unilateral use of military power ... (to ensure) ...uninhibited access to key markets, energy supplies and strategic resources.

That is, having the weapons breeds the belief that using them is justified. But having one gun quickly leads to the urge to get another, and another, and then the race is on. The central problem is that nobody wants to be the first to back down. Nobody wants to be seen as weak because everybody knows it feels bad *and* it encourages the other side to greater demands. Implicitly, we all know this from the earliest age, from the schoolyard, even from kindergarten.

Inherently, humans are not reasonable creatures. We are not rational beings halfway between angels and animals, and a major factor in our emotional instability lies in our animal heritage, our testosterone economy. And that could well be humanity's downfall because the urge to get to the top, to gain an advantage by any means possible, is so strong that it ruptures whatever moral restraints may have been in place, it drives people to do evil things. But changing it requires people to stand back and question something that intuitively feels good. People at the bottom of the hierarchy can tell when a superior enjoys pushing them around but the real problem lies in getting the superior to see his motivation. He won't believe it. He will find endless excuses as to why he should act the way he does because he perceives every objection as another challenge to his higher status, and reacts accordingly.

3.5: Conclusion: The challenge of human biology.

To summarise, humans are no different from any other animal in that we need to breed to survive, and success in breeding depends on competing for a mate. Testosterone, the hormone needed for success in the sexual competition, is also necessary in any other sort of competition. Winning produces a surge of testosterone which feels great; flush with the hormone, the winner stamps around, looking for other opportunities to prove how amazing he is, looking for the chance to put men down and get all the women for himself, seeing challenges which he then refuses to ignore. For a hormonally-charged male animal, there is no such thing as a minor challenge, or something that can be overlooked, or the other side being silly or making a mistake. Every potential challenge to his authority must be crushed by overwhelming force, and the opponent either taught a lesson he won't forget, or destroyed. Testosterone closes the options, closes the mind. But of course, each new challenge produces a further hormonal response, always ratcheting up but never down.

On the political field, that translates into always wanting more, of swaggering around issuing challenges, as Clinton did, which the other side see as threats to which they must respond firmly or suffer humiliation. But humiliation hurts so they respond in kind (as they are entitled to do) and so the spiral into yet another unnecessary fight gets under way. All because we can convince ourselves that yes, God is on our side so it's reasonable to attack somebody who won't do what we want. Without a moment's thought, we are sure that they should submit even though we wouldn't do it ourselves, and even though, as a question of biology, we are all acting at the level of dogs in the street, snarling and squabbling to sort out who's boss.

References:

1. McLaren N (2012). Testing the Biocognitive Model: Testosterone and the Challenge Hypothesis. Chapter 8 in *The Mind-Body Problem Explained: The Biocognitive Model for Psychiatry*. Ann Arbor, MI: Future Psychiatry Press.

2. Wingfield JC, Hegner RE, Dufty AM, Ball GF (1990). The 'Challenge Hypothesis': Theoretical implications for patterns of testosterone secretion, mating systems and breeding strategies. *Amer. Naturalist* 36: 829-846.

3. Milgram S (1974) *Obedience to Authority: An Experimental View*. Republished: New York/Harper Perennial, 2009.

Chapter 4: The idea of control.

If you want a picture of the future, imagine a boot stamping on a human face— forever.

George Orwell

4.1: That's not narcissism, that's show business.

In the first chapter, we looked at the psychology of self-centredness, the idea that I am so fascinating and so important that everybody should pay exclusive attention to Magnificent Me. We also touched briefly on the role of fear in shaping human behaviour. For narcissists, the greatest fear is being seen as boring and insignificant because, deep down, this is what they believe of themselves. In the second chapter, we considered the concept of fascism, which emerges when a number of powerful innate human drives combine as one political force. These primitive drives are universal, the essential features that define us as the creatures we are. First is the social drive, then the urge to form dominance hierarchies, and third is xenophobia, fear of The Other. In fact, this fear most often takes the form of hatred, the third leg of the four that implement tribalism, the last being territoriality. The social drive, the drive to dominate, xenophobia and territoriality. These are the ingredients of tribalism. Fascism is tribalism on a grand scale, but that is all. It has no deeper intellectual content; it is show, and show only. In Chapter 3, we looked at the biology of dominance, the underlying physiology of our apparently insatiable urge to organise ourselves into hierarchies, with me at the top and you down below, doing as I tell you.

In this chapter, I want to start to bring these ideas together, to show how these three ideas merge, producing a mania to control our fellow humans and our environment to our individual advantage. Lurking behind this positive drive is its reciprocal, the fear of losing control and being seen to be nothing.

By itself, narcissism is of no more significance than any other abnormal personality. If the woman down the street wants to join the local repertory club, and spends all her housekeeping money on clothes and hair styles, that's up to her and her family. Similarly, if the young man at work buys an old V8 car and spends all his money on expensive accessories for it, that's his problem, not mine. Difficulties arise when the narcissist gets ideas above her station and takes control of the repertory club so other people leave, or he steals money from work to pay for an extravagant sound system for his dream car. However, these are local issues, the society can contain them. It becomes a matter for the larger society when the narcissist manages to get control of a political party, or a large company which affects millions of people, or even a government, because the true narcissist is not there for the good of the party, or the company or the people. Instead, the narcissist is there for Number One, and looking after Number One requires control of Numbers Two, Three and so on, all the way down to the last soul in the country. But for Numero Uno to sleep well at night, secure in his sense of control, it follows that he also needs to get rid of any competition before it develops.

The essence of the narcissist is self-obsession. The actual mechanism by which this is put into effect is by control of the environment: if you want somebody to pay attention to you, you must find a way of controlling that person to make it happen. Initially, this means control of the immediate social environment, then the larger scene, then the natural environment as well. Do you want him to look at you? Fine, well you just have to be more interesting than the football match on TV. You want the crowd to look at you? You need to put on a star performance, keep them interested, keep them paying, keep them coming back. More to the point, you have to keep in front of the competition, and that's hard work. But there is a limit to how long you can fascinate the crowds; a new generation will arrive that isn't interested in the entertainers their parents adored, the kids want something new. Narcissists in some fields of religion discovered the answer to that thousands of years ago: keep 'em terrified. Politicians have long done the same, but they both seemed to have discovered the ultimate solution at about the same time: if you want the nation's undivided attention, you simply order everybody to watch and listen, leaving dissenters to the secret police.

All is grist to the narcissistic mills. Everything that can be done to reflect the glory of the Great Actor or Great Sportsman or Great Leader will be done, because the tantrums of frustrated Greats know no bounds. Henry Mencken said puritanism is the haunting fear that someone, somewhere, may be happy, but narcissism is the haunting fear that someone, somewhere, may not be paying attention, with the emphasis on fear. It starts by trying to attract attention; next step is to demand attention, and finally the Grand Narcissist orders people to pay attention under threat of punishment. Narcissism and what is now known as 'control freakery' go hand in hand; all that varies is how the control is exerted, and how intensely. A genuinely talented narcissist may try to keep his audience by doing better and better, but even talent has its limits, and somebody else may be better at it still.

Much more commonly, the narcissist reaches his or her limits; the fans demand more; it isn't forthcoming so they drift off, leaving the performer in a state of permanent frustration. They then turn to alcohol or drugs, weird religions or even weirder psychologies and carry on driving their families mad. So, you say, isn't that just Hollywood? Indeed, it's axiomatic that show business attracts narcissists, and as long as their affliction stays in Tinseltown, no harm will come, but it doesn't. Unstable and impressionable teenagers take the drama seriously and try to model their lives on it, even to the point of copycat suicides. It would be far better for parents and schools and everybody to impress upon the young that they shouldn't believe a word that comes out of show business. If that works, good, but there's another form of show business which attracts narcissists in droves, where they reign supreme, where they cannot be reined in and they do real damage to very large numbers of people just because every word they utter is taken as gospel. I refer, of course, to that ancient branch of show business known as religion.

4.2: That's not narcissism, that's religion.

The core of organised religion, any religion, is control, as in: "God in His eternal wisdom gave you free will but if you exercise it, you're in serious trouble." Before salvation, before deliverance comes the catechism: You must believe this, you must practice just this and nothing else or punishment will surely come your way. In the past in

Western countries, and in distressingly many others today, punishment meant just that: a quick death if you were lucky, the torture chamber followed by a bonfire if you weren't. Why is religion so violent? Why does it matter whether I face east or west at dawn, or eat beef on Friday or prawns soused in gin on Saturday or work on Sunday or, indeed, whether I believe anything you say at all? Surely it is a matter for me and the divinity? No, it never is. Religion is about humans controlling other humans, and the more absolute the religion, the more absolute the control. And religion is, and always has been, about show business. It is about impressing the oiks in the pews to shell out more money, or more labour, or more of their sons and daughters, anything, for the greater glory of the divinity and his (never her) emissary on earth, the pope or caliph or grand panjundrum or whoever it is this week. So there are always two faces to the divinity, love and hate, joy and rage, the happy-clappy show business and the iron hand of control, the pastures green and the sulphurous pits. Janus was heading in the right direction, both of them at once.

Now this is a bit of a problem because most, maybe all, great religions started with a simple message delivered by a rather gentle soul who wasn't much interested in power games. Indeed, most prophets spent their careers sitting under trees, while not a few have even ended dangling from one. Not for them soaring cathedrals and mighty temples nor, begowned in gold-shot robes and jewel-encrusted crowns, supping from silverplate with kings and presidents. Most religions are about leading a quiet, kindly and sober life, treating everybody fairly, not cheating or philandering, and laying off the plunder, rape and murder. Somewhere, somehow, it all changes; forgiveness and humility lose their appeal and the masses look longingly at where the Golden Calf last appeared. Gradually, the Sermon on the Mount transmogrifies into the horrors of the Inquisition, or the Prophet's message of treating other religions with respect becomes videos of ISIS beheading people on a beach. Far from opposing plunder, rape and murder, priests in uniform bless armies; many even had armies of their own.

How religion changes, why it changes, would be a major study in its own right but I will suggest it happens when people of a narcissistic bent realise that there are great opportunities to be exploited, and they move in. Narcissists will never be the first to enlist in a new religion as poverty and martyrdom have limited appeal to them. Wealth, power and glory are more their scene. In Christianity, perhaps this happened as late as when Constantine made it the state religion and bestowed great lands and wealth on his favourites, or perhaps it was earlier, that they had already impressed him with their knack of separating the poor from their pennies. In any event, over the centuries, churches became wealthier, more corrupt and more brutal; the paths of equality turned into marble staircases of power; their buildings slowly changing from places of quiet worship to palaces designed to awe the masses and to reflect the glory of the crimson-robed princes within: had he been offered, would the Nazarene have worn scarlet gowns and lace? But when it comes to a struggle, as eventually it must, the flamboyant and self-indulgent will be pushed aside by the coldly efficient plotters. In time, show business becomes just plain business.

Over the centuries, Christianity in its many forms has turned into a very large and successful conglomerate with a sideline in exploiting children. Almost unnoticed, it has abandoned the battles against wealth and violence, focussing its efforts on what are now called the culture wars, the subtle process of elevating trivial doctrinal squabbles to furious battles of life and death which distract attention from real life and death. Today, the church has very little to say about mass murder, as long as it is done over there by our armies, and not over here by their irregulars. Thus, the new US President, Mr Biden, an observant Catholic, was refused Communion by his parish priest in DC because he did not take a public stand against abortion. Had the priest refused the Sacrament to the many military men, both serving and veterans, who attended the same church, on the basis of their being merchants of mass murder, then he would very soon have found himself serving a parish on the Yukon.

But these days, the established churches are not where the excitement is; for that, we must cross the road to where the ecstatic franchises are rapidly building their empires. Lacking the rigid hierarchy of the two thousand year old branches, the charismatics of evangelical and pentecostal Christianity are building their own, a hierarchy of success. While most of their preachers have had some form of ecclesiastical training, it amounts to very little as all must compete in the open market to win a flock, not by godliness but by their performance. What the pentecostals have learned from the establishment is that their regular offering of repetitious sermons punctuated by ancient hymns wheezing in chill and echoing halls isn't winning the hearts and minds it used to. It is no longer simply a matter of parishioners arriving at their usual church to meet the new minister or priest sent by the Archbishop, as though the building is more important to them than the reverend gentleman; instead, evangelicals have adopted the Hollywood approach that, just as people would choose to hear a particular singer, so they will choose to hear a particular preacher. But, like a pop singer, he has to tailor his message to his audience; if they don't like his style, they will go elsewhere. He must speak to them in a way that satisfies them, in words they want to hear. In the ultra-competitive market of today's hi tempo, upbeat Christianity, the *style* of Christ's earthly messengers is now more important than Christ's message.

People no longer go to Church to wallow in guilt, to be warned they are miserable sinners and need to mend their ways before they get a one-way ticket downstairs. They don't want to sit on cold, hard pews guiltily sniffing hints of sulphur while listening to a distant man droning on about the wages of sin and masturbation. No, they go to be thrilled with the idea that they are special to God; that they are of the anointed and glory awaits them while all the bad people (yes, even the relatives they don't like) are already marked for the big meat grinder. The central message of Christianity, eloquently summarised in the ten brief verses known as the Beatitudes [10,] has somehow been lost in the hubbub of modern megachurches. People no longer want to hear about camels and eyes of needles, or being kind to widows and orphans. Instead, they want to jump up and down, to shout and sing and babble and weep while a prancing floodlit figure on a distant stage shrieks over a vast PA system that they are special and unique in God's eyes and they alone are the beloved of God.

The essence of new Christian revivalism is the suspension of the Christ's message of love, humility and respect for the other and its replacement by an ultra-tribal notion of 144,000 Chosen People. As promised in Revelations [11], only these will survive while the rest of us

---

[10] Matthew 5: 3-12. A somewhat different version appears at Luke 6: 20-26 but the message of kindly restraint and humility is the same.

[11] Revelations 7: 4: "And I heard the number of them which were sealed: and there were sealed an hundred and forty and four thousand of all the tribes of the children of Israel." This meant 12,000 from each of the twelve tribes of Israel except it probably just means "a lot." However, to literalists, that is the exact number who will be chosen from all the people who have lived since Pentecost, in AD35. Considering there are about 200 million Pentecostalists in the world, the odds are not looking good. Rev. 14: 3-4 adds that they will all be celibate males

will be cast into the Lake of Fire for eternity. This "interpretation" of Christianity assembles a hierarchy of worthies (the 144,000) and loathes and despises the rest; it sees itself as perfect and chosen, and all others, willfully wicked and condemned, as the enemy. It licenses greed, domination, selfishness, individualism, abandonment of community and even of family. It is used to justify destruction and despoliation of the natural environment. And a fringe benefit of being chosen means never having to bother with loving your enemies because they're doomed anyway. All you have to do is recognise them as satanic agents and you're free to hate them as much as you like. In one word, people go to luxuriate in the endlessly-repeated message of utter selfishness.

Suitably worked up, they are delighted to hand over large sums of money to pay for their entertainment. And who are the greatest performers? Narcissists, of course, but the whole thing is a gigantic confidence trick. Narcissistic preachers are daily pulling in untold millions just by delivering a message of reverse narcissism. Instead of the congregation worshipping God, they are told God actually pays attention to them. Yes, they are told, the Lord dotes on you, which is exactly what the worried, insecure or unhappy denizens of suburbia desperately want to hear: You're great, you're wonderful; No, you're not boring and insignificant, you're special in God's eyes so you can go home feeling hyped up and important (in Megachurch speak, inspired), you're forgiven (stop feeling guilty about all the stupid things you've done) and keep doing God's work (meaning do whatever you like and never feel guilty as long as you come back next week). By the way, I need a new private jet so be sure y'all slip a bit more into the collection plate.

Predictably, today's self-appointed heirs of Martin Luther, who rebelled against the venal, sybaritic (and syphilitic) Church of Rome, lead lives of breath-taking self-indulgence and immorality for, as Eric Hoffer noted, "Every great cause begins as a movement, becomes a business and eventually degenerates into a racket" [1]. To see the racket in action, there are dozens of TV channels showing hundreds of preachers working their gigs day and night, pulling in the loot by the truckload, thereby adding new depths of meaning to the word "shameless."

---

who have never told lies, which appears to exclude Pentecostalist preachers on both counts but you never hear that bit.

Of course, their message is multifaceted, it's not just about money. A big part of the appeal lies in what is known as dominionism, a doctrine which appears to anchor the concept of domination centre-stage in the Judeo-Christian tradition:

> Genesis 1:28: And God blessed them, and God said unto them, "Be fruitful, and multiply, and replenish the earth, and subdue it: and have dominion over the fish of the sea, and over the fowl of the air, and over every living thing that moveth upon the earth."

This is taken as authorising humans to use the world with no restraint, which is more or less how it has been in the past. However, it goes further. It has been used to justify Christians of a particular inclination taking control of government and then using their power to enforce their ideas of sin and human failings on the rest of the world, the idea being to eliminate all sin as a major step on the path to the Second Coming. All of these ideas swirl in the furnaces of right wing ideology, especially in the US, blurring, merging and demerging with the most virulent brands of racist, capitalist, supremacist politics until all that unites these diverse movements is their burning ambition to dominate other human beings, i.e. the central theme of fascism. And that is how they define their enemies. Egalitarians, who oppose the idea that one group of people has an inalienable right and duty to dominate others, are the true enemy. *Homo tyrannicus* immediately knows his *irreconcilable* enemy is *Homo pacificus*. This is how, during the January 6th attack in Washington, DC, we saw placards reading "Jesus Saves" held aloft next to Nazi, white supremacist and other hate-filled symbols [12]. Donald Trump actively fostered and enabled Christian fascism, not because he is Christian but because he is fascist by inclination. Intuitively, he feels an affinity with the inner fascist in every heretical Christian, the sense of kindred souls that he never felt with the urban elite of the North-East US, who despise him. Christian fascists

---

[12] How can they work together? Partly, they submerge their differences in pursuit of a common enemy, as the Western nations did in World War II when they allied themselves with their formerly mortal enemy, the USSR. However, I suspect they all believe that once they have eliminated their common enemy, the tolerant, internationalist egalitarians, they will be able to take over the movement themselves, perhaps via a divinely-sanctioned "night of the long knives." For fundamentalist Christians, "dominion over every living thing that moveth upon the earth" extends to the 7billion non-Christians on earth. And Catholics, of course.

and white supremacist fascists are *reconcilable* enemies, at least temporarily.

If right wing religious politics were just a vast pyramid scheme where all the money finds its way to the top and disappears, then there would be no harm but it doesn't stop there. The crucial point of *any* narcissistic show business is that the crowds will always want more. And more. Yesterday's message no longer sends the same shivers down the spine since, like booze and all the other fun things in life, its effect wears off. It has to be spiced up. It was no longer enough to tell the flock that God loves them; they had to be told that He will show his love by making them rich because that's what He does, He sends gifts to his favourite children [13]. If people are rich, the breathless punters are told, it proves they are favoured by God. "All you poor people will just have to work harder but if you send me $10, you'll get $20 back next week. Do you doubt me?" the preacher thunders. "It's in the Bible, do you doubt God's word?" The sad and lonely, the insecure and easily intimidated, the vague and uncertain shudder and, to prove they don't doubt the Lord's word, slip in an extra $5. This heretical reworking of the Christian gospel is called prosperity gospel, and it has a strong following among poor people with no job and not much education. Trouble is, even that is no longer working (meaning it no longer attracts people with spare money in their pockets) so charismatic preachers have found a new line to sell, conspiracy.

More and more, preachers are supercharging their sermons with the news that The Evil One is everywhere, he never sleeps, his agents are prowling your street, watching your house right now. "Yes, brothers and sisters," the sweating preacher whispers hoarsely, "these are surely the End Times. The signs are everywhere, the plague is visited upon us, the enemy is everywhere. Government has been taken over by unbelievers, you can see it in their eyes, there is no evil too debased for them to force on God's chosen people. The virus is a communist hoax, the vaccinations are to turn y'all into zombies or to insert tracking devices, masks are to stop you recognising Satan's agents. They want your soul," he screeches, "your children's souls, especially children, yes it's true, they want your children to indulge their sick and satanic appetites, their evil animal lusts, and when they have finished, when

---

[13]   The Matthew Effect, after a misreading of Matthew 25:29. "For unto every one that hath shall be given, and he shall have abundance: but from him that hath not shall be taken away even that which he hath."

their foul sulphurous seed has penetrated your children's souls and they too have been captured, they will sacrifice them and drink their blood and then your beloved children will be reborn as Satan's agents, and they will be damned forever. So love your nation, hate homosexuals and vote for Trump /Bolsonaro /Kyszinski /General Ovumbo etc," whom God has appointed as his personal warrior to lead the army of the righteous on earth.

Theatrical? Yes, deliberately so, but insecure and unhappy people can easily be frightened into believing it. What is happening is that the heretical Christian cult known as prosperity gospel is melding with the ultra-right, white nationalist (i.e. fascist) cult known as QAnon. This movement played a large part in the January 6th insurrection against the US Capitol building after Trump was defeated in the 2020 election. The most far-fetched, the most ridiculous and frankly insane conspiracies pushed by the most unhinged rabid ultranationalists have now metastasised to, have infected and infested, the evangelical and pentecostalist churches. An extremist political movement which ordinarily would mean a spell in a strait jacket is finding new converts among the holy jumpers. This message of fear and hate whips the crowds to a frenzy, they are shouting and screaming in artfully-induced terror, throwing money at the preacher so he can continue God's work and save their children and their nation.

But again, who cares? So the religious crackpots and the political crackpots are in bed together? Society can cope with a few more Jonestown Massacres. The last one didn't slow things down, it didn't convince presidents to keep away from lunatic preachers or stop preachers fleecing the poor and gullible, so another half dozen won't change much. What does matter, though, is that the ultra-right wing churches (an oxymoron) believe they are on a mission from God to spread the word through the world. They believe that by proselytising, they can store up loyalty points in heaven, so that's what they do. Financed by the fortunes skimmed from the poor and a few gullible and/or deranged wealthy patrons, evangelicals and pentecostalists are actively spreading their message all over the world. Wherever there is despair or fear, poverty or disease, in Africa, Latin America, Asia, there you will find evangelical missionaries beating the drums of hate and intolerance: "Yes, brothers and sisters, we are in the End Times now, the signs are everywhere, the enemy is everywhere. Government has been taken over by unbelievers, you can see it in their eyes, the virus is a hoax, there is no evil too debased for them to force on God's chosen people, they want your soul blah blah…" When a white man goes into a black slum, say in Kenya or Nigeria, and starts spouting this sort of stuff, people believe him. Why should they not? Would a white man lie to black people?

The same sort of message is spreading in the Muslim world via groups such as ISIS and Boko Haram; in India via the fascist Hindu organisation, Rashtriya Swayamsevak Sangh, long-term patrons of Mr Modi, and in many other places: "Beware, the enemy is inside our citadel, he is the stranger in your street, the woman who mutters to herself, the child with white skin and hair. The enemy is The Other and God wants you to destroy his enemies." So they do. As wars spread, as the effects of climate change spread, then fear will spread. Where seeds of fear take root, the opportunists, the scoundrels and the crackpots are waiting, ready to harvest the fruits of hate. And that is very, very dangerous. End Times? More like Dangerous Times.

4.3: That's not narcissism, that's the military.

In 1975, the mighty US military was defeated by men wearing sandals made from rubber tyres. Despite the overwhelming firepower and technology derived from their vast military-industrial complex, the US Army ducked and ran; the armadas in air and sea picked up their bits and pieces and scuttled home to lick their wounds. Of course, it wasn't defeat, it was Peace with Honour, although peace was slow coming to Vietnam, and honour did nothing to fill the bomb craters, the empty stomachs or the empty limb and eye sockets. Just this week, after twenty years, the US military literally turned off the lights at their gigantic Bagram Base in Afghanistan and, without telling anybody, flew off into the night. When the locals realised there was nobody home, they quickly broke in and began looting the Forbidden City until chased out by the Afghan military, who are no mean looters themselves.

What, you may ask, does this have to do with narcissism? With fascism? With dominance? Everything, but often the threads don't seem to be connected, or perhaps people just prefer not to see them. Every culture has its mythology, and most of it involves soldiers and fighting. The military is so much part of life that we don't even notice the utterly bizarre premise on which it is based:

Q: Why do we have an army?
A: Because everybody else has one.

Armies are horrendously expensive, with military activity costing the world something like $13 trillion a year, not to mention the incalculable heartache from the deaths and human destruction armies wreak, so why do we put up with them? Because everybody else has one. End of story.

The most fundamental imperative in our lives is that we are social animals. That much is hard-wired in us, probably mediated by fear of separation on the one hand and a strongly positive, hormone-mediated sense of comfort and security when surrounded by kith and kin. As soon as we form a little group, we identify ourselves with the group, mentally and physically, via songs, badges and flags. We can see it very clearly in children, we actually encourage it. In adults, it takes a slightly different form as the picture is camouflaged by our tendency to believe pleasant lies about ourselves. The second imperative is our need to dominate each other. No sooner have we formed a group than we sort ourselves into a dominance hierarchy. The third imperative is xenophobia, fear of the other, which all too often morphs into hatred, and the fourth is territoriality. Of these four imperatives tribes are born.

The first thing a tribe does is try to dominate the neighbouring tribes. This is innate: the urge to dominate has such a powerful biological basis that we don't question it, it is self-evident and satisfying, like keeping warm, choosing tasty food and avoiding bad smells. Nobody who is fighting his way up a hierarchy ever stops to ask why he is doing it. He is doing it because, as we all know, higher feels better, it is its own reward. Granted, a few mimsy priests like to mutter about equality, fairness and forgiveness and all that, but tell me the last time equality won a war?

Only the most determined get to the top but, once there, the winner doesn't ask: "Do we really need this pomp and paraphernalia? It's all a bit silly, let's get rid of most of it." That almost never happens. For years, reaching the top has been his goal and his purpose so, having made it, he owns the pomp and ceremony. Now it has become the sign of his supremacy, he will never get rid of the trappings of power just because he wants people to see and marvel at him. The hierarchy has become a reality that gives his life meaning, it *is* his life. Without his status, who is he? Strip away the charger or the limousine, the big chair, the hat and braid, the palace with fanfares echoing through grand chambers, and what is he? All too often, he is nothing. His obsessive quest to force his way to the top was driven only by the need to have people sing his praises, to bathe in their regard, to wallow in their adoration. In the narcissist, the two drives, to dominate for domination sake, and to seen on top for the sake of being on top, fuse. As a combination, they are all but unbeatable; but, as mentioned before, when it comes to a struggle, as eventually it must, the flamboyant and self-indulgent always lose to ruthless plotters.

If we watch a military parade, we see squads of fit young men stepping briskly past, ramrod straight (itself a military metaphor), every boot and arm swinging in tight unison, weapons glinting, flags fluttering, bands thumping, engines throbbing and jets screaming overhead, but what is it for? Does the spectacle serve a military purpose? Indirectly, it does, it helps weld the motley collection of recruits into a unit, gives them a role and function, a place and relations so they feel part of the larger whole. They swell to fill their boots and hats, their chests expand to fill their tunics, they feel stronger and more self-assured, more in control, more powerful. That is, they feel more powerful than they are, more inclined to react aggressively to challenges or threats; through their shared sense of power, they feel the urge to dominate, which is what a hierarchy is all about. It is about exerting dominance, and dominance is mediated by testosterone, so anything that gets it pumping will boost the sense of dominance. That's what the general wants, he doesn't want his men scattering at the first sight of the enemy, it would reflect badly on the him and would kill his post-service career as a lobbyist.

Over thousands of years, the military have perfected the art of pomp and circumstance, of making skinny, wobbly recruits stand tall and proud. Nothing is left to chance. Everything is designed to make them feel better about themselves, everything they wear, the colours, the sounds and smells, every movement, every barked order, every tone of voice is honed to get the feel-good masculine hormone working overtime. Marching behind a band, crowds cheering does it, it makes the troops feel better about themselves and as a result, feel superior to civilians. The other part is that watching his army swing past makes even the general's elderly blood flow again, his sagging flesh feels tougher; it makes him feel stronger and so much more important. Of course, it has exactly the same effect on politicians, especially if they had no military service themselves (as most don't, they're not stupid).

Needless to say, none of them know this. Nobody in the military knows anything about hormonal feedback loops or Challenge Hypotheses, and they wouldn't care to be told. All they know is what the lowliest private knows: that a parade through the city with the girls waving and cheering is much more fun than playing a lonely video game in a chilly house in the distant suburbs, or driving a delivery truck through a rainy night. Over thousands of years, the business of war has been honed to its essentials, of fooling young men into thinking they're tougher and more important than they are.

We don't question any of this. We watch the Coldstream Guards marching along in their bright red tunics and towering bearskin helmets, and what's it for? To impress, that's all. The uniform has no functional value whatsoever but it makes the troops feel good about themselves, makes ladies' hearts swell, impresses men and thrills politicians. If we told one of the Guards to go to the beach alone, to march up and down dressed in full regimental regalia, he would refuse as he would know immediately he would look ridiculous and pointless. But if it's ridiculous in one setting, it's ridiculous in all, even though not always pointless. The point of a uniform lies in its name: uniform, meaning one-ness: I'm part of the group and together we're powerful. It builds a sense of superiority, strengthens the hierarchy. Imagine the same squad ambling along in their underwear and bare feet; even armed, would they have the same impact? Not at all, onlookers would laugh and turn away leaving the troops feeling humiliated, painfully conscious of their loss of status. In a dominance hierarchy, status is all.

The ideal of the handsome young soldier is universal, every mother's son looks great in uniform. It is true of every culture at every age in every country around the world: men decorate themselves so they can dominate on the field of war. They do not decorate themselves to plough a field on the farm, to take the fishing boat out or to stand at the factory bench. Instead, workers mock men who over-dress: show-off, skite, attention-seeker, they will say, and push him away, excluding him from their group. But that is because they are actually on the same level and they resent anybody trying to elevate himself by overdressing. They don't want anybody appearing to look down on them, so drably-garbed workmen are the exception that proves the rule.

In fact, every hierarchy does the same. Academics dress themselves in gorgeous gowns and silly hats to elevate themselves over mere students. Judges wear crimson robes with lace gorgets and archaic wigs to convey the limitless power and reach of the law, intimidating and belittling the shackled defendants who, increasingly, are dressed in bright orange clown suits. The American "perp walk," where a harmless businessman is led out in handcuffs, serves only to humiliate. The Nazi judge, Roland Friesler, was an expert in this. He ordered that all defendants in his courts be given overlarge trousers and no belt, so they spent their time in the dock trying to hold their pants up. This gave the ghoulish Friesler the chance to mock them before sentencing them to death. Priests, of course, have wardrobes of elaborate costumes but nobody does it as well as the military. Soldiers cover themselves with badges, braids, medals and ribbons known as ... decorations. They decorate themselves with pretty but useless things designed for self-inspiration, to make them feel proud and inspired by the heroic vision of themselves so they will go to battle charged with testosterone. As Napoleon said "All men are enamored of decorations . . . they positively hunger for them." If nothing else, it makes for more beautiful corpses.

The Nazi Party took military uniforms and regalia to the level of an art form in its own right. *Triumph of the Will*, Leni Riefenstahl's remarkable documentary of the 1934 party congress at Nuremberg, shows the breath-taking attention to detail in the service of boosting the unrestrained militarism of the new German government [14]. For the downtrodden and unemployed, the celebration of mythic masculinity promised heaven on earth. The individual, as Riefenstahl showed, is lost in a sea of uniforms, submerged in the aura of power: Come and join us, it says, all you who are lonely and despair. Bring your sense of high drama and your lust for power, or just your insecurity and your need to feel wanted, our tent has room for all. Borne down by a sense of persecution, or just itching to smash your enemies? We're your men, so bring the excitable and those enthralled by mythology, come one come all but no Marxists, queers or weaklings.

As propaganda, her documentary remains unmatched even today, an astounding mating of the human lusts for power and glory producing a frightening exercise in national discipline. For discipline, read control. The Gestapo were watching every move.

---

[14]   The Nazi government had been in power barely eighteen months during which it had built the arena, produced uniforms for hundreds of thousands and resurrected the transport system, not to mention having enough toilets for all those people.

4.4: That's not narcissism, that's authority.

Authority, discipline, domination, control, these are aspects of the same thing, a small group of people exerting power over the larger mass. The sense of being in control is important to all of us, we don't like to feel dominated, powerless or ignored. One of the slogans central to the Brexit campaign, the rush job to drag Britain out of the European Union, was: "Take back control. Our money, our borders, our laws." This, of course, was arrant nonsense, a patent falsehood because it implied that the UK had no control over its destiny in the EU. As the second biggest economy in Europe, it had a much greater degree of control than the many minnows, such as Estonia or Malta. But it hit home: the mere suggestion that Britons were being told what to do by foreigners was enough to make them stampede to the ballot box to perform one of history's great exercises in cutting off your nose to spite your face. Now, having left the EU, Britain has lost a large measure of control over its destiny, and its financial position is worse but the Brexiteers are happy.

Why does their *faux* autonomy matter so much? Because while we all like to join with other humans, we also like to be in charge. Given its unequalled history of dominating lesser nations, Britain was deeply resentful of not being in charge, a case of "If we can't be boss, we're out." The late and purblind imperialists thought that by not being in charge (the EU is an egalitarian system), they were being dominated by ghastly continentals. So, against the wishes of the younger generations who would have inherited the EU, swarms of myopic elderly voters forced Brexit. We humans don't like feeling dominated and even in our dotage we like to dominate, which comes directly from the principles explained in Chapter 3. This is also true of the US which, after 75 years of being "Most powerful nation in the world," can't stomach sharing the podium with China as "Equal most powerful nation in human history." In his first State of the Union speech, former president Barack Obama said "I do not accept second place for the United States of America." This was echoed by Mr Biden, addressing Congress in April 2021, who said: "We're in competition with China and other countries to win the 21st Century." The fact that the US is now far richer and more powerful than it was even twenty years ago doesn't register. What counts is their *sense* of being strongest, of looking down on everybody else.

In Chapter 1, I clarified that narcissism is a personality disorder, and personality disorder is not mental illness in any sense of the term. Personality is a set of rules but, because there are so many rules involved, all of which arose in unique circumstances, no two personalities are alike – fortunately. A person can score high on narcissism, meaning a lot of his rules of life are directed at self-promotion, or low, meaning he prefers to avoid attention. I described the psychopathic personality as heartless, self-serving, unable to form stable relationships based in mutual respect, dishonest, manipulative and possibly aggressive but very, very controlling. Again, people can have few psychopathic traits, in which case we'd say they're normal, or lots so that psychopathic behaviour dominates their lives. Two other traits we need to mention are obsessionality and paranoid thinking.

Obsessionality means attention to detail. The obsessional person wants everything in order, done by the book, tidy, on time and put away afterwards. A place for everything and everything in its place, as they say. They want the rules followed precisely, the clock controls everything; cleanliness, tidiness and efficiency are their bywords. They abhor waste of any sort and will often horde material "just in case." Ideally, meaning if they can control things, they want everything done by a ritual; if it isn't done their way, they'll insist on doing it again. But what drives this? Disorder frightens them. They believe everything must be under total control otherwise some sort of trouble will erupt and their world will fall apart. Even though most won't admit it, they fear trouble of any sort because they fear being held responsible, of being blamed when things go wrong. Thus they spend their lives fussing over the most trivial or even imaginary detail, making sure nothing can go wrong, all directed at making sure they don't get into trouble. Trouble terrifies them, they feel they have no defence. The thought of saying to somebody: "If you don't like the way I did it, do it yourself," sends them into a panic and makes them redouble their efforts to get everything under control.

Unfortunately, the world doesn't control very easily, so they often retreat, mark out a small territory (home, the office or bench at work, a garden or hobby) and put all their obsessionality into it. Some, however, aren't content with just a small zone of control, they have to manage everything and everybody. These are the control freaks, the person at work or in the club who insists you follow his way, who demands to be in charge of everything just to make sure nothing can possibly go wrong. But control is self-reinforcing, it feels good so people are never satisfied with "a measure of control," they want the lot. Obsessional people tend to join clubs, groups or companies and, as they like fussing around and can be trusted to get the job done with no bits unfinished, they quickly get themselves into positions of power. Trouble is, once they have a measure of power, they start to make everybody's life miserable. Often, they are destructive in that if things aren't going the way they want them, they become irate and start yelling and threatening people. They are killjoys. Humour exasperates them, partly because they have no way of controlling a comic, no way of stopping people laughing, but also because they don't get jokes. In their dull, pedantic and literal way, they just don't get jokes: "But why would anybody leave the keys in his car? That's silly, I don't get it."

As the obsessional personality becomes more extreme, the need to control takes control, as it were, the need to dominate for domination's sake slips into the driving seat. The true obsessional is cold, humourless, obsessed with rules and detail to the point of mania, and controlling. Sometimes it's passive-aggressive control, others it's fullblown, destructive and endless rage over the paper cup left on the desk. At the extreme, the destructive bit is overwhelming; the anankastic personality, as it is known, is completely incapable of seeing that screaming at a small child (or hitting them savagely, as was the case years ago) over a spilled glass achieves nothing. In the old days, it seemed that every school principal was anankastic, every sports master, in fact most teachers. Certainly, there were plenty of church ministers and priests who filled the bill, as were a lot of the bitter old nurses left over from World War II.

Authority, discipline, domination, control. Some dominate because they are terrified of getting into trouble, others because they want to dominate, they actually get a kick out of ordering people around or having people frightened of them. It feels good, but the worst thing for them is the thought that somebody could dominate them, so they are constantly watching for threats, they worry what people are thinking or planning, they don't trust because they never know who's up to what. This is paranoid thinking, of which the old German psychiatrists recognised five themes:

1. An intense preoccupation with justice and vengeance;

2. An intense preoccupation with the supernatural;

3. An intense preoccupation with conspiracies;

4. An intense preoccupation with persecution;

5. Intense jealousy.

Now intense means intense. I know that these days, everybody uses the word "extremely" to mean "somewhat, quite a lot, more than I want," but it actually means "at the limits of human experience; the point beyond which there is no return." You should use "extremely" extremely rarely. Similarly, intense doesn't mean "a fair bit, more than me." It means "dominates the mental life to the exclusion of rational thought; at a level rarely seen; unjustified." People who misuse "intensely" are intensely annoying.

The word "paranoid" is an adjective, it describes our mental set and behaviour but there is no such *thing* as paranoia. We are all paranoid to some extent, we have to be because things can go wrong and we have to be prepared for trouble. But this can reach the point where a person shows a paranoid personality disorder, meaning mental life is dominated by one or more of the five themes listed above. It is normal for these people to show signs of all five variants but mostly, a particular one tends to control their thinking although it can change from week to week.

It is also possible for people to show a paranoid psychosis, in which the beliefs are manifestly false and outlandish but they won't budge and are enraged if anybody tries to show they are wrong. It is common for people to develop paranoid ideas, even hallucinations and delusions, due to drug intoxication such as cocaine and amphetamines, and in chronic alcoholism. The same thing can happen in brain damage or early dementia. The last feature on the list, jealousy, is more common than people think. Full-blown pathological jealousy is probably the most dangerous of all psychiatric syndromes but it is difficult to know where "normal" personality-based jealousy stops and delusional jealousy begins. Clearly, the paranoid disorders generate a lot of work – and angst—for psychiatrists.

It should be clear that there is overlap between the obsessional personality and the paranoid: they both want to be in control; they don't like anybody disagreeing with them; they are preoccupied with rules and procedures and want things done their way; but if anything goes wrong, it isn't their fault. There are many paths up the mountain called Control. In first place is the normal, hormonally-based human drive to dominate, definitely more pronounced in men than women but otherwise universal. This can be weakened by high levels of anxiety, which inhibits testosterone secretion, as in the anxious personality, or by chronic depression, of which anxiety is the most common cause. However, the urge to control can be intensified by personality traits, especially the narcissistic, obsessional, paranoid and the psychopathic. A person who has a high score on one abnormal trait is likely to have high scores on others. An obsessional person can be paranoid; psychopathic people tend to be both narcissistic and paranoid; the true paranoid is very narcissistic as they are unconcerned over how their behaviour impacts others, or may have no awareness that other people are entitled to a point of view. Narcissistic people are often psychopathic, they use people and discard them, they are often dishonest and manipulative, sexually aggressive, intensely controlling of people close to them, and vengeful. Fortunately, while narcissists can be controlling and psychopathic, it's often not for long; something else gets their attention and they rush off after it.

There has been a lot written about something called the authoritarian personality, especially in the period after World War II, which some people still believe was caused by a few deranged personalities. The problem is that most of that work was based in whole or in part on Freudian theories of psychoanalysis. As mentioned, this is now regarded as non-scientific but in any event, I am saying there is no single, unique category of personality called "Authoritarian." Personality is far too complex to be reduced to a single factor. Authoritarian *behaviour* can emerge from many different contributions, some in the individual, some in the society and some in circumstances. The notion that there is a "thing" called authoritarian personality encourages us to look for authoritarianism, which we always find in somebody else, not in ourselves.

My case is that, as the experiments by the psychologist, Stanley Milgram, showed as long ago as 1961, we all have the potential to act in an authoritarian manner, it is built into us. Similar experiments have been repeated and confirmed since but, to my mind, they were all a waste of time and money. We have ample evidence from real life to say that perfectly ordinary people will readily act in a cruel manner if encouraged or forced to do so, if they have the opportunity, if they think they can get away with it and, finally, if they feel like it. There have been enough variations on Milgram's theme, plus we have the evidence of the evening news, to leave no doubt on this point: the Authoritarian Personality, *c'est moi*.

People join political parties for all sorts of reasons. Some join just because they want to see certain changes in the society, such as better health or education services or more active conservation, or more laws to reduce crime and so on. Some join because they want to feel they belong to something big, they like the sense of being close to power, even if it's only folding newsletters for the local councillor. Others join because they believe the country is going to the dogs and it has to be stopped; some join for other reasons and some for all of the above. When it comes to extremist parties, meaning parties at the limit of political tolerance, certain reasons dominate, including the need to be in control, the need to gain attention, and the need to get even with other people.

By the vague breadth of its political program, fascist parties attract abnormal personalities, particularly those with an overdeveloped sense of persecution, those who love to control, and those who glorify in militarist and mythological memes. By definition, extremist parties attract extreme personalities who then use their particular talents to force their way to the top. An extremist party will only get worse, it can't recant and revert to a more moderate stance, which is exactly what we see in right wing parties the world over. But repression breeds extremism, as John F Kennedy observed:

> Those who make peaceful change impossible make violent change inevitable.

That is, if reasonable people are denied their fundamental human rights of security and of expression, then extremists will gradually take over their political movements and fight for them. This is what happened in Vietnam after World War II, when the legitimate national ambitions of that proud and independent people were frustrated by the Western colonial powers. Eventually, the highly organised Marxists took over and the rest is history. The same thing happened in Iran in 1953, after the moderate socialist government of Mohammed Mossadegh was overthrown by the British MI6 and the American CIA for daring to nationalise the Iranian oil industry. Under Shah Reza Pahlavi, a brutally-repressive right wing government was installed which took no notice of the wishes of the people until, as they always do, extremists overthrew it.

This problem has become a major destabilising factor throughout the world because, while mild-mannered centrist citizens were distracted by the Global Financial Crisis (GFC) and climate change and everything else, paranoid obsessionals and narcissists slipped in and took control of governments. They are now actively engaged in programs to entrench their control. As we saw in Washington on January 6th, extremists are most reluctant to follow the rules and cede power, just as John Dalberg-Acton, predicted:

> Power tends to corrupt, and absolute power corrupts absolutely. Great men are almost always bad men ... And remember, where you have a concentration of power in a few hands, all too frequently, men with the mentality of gangsters get control.

David Brin saw the same risk in the concentration of power, which is the essence of fascism:

> It is said that power corrupts, but actually it's more true that power attracts the corruptible. The sane are usually attracted by other things than power.

One of the defining elements in the paranoid personality is the indiscriminate and insatiable suspicion, the complete inability to take things at face value. For the paranoid, nothing is as it seems to be on the surface. Hidden from sight, he is convinced, are plots, and plots within the plots. Starting at the top, mistrust soaks through fascist movements like a miasma, contaminating everybody it touches. Since fascism needs enemies, the logical place to look for them is under the bed. Or at work, or in the neighbour's house, in the same platoon or on the same ship, at school and university, everywhere. The fascist doesn't doubt that there are enemies, that much is a given in his life; nor that those same enemies are planning a mischief, trying to bring the fascist party down because that's what enemies do. So no sooner does he form an alliance with a similarly-inclined person than he begins to worry what the new friend is up to: is he genuine or an agent of the Comintern, Satan, the Zionists, capitalists, Al-Qaeda, the masons, papists or whatever? There is no end to suspicion, it only ever ratchets up, not down, because the only way out is to admit that one was mistaken, apologise or laugh about it and get back to normal business.

For a committed narcissist, or paranoid, or psychopath or obsessional, admitting error is anathema.

But the problem is, anybody who looks for evidence of plots will find it. There are so many dots happening around us each day that we can connect them in any manner we like. For a person who believes randomness is real, then most little events can be dismissed as of no account; for a person looking for evidence of hidden enemies, the dots can always be connected in such a way as to reveal them. Pareidolia, the habit of finding patterns where none exist, as in seeing warriors or wombats striding across the starry skies, is the hallmark of the well-developed fascist state. Dominicans and Puritans searching for witches, OGPU and NKVD looking for traitors in the factories, McCarthy's crew ferreting out communists and sleepers, Mao's Red Guards finding capitalist roaders, evangelicals and Wahhabists looking for demonic tempters, suspicion is limited only by human ingenuity in digging up evidence to support an accusation.

The ultimate form of control is making sure nobody thinks independently, which is why the first people a new fascist dictatorship kills are the government they have overthrown, but the next lot are the comedians. Talking of repression, Orwell said:

> No spell, however potent, can withstand for long the assault of a sceptical reflection. That is why it is the sceptic and not the believer who is in the end our saviour.

Marked on the door to the local fascist party recruiting office is a sign: Sceptics need not apply. The ultimate state is not just where every citizen fears that the secret police may suspect him, but that his neighbour may and, through fear of not reporting a potential traitor, will report him.

4.5: Conclusion: The mania of control.

To summarise, personality is the vast and complex set of rules that govern how we think and thence our behaviour and our reactions to the world. Each of us has a personality, which means more or less what we believe is true of ourselves and the world, and how things should be done but a lot of this is only marginally conscious, if not outside awareness. Each person's rules can be sorted into clusters whose members are more like each other than like the members of another cluster. Depending on how they are sorted, we can have three, or five, or sixteen or dozens of clusters, each of which gets a name and allows somebody to build an academic career. We call these clusters "traits" and give them fancy names, usually Latin or Greek, which everybody misunderstands. What we must not do is reify those clusters, turn them into a "thing" in the head or talk about them as though they were real entities which exist somewhere. They don't, it is just a manner of speaking.

We all show the features of all clusters, the only difference being the extent. If one particular cluster dominates a person's behaviour, we will often say he is a _____ (fill in the blank) but that's actually wrong. There is no such 'thing' as, for example, a psychopath, it is just shorthand for saying he shows more psychopathic behaviour than is good for the rest of us. An obsessional is a person whose life is dominated by rules the rest of us prefer to ignore, while a narcissist is a person who hogs the limelight when we would like a bit of it ourselves.

The title of this book is Narcisso-Fascism, but it could equally have been "narcisso-obsessional-paranoid-psychopathic-fascism," because, in the mass or socio-political setting (as distinct from individual psychology), these personality types blur and run together. They resonate with the most basic human urges, to form societies, to build dominance hierarchies, to hoard stuff and to fear or hate everybody else, which combine to give us the social picture called tribalism. When translated into the political scene, tribalism assumes the form we call fascism but, at base, it is actually a confederacy of disordered personalities. In politics, fascism is the licence everybody has been waiting for, to drop their inhibitions and bring out their worst but in the service of a greater good, the tribe. Fascism is tribalism writ large, which is why, as Edgar Doctorow commented, "The right wing politician has less of a distance to go to exploit our tribal fears and hatreds than his opponent, who would engage our better selves." Each of the impulses we should keep under control, like dominating everybody in sight regardless of their needs, their wishes or their rights, is given a grandiosely sanitised name like "exceptionalism," or "bringing Christianity/ democracy/ modernism to the unenlightened," or the "international rules-based order," etc., when what it really means is "Might is right, so if you know what's good for you, you'd better do exactly as we say."

Fascism is not a single doctrine but is a set of elements that can be applied to any political movement, a bit like decorations that can be applied to any tree to make a Christmas tree. It is about that most intoxicating of drugs, power, meaning what to do to attract and retain followers, how to gain and keep power. Ultimately, fascism must fail. It consumes itself: if there are no enemies massing over the border, then they must be a hidden fifth column; if they've been wiped out, then there are traitors among us so we need a purge to burn them out of our midst. This has happened countless times in human history; Rome, France, the USSR, McCarthyism in the US, Mao's Cultural Revolution, the Khmer Rouge, Islamist Iran, Ruanda, Ethiopia, ISIS, on and on. It is not a weakness of that country, it is human. We all like to be in charge, we all like to do what we want to do and we want others to do things the way we like. *Le fasciste, c'est moi.* That is the danger.

References:

1. Hoffer E (1967) *The Temper of Our Time.* New York: Hopewell (2009)

Chapter 5: Facets of fascism.

Totalitarianism and homosexuality belong together.

Theodor Adorno

Our legal machinery has become little more than an engine for protecting the few owners against the necessities, the demands, or the hatred of the mass of their dispossessed fellow-citizens.

Hilaire Belloc

5.1: Boys will be boys.

For the Nazis, Fascists and Phalangists, life was uncomplicated. Men were warriors and women sweet, mild creatures fit for *Kinder, Küche, Kirche*. Children, kitchen and church. Men dressed in manly uniforms, often for office work as well, and spent their spare time in masculine pursuits like tramping up and down behind a flag, singing martial songs or learning how to shoot. Women dressed in homely, modest clothing and conducted themselves in a homely, modest manner while caring for home and children. Fascism glorifies masculinity: with occasional nods to women, men are what count, men know what they're about and men are where it's at. Men must to be lean and tough in body and soul, they work diligently to rid themselves of what would now be called their feminine side. Traditional fascist groups worked and trained hard to weld them into a single-minded fighting machine. Individuals coalesced in the work unit, be it military, factory or in the office or fishing boat, the goal being to eradicate differences, to produce a standard and uniformly reliable human resource unit. This phenomenon of total control of the individual is also seen in communism, both past and present, in churches, cults and in all other absolutist organisations.

Despite their obsessive worship of the gloriously-developed male body [15], fascists reserved a special hatred for homosexuality in any form, yet their obvious androphilia led many people to conclusions similar to Theodor Adorno's, above. Adorno, who was heavily influenced by Freud's psychoanalytic theory, explains it thus:

> In organized groups such as the army or the Church, there is either no mention of love whatsoever between the members, or it is expressed only in a sublimated and indirect way, through the mediation of some religious image in the love of whom the members unite and whose all-embracing love they are supposed to imitate in their attitude towards each other. ... It is one of the basic tenets of fascist leadership to keep primary libidinal energy on an unconscious level so as to divert its manifestations in a way suitable to political ends.

Libidinal energy is a Freudian term with mystical overtones which roughly means a combination of sensual/sexual drive and "life force." While the men in the units were tightly bonded to each other, no hint of sensuality was permitted. Their sexual urge was channeled in the approved direction only, very often violently so. Yet, while homosexuality itself was severely punished in the Third Reich, it was never very far from the surface because Nazism appealed to androphilics. Ernst Röhm, leader of the SturmAbteil, or SA, the original Nazi militia, and a number of his senior officers were murdered on June 30th 1933, on Hitler's direct orders, ostensibly because of their "depraved conduct," meaning they were gay. The real reason was to be rid of the competition from the SA but subsequently, homosexual men were brutally suppressed. In the twelve years of Nazi rule, perhaps 100,000 men were arrested because of their sexual orientation and many died in concentration camps. That was the overt message; at the same time, Nazi racial propaganda heaped praise verging on adulation on the

---

[15]   The implicit reasoning is something like this: Life is a Darwinian struggle; therefore, only the fit survive; in order to survive, we must be fit; fit means strong; men are stronger than women; strong men are essential for survival; strong men need weapons; therefore lean, well-developed men are desirable in the sense that a weapon is desirable, because it leads to survival; survival is beautiful; therefore weapons and well-developed men are beautiful. Or something, my limited experience is that fascists are enraged merely by raising the question of their homoeroticism.

ideal of the beautiful Aryan male. Perhaps envy played a part in it because the Nazi inner circle were mostly, well, unbecoming.

This, as Adorno noted, is not unique to right wing movements but is part of totalitarianism in the broadest sense. In general, the more extreme the government, the more effort it puts into presenting huge displays of martial splendour, with dazzling uniforms and amazingly choreographed performances of vast bodies of troops wheeling past in faultless synchrony. It was true of the USSR and is true of militarily resurgent Russia today [16], although China and North Korea are their equals. Why does this happen? I suggest the reason is a set of contradictory imperatives which contribute to the inner tension of fascism and ultimately contribute to its collapse.

In the first place, fascism is about domination, as was recognised by the writer, George Orwell. In an essay published in late 1945, he distinguished between patriotism and nationalism:

> By 'patriotism' I mean devotion to a particular place and a particular way of life, which one believes to be the best in the world but has no wish to force on other people. Patriotism is of its nature defensive, both militarily and culturally. Nationalism, on the other hand, is inseparable from the desire for power. The abiding purpose of every nationalist is to secure more power and more prestige, *not* for himself but for the nation or other unit in which he has chosen to sink his own individuality [1].

He used the term nationalism broadly, more akin to the way I am using the word fascism, but he tried to distinguish between the two [17]. He was quite clear that what he called nationalist elements could be seen in such diverse movements as Communism and religion. Nationalism as he understood it was not a social program, just a cluster of primitive impulses, a tribal drive for domination that could be grafted on to any private or personal attachment. As such, it was hollow, devoid of constructive features to advance humanity in general, as he said: "A nationalist is one who thinks solely, or mainly, in

---

[16] See videos of the Russian May 9th Victory Parades, including synchronised juggling with rifles.

[17] He saw common elements in the two great dictatorships of his day, Fascism and Communism. He attributed those elements to 'nationalism,' because he didn't want to label Stalin as a fascist, whereas I do. That is exactly what he was; Stalin's socialism was justification for his taking power but became little more than window dressing for his paranoid egomania.

terms of competitive prestige." And this is what lies behind the emphasis on male perfection which is so characteristic of fascism: lacking a formal social program, such as socialism has, it justifies itself as advancing the mystical tribe whereas, in reality, all it is doing is licensing the male impulse to domination.

Why is the tribe so important? Because it is based in the fourth great imperative that drives human behaviour, territoriality. We may call it patriotism but we are territorial animals, just like cats and crocodiles, and at the same primitive, reflexive level. We own things, we possess them and because they belong to us, they are somehow both better than everybody else's yet so delicate that they must be guarded with life and limb. Territoriality is utterly unreasoning: people fly into terrible rages if they see anybody on their land. We actually have laws to prevent landowners murdering intruders, because that is what used to happen, and still does in many places. The sense of possession doesn't stop at land, it covers all sorts of goods and, of course, the most precious goods of all, sexual partners. It is a blind, unreasoned and unreasoning trigger for instantaneous fury and aggression as in so-called crimes of passion. Again, it may have its origin in evolutionary pressures, guarding precious resources for the tribe but it goes back a very long way. Even though it takes different forms, humans are among the most ferociously territorial of all animals.

Men in fascist working units, mainly military but also agricultural, industrial, the bureaucracy, etc, are expected to work together at the most intense level, to belong to the unit and to own it, to support each other through thick and thin. They must indulge in regular displays of joint male competition but also try to outdo each other in loyalty to the cause, whatever it is. Their uniforms are designed for dramatic effect, to focus attention on them and enhance their image as eminently desirable but also slightly unreal embodiments of male perfection. However, and this is important, the intense emotion thus engendered is necessarily heavily sexualised just because it is driven by the male sexual hormone, yet it must never be expressed physically. That would represent the betrayal of the fantasy fascist male. The state is all; if men engage in sexual activity, then it must be in the service of the state, meaning breeding children to serve the nation and the military, but not for their selfish pleasure.[18]

Arrayed in their extravagantly-decorated uniforms, scrubbed and polished, the precisely-ordered, strutting legions are drones, idealised males as perfect as peacocks but devoid of their sexuality. Given this entirely artificial ideal, homosexuality is treason. Yet again we see a contradiction at the heart of fascism, a tension which, ultimately, must fail. With one hand, fascism boosts androphilia yet, with the other, shoots any man who got a bit too overwhelmed with one of his beautiful peers. The only outlet for the artificially-elevated sexual arousal is aggression, almost invariably directed at women.

5.2: Lies will be told.

And this brings us to a point about extremism which Orwell understood well:

> Nationalism (read: fascism) is power-hunger tempered by self-deception. Every (fascist) is capable of the most flagrant dishonesty, but he is also—since he is conscious of serving something bigger than himself—unshakeably certain of being in the right [1].

As he showed later in his novel, *1984*, dishonesty is the stock in trade of fascism. I don't mean stealing from shops, robbing banks or even looting museums in conquered countries. I mean the deep-seated sense of willingly, eagerly surrendering all morality in the service of a greater cause (the nation, the race, the church, the dictatorship of the proletariat etc). The cause is holy. For the extremist, any action done to advance the cause is *ipso facto* justified and unselfish, regardless of its immorality. Because it is justified, then it is right and proper, so anybody who opposes it is necessarily evil and must be annihilated. Thus, religious groups justify the most appalling cruelty toward their opponents: because God is on their side, anybody who opposes them must be on Satan's side and, as everybody knows, God wants His loving followers to destroy all evil. QED. By this means, ISIS justified slaughtering tens of thousands of Shia Muslim, Yazidi, Hazara and

---

[18] In the main, the great dictators of the last century put little public emphasis on themselves as sexually capable adults; Mussolini, the exception, probably made up for them all.

B'hai civilians, as well as their usual harvest of Christians, gays and spies.

If that were all, it would be bad enough but it isn't all. The violence of fascist movements and their inherent dishonesty go hand in glove. The violence follows from the urge to advance the state, race, religion, etc, just because it is seen as "the best" of the field. But the quality of what is being advanced has nothing to do with the issue: by any objective standard, when we look at the endless conflict in Northern Ireland, the relative qualities of the Catholic and various Protestant sects of Christianity are irrelevant to the strife. Religion is the excuse but the real nature of the conflict is the two groups yelling at each other "You're not going to dominate me, and I'll dominate you to prove it." This is not a recipe for peaceful coexistence but the tribal human isn't interested in coexistence. Over hundreds of years, each side in Northern Ireland has defined itself negatively, in terms of whom they love to hate, in terms of not being their enemy. Religion is irrelevant as the drive to dominate is a primeval urge that was designed into us long before there were countries or religions. Take away the nation or the religion, the football club or whatever, and they would still find an excuse to fight. It is not that football produces louts; it is that louts use football as the excuse to wind themselves up to fighting pitch, just because it feels better than weeding the garden or visiting the grandparents on Saturday.

But nobody is allowed to say this, and nobody involved in the various movements would do so. Instead, people shout: "I want our nation to win at the Olympic Games because it's the best and we'll fight anyone who says otherwise." [19] But that of course is a lie, the falsehood at the core of fascism. The truth is people want their lot to win because they don't want anybody looking down on them. It has nothing to do with the merits or activities of whatever group they identify with. The stronger the need to dominate, or the more desperate the need to avoid being dominated, the more likely people are to believe that violence in the service of their nation/religion/football club is justifiable. Not violence or treachery from the other side, of course, that's never justifiable but they're dirty dogs anyway and if they want to play dirty, well, we'll show them dirty, then they'll be sorry. And thus a further round of the endless cycle of violence is initiated and justified.

---

[19]   As the Nazis realised in 1936, international sport is yet another activity that eagerly lends itself to fascist ends.

To use Orwell's expression, fascism is "power-hunger tempered by self-deception." At the very heart of the fascist enterprise is an enormous deceit, that the wild excitement I feel from cheering our troops or marching behind our sacred flag is based on the merits of my country/religion/football team etc. It isn't, and beneath all the festivities, we all know it isn't. We know that the other side are saying exactly the same thing about their country/religion/football team etc, and we both can't be right. We could settle the matter by agreeing to disagree, or by asking an independent judge to look at the strengths of our respective cases, but that never happens. Deep inside, we know that all we want is to smash those cheeky pricks into the ground, we want to show them who's boss so they learn some manners when we're around. To hell with turning the other cheek, I say, I just want to kick arse, I want to win. And that, of course, is precisely why the Nazarene felt it necessary to urge that principle on his tempestuous followers.

Everybody knows this but the thrill of domination is sanctified. Before the game, parents tell their offspring: "Don't worry whether you win or lose, you just go out there and do your best." But at match end, everybody can tell the winning side by watching which group of parents is jumping up and down, hugging each other and cheering. And that tells the children loud and clear: Forget the schmalzy stuff junior, winning is everything. Practically every religion enjoins its adherents to proselytise, to preach to the pagans and bring them into God's embrace. It doesn't say: Live and let live. No religion teaches that other religions are just a different way of seeing things, that we should be tolerant and perhaps even learn something from them. What each religion teaches, and what we accept (as gospel, in fact), is that only we are right. Everybody else is an agent of the devil working assiduously to destroy us, so we'd better get in first.

In fact, every person has the option of choosing to believe his country is preeminent, or of saying "All countries have a mix of good points and not so good points, it's much of a muchness." Nobody chooses that option because we are told from infancy that the thrill we feel from saying "My country is the greatest" is justified. In so many ways, we are told that it is a sacred duty to burst with pride when seeing the flag raised or on hearing the national anthemn. Triumphalism is inherent, it is not taught but can be amplified and exaggerated by education: it *feels* good to gloat over defeating another person. People accept it as normal and desirable because all we want is to dominate The Other in order to get that wild joy. Ecstasy doesn't come from growing cabbages, setting bricks in a wall or hanging out the washing, we have to get it elsewhere.

After so much indoctrination by word and deed, it isn't clear how far the dishonesty in fascism is simple self-deception. Most people are not sufficiently self-aware to question why they support a particular code of football or why they believe their country is best or their religion the Revealed Truth. Fundamentalist Christians are utterly incapable of explaining the myriad contradictions in the Bible, they just start ranting about Satan's agents being everywhere. The indoctrination started too early, it is too pervasive – and too subtle – for the great majority to consider dispassionately, but it is indoctrination in what they were going to do anyway. People don't need to be taught to hate different coloured skin or different religions or poor or disabled people, they were going to do it anyway because they like it, it feels so good. God does play dice with us. He randomly allocates each child a different skin colour, different intellect and appearance, a different language, religion, favourite sport, food, music, clothes and so on, then waits to see whether we can overcome the handicap of having so many things to hate about other people. Mostly, we don't, and not just because there are so many people telling us to look down on our neighbours. It's natural, it's inherent to fear and hate The Other so we don't even try to be nice. We are tribal animals and xenophobia is a *sine qua non* of tribalism. Eric Voegelin said "Tribalism is the answer to immaturity because it permits man to remain immature with the sanction of the group."

Moreover, in most parts of the world, merely questioning whether one's country or religion is the best is seen as incipient or actual treason, and treated accordingly. Certainly, our politicians, who have completely surrendered to the drive to dominate, never question or look objectively at anything they do. For them, winning is more than just everything, it's the point of life itself. Politicians show no inclination to distinguish between what is good for them and what is good for the country, they see them as essentially one and the same thing: *L'etat, c'est nous.* They can justify any move they make as being for the good of the nation, even when a moment's reflection would show it is dishonest or damaging to others. Therefore, they don't take a moment to reflect because, behind the façade of administrative integrity, they know that when push comes to shove, all that counts is who can shove hardest. As Stalin asked, "And how many divisions does the Pope have?"

In 2001, Americans weren't concerned whether the Taliban had anything to do with the attack in New York on September 11th, they just wanted to smash a few troublesome Arabs over there (and no, not one American in 10,000 knew that Afghans are not Arabs, but if they had all known, it wouldn't have made any difference because the US had been humiliated and somebody had to pay). When the Taliban offered to hand over Osama bin-Laden and his motley crew, the Bush administration refused because they had already decided they were going to invade. Bin-Laden was the excuse for the invasion but not the reason. The same happened in 2003. All politicians in the world were aware that Iraq did not have weapons of mass destruction; 90% of them knew that Iraq had nothing to do with Al-Qaeda; and all of them knew, or should have known, that, after years of sanctions, the country was on its knees; that the poor were suffering dreadfully; that an invasion of Iraq would be resisted bitterly, and that it would unleash the most dreadful sectarian hatreds. In Vietnam, the West's political war (to determine the form of government for the Vietnamese) was won by the locals, for whom it was a war of national liberation as well as a war of racial survival against foreign colonialists. Iraqis, as every Western politician knew at the time, would be fighting a nationalist war, a race war and a religious war. That combination is unbeatable, as the West should have known all along (and does now) but the need to avenge the humiliation of 9/11 by crushing Arabs overwhelmed common sense. Into that vacuum strode the Siamese-twin wolves of dishonesty and violence, clothed in the sheepskin of self-righteousness. And they are still there.

Further down down the ranks from the politicians and generals, the violence is closer to the surface. Football louts don't know anything about how clubs are ranked and care even less whether their players come from Outer Ruritania: all they care about is jamming it up the other side. Meanwhile, down at ground level, not only is the primeval urge to dominate closer to the surface, untrammelled by genteel considerations of fair play, but the opportunities are so much greater: "Nobody's looking, so let's rape that woman before the sergeant comes. She'll report us? OK, a bullet will fix that but none of us saw anything, got it? Anybody who blabs will join her six foot under."

There is no recrimination from the higher echelons, and no redress for the victim.

People know when they are deceiving themselves but if the social climate sanctions their wildest impulses, justifying extremism, then the essential questions are never asked; if the questions aren't asked, nobody needs to bother themselves over the answers:

> Why should I salute the flag, sir?

> Isn't this stuff about turning water into wine all a bit silly, Father?

> Nein, mein Führer, Ich habe keine Probleme mit Juden, ich habe gute jüdische Freunde.

> Excuse me Imam, but we are required to care for the strangers in our midst, not behead them.

People would rather grab the flag and bash somebody, or kick the Jews sooner than help them, or invade the Arabs to free them, just because it feels so much better than pondering complex moral questions. This is especially the case when merely asking those questions carries the risk being of expelled from the tribe, or worse. This point helps explain the outrage we all feel when we uncover hypocrisy. Being ordered what to do or how to act, what to believe or profess, puts us in an inferior position. If we later learn that the teacher or moral busybody was dishonest, perhaps we may laugh but mostly we are deeply offended. We had to defer to that person, we had no response other to fall into line, and that is humiliating, meaning it lowers our status. Nobody likes that, we are programmed to respond angrily to losing status, and we do.

5.3: Don't tread on me.

During the 2021 attack on the US Capitol Building, many of Trump's carefully wound up "very fine people" carried a yellow flag bearing a coiled rattlesnake and the insignia "Don't tread on me." The Gadsden flag, as it is known, is a prominent meme of the ultra-libertarian right wing, many of whom also carried Nazi symbols which, we can presume, demonstrates a measure of sympathy with fascist ideals. On the basis that the snake never backs down when provoked, the flag is taken to mean "Don't tell me what to do or I'll hit back." Apparently, its bearers didn't know that Hitler was rather strong on discipline and had his own ways of dealing with people who didn't follow orders, but that's not the point. The point here is the apparent contradiction of people on the extreme right wing who are both fascist in orientation (wanting to build a massive, powerful, militarised state) and, at the same time, fanatically opposed to anybody ordering them around. Taxation is theft, socialism is slavery, government is oppression, freedom is sacred and the individual is god [20]. This calls to mind a comment by the author, Kurt Andersen:

> Americans have always been magical thinkers and passionate believers in the untrue [2].

It's not just Americans, it's all of humanity. We have to explain the facts as they are, that a highly visible segment of the US population, with outliers in many other countries, seems to believe that all problems in society and in their lives will be fully resolved by the complete deconstruction of society. With an axe in one hand and a gun in the other, we should all cut ourselves free of the stranglehold of modern life, head for the hills and build ourselves a log cabin. Putting aside the slight contradiction that axe heads and guns are made of steel, and that there aren't that many hills or trees in the world anyway, what are they actually saying?

It should be clear that everything we wealthy westerners enjoy in our rather easy lives today is the result of a great deal of highly disciplined and cooperative effort by very large numbers of people in different countries over many years. Presumably, we could say to a man carrying a Gadsden flag, "We gather you would like to shoot your enemy, as distinct from merely club him with your gun, or throw it at him? That will require bullets, which are made from chemicals and metals extracted in a dozen countries, processed and manufactured in another dozen, brought here by ships built in one more country, fuelled by oil from yet another, financed by banks in several more, and all this has to be coordinated and timed exquisitely, and still allow the manufacturers to make a profit. What is that ineffably complex process if it is not the society that you affect to despise?"

---

[20] Without wishing to spoil a good story, Christopher Gadsden, the South Carolina politician who devised the snake emblem, was a wealthy slave owner and slave trader (i.e. he was totally opposed to the concept of personal freedom). Actually, when I first saw the flag waving over the crowd of insurrectionists, I thought it was an emoji for a turd.

In fact, asking these questions of such a person is a complete waste of time and, if he is carrying his gun, potentially quite dangerous as his beliefs are not rational. They are entirely the product of primitive emotional drives and impulses of which the owner is all-but-unaware, but which he accepts without question as being the proper foundation for an ideal life, just because they feel so good that they can't possibly be wrong.

Once again, the primary motivation is as described for all humans: the testosterone-driven need to dominate. This time, however, we are seeing the reverse face of the Challenge Hypothesis. Rather than saying "I am determined to dominate you," the libertarian is saying "I am determined that nobody will dominate me and I'll fight anybody who tries." This is, of course, a form of domination in its own right. For example, when the council inspector comes to check the drains, the libertarian orders him off his property at gunpoint. "Aha," crows the libertarian to his friends, "I showed them who's boss. Next time, they'll know better than to mess with me." That is, he was able to dominate the council officer, showing what happens when gross narcissism and the compulsion to dominate synergise and, amplified by a gun, produce a single antisocial outcome. In other words, their ultra-libertarianism is no more than conceit, a sort of *Fascism for Beginners*, a *faux* independence whose members are utterly reliant on modern technological society in order to survive in the wilderness [21].

Before we leave this sector of the far right wing, we should mention again how they use conspiratorial thinking to establish their case. Among their many other irritations, libertarians are currently railing against government directions to wear masks, to stay at home and for everybody to have Covid immunisation. The first two are typical cases of obtuse reverse domination: "This gun says you can't tell me what to do." The third, arguing against immunisation, is more subtle. It relies on the concept of weaponized doubt, which was introduced by the tobacco industry in the 1950s and 60s (and is still called 'the tobacco shuffle'). Subsequently, it was honed by the asbestos, pesticides and pharmaceutical industries and, starting with acid rain and the ozone hole, the fossil fuel interests in their battle against the idea of anthropogenic climate change. The notion is to use the crucial concept of doubt in science to prevent people drawing the correct conclusions

[21]   It's a bit like Ghandi's vow of poverty. Nehru reportedly commented: "It costs us a great deal of money to keep him in poverty."

from the evidence. Empirical science is about doubt; all results are accepted pending another set of results that overthrows them. That's what makes science so exciting, as distinct from, say, religion: the elusive truth is "out there" waiting to be snared. Conspiratorialists misuse this notion by insisting that established and accepted areas of science are still open to doubt, which is logically true, but they go further. They argue that doubt equates with unreliability, and unreliability equates with falsehood, therefore the science is all a big lie.

The ploy was developed by capitalists for their own purposes but has now been taken up by people who, unlike the immensely powerful industrialists who developed it, have no knowledge or understanding of how science works. What has been called strategic ignorance relies on the audience assuming that if something isn't 100% true, it's false. This assumes there are only two truth values, True and False, when there are in fact three: True, False, and Indeterminate. I can make a statement: "It will rain tomorrow." As a question of science, its truth value is indeterminate (neither true nor false): tomorrow hasn't happened yet, so no truth value can be assigned. The passage of time will assign one.

I could also say: "If you don't wear a mask, your risk of catching Covid-19 is very high, so you must wear a mask." The libertarian's response is: "You can't prove I will catch it, therefore your conclusion is false and you can't use it to make me wear a mask." Of course, none of them understand Bayesian probability but that's not the point. This black and white interpretation of complex issues is widely used by propagandists. For example, libertarians fulminate against anything that might be called socialism. This is based on the notion that absolute freedom is the highest human ideal; socialism reduces freedom; unless you are totally free you are enslaved; therefore socialism is slavery and must be fought to the death. This is held to be true even when, as in the sort of slightly-socialised health services that other countries enjoy, the benefits to working people are very real. Granted that slavery is beyond abhorrent, but it is rather difficult to know why so many Americans say they will fight to the death to prevent themselves being enslaved, yet they have no problem lauding slavers (such as Messrs G Washington, T Jefferson and C Gadsden), excusing historical slavery as an institution in US or in keeping descendents of slaves in subjugation.

However, as so often happens, the working man's libertarian movement has been coopted by the big end of town. The ferocity with which poorly-educated, poor or working class white people will rush to grab their weapons to fight the slightest hint of socialism-cum-slavery is used by big business to scare politicians from voting for anything that the wealthy don't like. All they have to do is rattle the libertarians' cages with some dishonest sound bite ("Covid is a hoax," "Socialised medicine = death committees") and the politicians panic like rabbits that think somebody is about to lock the gate to the carrot patch. A C-Span poll, reported on June 18th 2021, asked people in the US: Would you pay more taxes for free education and health care? Of responders, 33% said Yes, 67% said No. These were people who would definitely benefit from cheaper education and subsidised health care, such as the working class people whose average life span is actually going down. It also included veterans who perhaps didn't realise they benefit from one of the world's largest socialist health schemes, the US Veterans' Administration. Similarly, it is difficult to know why libertarians, in any country, are so antagonistic to socialised systems when they fall over themselves to support the world's single most expensive socialised government program, the military. Being a libertarian means never having to admit you're wrong. Everybody else is.

5.4: "Socialism is slavery."

> "The problem with socialism is that eventually, you run out of other people's money."

No doubt Margaret Thatcher thought she was being frightfully clever with this remark but she was wrong. The socialist responds: "Actually, it's our money we're spending, it's just that rich people stole it." This points to the ideological dispute which is doing as much as any to split modern Western society, the question of tax and spend. On one side stand the traditional leftists who believe the wealthy should be taxed to support beneficial social programs (which does not include the vast and ever-expanding military-industrial-spying-policing-incarceration complex); on the other are so-called neoliberals, who argue that society should do nothing to limit the ability of any person to make money because concentrations of wealth will eventually trickle down to enrich those at the bottom of the social scale. Where did this idea come from?

As recently as 250 years ago, the great majority of humans lived in essentially static societies where paramount authority rested with god, king and country, in that order. What was good for the king was ipso facto good for everybody. Most countries were firmly under the thumb of divinely-sanctioned, hereditary absolute monarchies whose citizens were told who, when and where they had to worship. Financial and other duties were imposed at the whim of the king or archbishop, and there were severe restrictions of speech, movement, association, trade, education and even of marriage. Authority and privilege flowed from god to the king and thence to his chosen nobility so by the time it reached the level of the tillers of the soil, the hewers of wood or catchers of fishes, there was very little of either left. For women, children and foreigners, especially the non-white races, there was none at all. In large parts of the world, peasants were bound to the land as serfs, a polite name for domestic slaves, and lived or died largely at the whim of their superiors.

The goal of liberalism, the political wing of the Englightenment, was to reverse all of this. God and king were pushed aside. The individual was placed at the pinnacle, free to grow, develop and express himself (*sic*) with as little restriction as was consistent with the idea of society. The idea of the common or social good replaced the notion that individuals were of value only as they related to the power structure. Basic freedoms were established as universal rights—speech, religion, movement, etc, guaranteed by a rules-based civil order with equality before law, including public trial by jury. Goals included restriction of inherited privilege (or guilt), representational government with universal suffrage, and recognition that, as they are essential to the well-being of individuals, the benefits of universal education, health, and other services were to be spread as widely as possible. In due course, the unrestricted right to explore knowledge lead to artistic, scientific and industrial revolutions.

Following the chaos of the two World Wars and the Great Depression, liberalism as an economic doctrine was in retreat, pursued by socialist ideals in the form either of the welfare state or the repressive communist governments. For workers in western nations at least, the 1950s and 60s were a golden era. National health services spread rapidly, state schools and universities expanded, war-damaged housing stock was replaced and roads and railways extended to all. In the US, senior levels of management earned only about twenty times as much as their median worker's salary, but they weren't satisfied. Greed intruded into the tranquil scene, defeating altruistic socialism and mild-mannered liberalism. The drive to dominate, to crush all possible enemies, led to ever-expanding military budgets, endless warfare and Mutually-Assured Destruction, and neoliberalism.

Neoliberals believe that an unrestricted market acting on nothing more than price signals will correctly allocate resources to investment, production and distribution, and will thereby fully and efficiently satisfy the population's needs with minimal interference in personal liberty. Their concepts and values are known collectively as the Austrian school of economics, as a group around Ludwig von Mises was influential in spreading the ideas. In 1944, Friedrich Hayek, an Austrian economist who had been working in the UK since the early 1930s, published *The Road to Serfdom*, which is probably the best-known outline of neoliberal principles [3; see end note this chapter]. From 1950-62, he worked at Chicago University, having a major impact on what is now known as the Chicago school of economics. In turn, this has heavily influenced national and international affairs over the past 70 years. Margaret Thatcher was a devoted fan of Hayek's and reputedly carried copies of his work in her handbag, to slap down on the table to end arguments.

Despite its influence, Hayek's *Serfdom* is not an economics textbook, nor a research report, an academic review or anything of that nature. It is a polemic, a political diatribe masquerading as a dispassionate analysis of socialist economics which the right wing has seized and used to justify ever-increasing inequality. Hayek's starting position is that there is only one social good, freedom. Nothing else counts. As J K Galbraith noted:

> The modern conservative is engaged in one of man's oldest exercises in moral philosophy; that is, the search for a superior moral justification for selfishness." But when they finally realise there isn't one, they reach for their guns, they resort to might as their justification.

In the concept of total freedom, Hayek thought he had found that justification. Anything that interferes with total freedom must be opposed because the slightest reduction in personal freedom means that the society is sliding into socialism, and socialism means abolition of private property, central planning, forced collectivism, government by committee and, ultimately, total mind control. But, and this is important, he believed that socialism leads to fascism, which is bad because it restricts freedom. The best that could be said of his argument to support this claim is that it is opaque and open to multiple interpretations; at its worst, it is pseudoscience on a par with Marxist dialectics, Lysenkoism or Nazi race science.

The first problem is that *Road to Serfdom* is badly written, so bad, in fact, that it is almost impossible for even a careful reader to be sure of what Hayek was saying. As prose, it reads remarkably like Hitler's *Mein Kampf* which, given their backgrounds, is not surprising. A critical reader can go over and over the same few sentences and still not be sure what the author intended. In practice, it means that anybody can read it quickly and feel assured that it supports his or her position. For example, having repeatedly said that all central planning is bad, Hayek then reveals that he believes the society must have laws and regulations to govern the market, and a degree of social planning and central control to provide welfare services for the elderly and disabled and the unemployed. He didn't mention the military, police and prisons but we know he meant these as well. Of course, these services have to be financed by taxes but he doesn't explain why these taxes and services aren't abhorrent restrictions of personal freedom. Freedom extends to the market (he was an economist, after all) where the basic principle is that, driven wholly by naked self-interest, markets are inherently self-righting and therefore don't need regulation or red tape. Any attempt to restrict them or any input other than price signals will produce distortions, and distortions lead to socialism, which is the same thing as Stalinism and morphs into fascism which is bad because it restricts freedom.

What Hayek doesn't explain, what he doesn't even address, is why a minimally-regulated market will necessarily be an honest market. Nothing in *Serfdom* intimates that market makers (i.e. the rich and powerful) are any other than people of the highest integrity; he accepts this without question. Where he got this idea is not explained but it certainly didn't come from reading the daily newspapers or from rubbing shoulders with the rich and powerful. Common sense says that every social or political program can be betrayed. Any system that relies on minimal regulation necessarily relies maximally on the bona fides of the operators, and that is the fatal flaw in the neoliberal project. Humans (especially the rich and powerful strain) are most assuredly *not* inherently fair and reasonable. The very expression "self-interest" means "placing one's own interests before all others; unfair and unreasonable to all but self." While the whole point of morality is

to constrain self-interest, a free-market economy demands uncon-
strained self-interest. We know that left unsupervised, humans will
soon start to help themselves to everything and anything within reach.
Self-interest says "Get it while you can (by any means necessary),"
whence it is but a small step to "I'll get the lot if I can but if I can't, I'll
make sure nobody else can, either." As shown by the unfolding saga of
the late Jeffrey Epstein and his endless webs of illicit contacts at the
highest levels of society, besides the odour of lucre, wafting through the
corridors of power is the intoxicating aroma of utter amorality.

However, also in 1944, an expatriate Hungarian historian and
economist, Karl Polanyi, published a long and detailed argument
against this model, concluding that an unregulated market economy
must eventually destroy society itself and the natural environment [4].
His case was based on the essential market principal that, in order to
function, a free market economy allocates a price to everything.
Otherwise, it would not be able to work out the relation between, say,
potatoes and workers' holidays, or the plans of a mining company
compared with the value of a national park.

For Polanyi, the neoliberal program of pricing everything meant a
price on precisely everything. In particular, the primary elements of any
human society—land, labour and capital—are to be recast as fungible
commodities, just like food, water, fuel and raw materials. Thus, the
basic structural elements of society itself are isolated so they can be
allocated a price and thence traded. If it doesn't have a price, it doesn't
exist, and a society split into its elements doesn't exist. This is what
Thatcher meant when she said "There is no such thing as society."
Society, in her view, was just ciphers sitting in their silos putting prices
on anything they deemed a commodity (i.e. anything they could
possibly make money from).

In Polanyi's view, the real issue is that there is no such thing as a
market. There are groups of people buying and selling goods and
services, all of whom make decisions on what they are prepared to pay
for an item or what they want for it but of the hypostatised Free
Market, there is no sign. In a traditional (read: rational) society, the
market is just part of society, a service like police, health, education,
road-mending, etc. that helps keep things ticking over. Markets serve
societies, but in a market economy, the society subserves the market,
meaning society exists for the benefit of the groups of traders who
comprise the market (i.e. a market economy puts supreme and

unassailable value on itself). But, and this is a very important *but*, in a market economy, the commodity known as labour is also allocated a price and traded by the market-makers.

What this means is that the price of labour is decided by the market-makers, not by the workers themselves who provide (and own) the labour. This is where Polanyi locates the central problem in neoliberalism: workers are treated as mindless work units who are told what their efforts are worth by the very people whose profits go up if the price of labour goes down. It is often said that workers "sell" their time and energy to the business owners but that is false: their efforts are, at best, harvested by the owners or, all too often, mined, meaning exploited until there is nothing left. In the capitalist system devised by the owners of capital, workers are deemed to be separate from their labour, they have no say at all and can be discarded like the straw of wheat after the grain is harvested, i.e. they are genuine non-entities. In particular, the owners of a commodity can decide whether to sell it or not. If they don't like the price, or change their minds, they can take it off the market with no penalty. But workers cannot take their "commodity" called labour off the market because that is a strike and strikes are evil.

But it turns out that all talk of a "free market economy" is self-contradictory. The market makers may be free to do as they please but workers are regulated unto their graves by the most powerful force of all: fear of their families starving. Workers, who act morally at all times (caring for their families and neighbours, going to church and school concerts, supporting their football teams, tending their gardens, attending funerals, etc.), maintain the contradiction by assuming that the rich and powerful will will also be morally constrained in their dealings with their labour force. But of course, they're not. The rich and powerful live in an anything-goes world with only one rule: don't get caught [22]. In reality, plutocrats carve up the world between them so that they don't waste time and money squabbling over the spoils. France never tried to muscle in on India, while the British kept their distance from the Mahgreb. But when the workers rebelled, France and Britain were as one in their loathing for Bolshevism.

So the market-makers push the price of labour down and gloat all the way to the bank. Safe in their gentlemen's clubs, they toast each

---

[22] And one more: Look after your mates if they get caught. See [5].

other as impartial vectors of rational but blind market forces when nothing could be further from the truth. Greed, as they say, is good, and it is: greed is exciting, exhilarating, endlessly intoxicating... but only if you're part of the 1% who are winning from it. For the rest, who are being traded like pork bellies, other people's greed is a meat grinder.

Thus, the effect of a market economy is three-fold: it eliminates anything that people regard as interesting, or important, or fun, or of spiritual or emotional significance, unless it makes a profit. Everything that exists must be commercialised, as has happened to Christmas, sport and children's hospitals. Second, it pushes at least 95% of the population into lives of servitude where they are at the beck and call of the moneyed class who, in turn, are profiting from keeping the workers in bondage. Third, it encourages the wealthy to abandon "bourgeois morality" in their pursuit of pelf. Gradually, then faster, the upper echelons of society turn away from the idea of a fair deal, toward an unbridled larceny driven by self-interested scoundrels whose contempt for the rights of the less-fortunate increases in lockstep with the inequality they are creating.

To Polanyi, writing nearly 80 years ago, that was a recipe for disaster because the workers must come to resent their lot and would eventually demand and then fight for their rights. But to the plutocracy, workers' rights, insofar as they exist, must also have a cash value which, as the market movers, the wealthy can decide without needing to ask the workers their opinion. Workers are seen as the vehicles of their labour, but not the owners, so the right of the rich to make money from labour overrides the right of the poor to withhold their labour if they aren't getting paid enough.

Needless to say, the governing classes place no value on workers' rights because they interfere with the pricing mechanism of the market, and produce distortions (i.e. limit profits). That is why the wealthy classes do their damnedest to break trade unions, and outlaw strikes as attacks on the very mechanism of the free market, i.e. they recast strikes as a *moral* crime. Strikes sabotage the well-oiled machinery of the market so, along with bank robbery, they must be outlawed because they both strike at the heart of the free market, which is Hayek's attempt at a "superior moral justification for selfishness." Any attempts by government to mitigate the workers' position, the wealthy sometimes argue, could leave workers worse off by exposing the economy to manipulation and corruption (by the wealthy market-makers, in fact, including their servants in parliament). That is not a moral argument: they don't care whether workers are worse off, as long as they can make their profits.

At this point, the concept of a "market economy" is exposed as a charade. For all commodities apart from labour, the owner of the commodity sets a price which buyers accept or decline. However, workers, the owners of one of the three basic elements in an economy, are not allowed to set a price for the only commodity granted to them by the market-makers. All profits from their sweat go to the wealthy.

In place of the old concept of *noblesse oblige*, i.e. that privilege imposes certain responsibilities or duties of care toward the less powerful or less fortunate, the privileged have now embraced *noblesse merite*, the notion that privilege always deserves more. The accumulation of wealth, they say, is morally sanctioned and must never be restricted; wealth naturally and efficiently devolves onto those who deserve it so governments must never interfere with this process in any way. Power and fortune, in their view, should always and in all ways be rewarded by the opportunity to accrue more power and more fortune, without limit. The more they have, the more they feel they are justified in taking as their due reward but, ominously, they also insist that morality doesn't enter the equation. If there are no rules, then there is no wrongdoing. QED. They don't believe they are greedy, they believe their good fortune is simply the outcome of the invisible hand of the market allocating rewards where justified. The corollary is that the lower classes don't deserve anything: the same invisible hand has them by the throat, but that's their problem, not society's, as there is no such thing as society. The trouble is that since Richard Nixon closed the gold window half a century ago, that is exactly the economic program imposed over most of the world – by the rich and powerful. That suits them very well: if the "hand" of the market is invisible, nobody can tell who is manipulating it.

Today, the "free market" financial tail wags the social dog. In neoliberalism, the privileged group of insiders who run the financial sector use their inside knowledge of the market gradually to take control of the entire society. The entire neoliberal project depends on a single falsehood: *that the wealthy and well-connected members of the financial sector are themselves neutral as to their influence over the market, the economy and thence over the society.* They are not in it for themselves, the story goes, they wouldn't dream of covertly manipulating the system to feather their own nests. Instead, they are technicians, approaching their task of efficiently allocating prices with the same dispassionate or impersonal attitude they expect workers to adopt when told their job is to be off-shored.

But, as we saw in the Global Financial Crisis (GFC), the direct result of decades of oh-so-clever financial engineering by the market-makers, this is pure fantasy. Of course financiers manipulate the market economy for their own benefit, that's what financiers *do*, that's what the free market *is*, that's what self-interest *means*. They are certainly not running the market as a charity for workers, that would be absurd, a contradiction of the entire concept of a market, that market-makers make markets to make themselves richer. A pig market does not exist for the benefit of pigs, it exists for the benefit of people who own and trade pigs. Similarly, a labour market does not exist for the benefit of the people who own labour, the labourers. Nobody questions that, it is self-evident. Not once in history have market makers created a market that could only spread wealth evenly around the community. Even without an actual conspiracy, the wealthy are able to turn the concept of a market economy into a charity for the wealthy. Perhaps we should rephrase that: in neoliberalism, the conspiracy becomes the market [23].

The market is only free for the 1% who control it but for the 99%, it is slavery. That's what humans do, that's how humans operate. This is because the insatiable drive to create a dominance hierarchy with Yours Truly at the top is not second nature, it *is* our nature. During the GFC, had the neoliberal financiers been true to their beliefs in an unfettered market, they would have accepted their collective fate as casualties of the free market and gone bravely to the bankruptcy courts – or jumped willingly from their windows. But they didn't. To a man (and quite a few women), neoliberalism's true believers fled squealing to the governments they affect to despise as "market riggers" and begged to be bailed out—at public expense. Adding insult to injury, they then calmly proceeded to pay themselves their productivity bonuses from

---

[23]   Following the publication of his critique of DSM5, the psychiatric diagnostic system, author Gary Greenberg was asked: "Could you briefly summarize the problem, as you see it, of the relationship between pharmaceutical companies and psychiatrists?" He replied: "I don't think there is a conspiracy in which drug companies pay doctors to create diseases for which they can then sell the cure. But who needs conspiracies when you have capitalism?"

the taxpayers' money. And as a final insult, they insisted that they were not responsible for the mess of the GFC and further regulation was not necessary, that's just the way markets are. Suck it up, and please send the bailout funds to our accounts in the Virgin Islands.

The reason for what is essentially psychopathic behaviour by the wealthy is that as wealth increases, so does the sense of entitlement. When their carefully-constructed money machine collapsed, they ran to the government for assistance because they were convinced they were doing an essential job and didn't deserve to go broke. Instead, and in spite of overwhelming evidence, they believed, to a man and without reservation, that society owed them a debt of gratitude, that they were doing something nobody else could do.

A neoliberal market economy will not work unless and until somebody devises a mechanism that unconditionally guarantees the impeccable integrity and impartiality of the market makers. It won't happen, of course, because the moment some such mechanism were instituted, the well-connected would immediately make superhuman efforts to sabotage it. So until that sunny day, neoliberalism remains little more than a jargon-laden licence for larceny on the grandest scale.

This is equally true of monopoly state capitalism, such as the brutal Stalinist, Maoist or Khmer Rouge collectivist socialist regimes. On practically all measures – human rights, scientific and cultural progress, corruption, inequality, environmental damage, etc. – monopoly state capitalism failed catastrophically. At the same time, and for the same reasons, neoliberal capitalism has encouraged warfare, corruption, inequality and impending total environmental destruction, but has failed to deliver the supposed benefits of "trickle-down economics." Every available figure shows that workers do not get richer alongside the rich. Monopoly capitalism, both state and private, contains the seeds of its own destruction. It disempowers the overwhelming majority while transferring power and wealth to a tiny, unaccountable minority who then use their privileged positions to entrench and enrich themselves further. That is biologically-driven human nature: the more people get, the more they believe they are entitled to have, the more they want, and the more they scheme and manipulate to get what they want. And, when frustrated, say by a workers' strike, their rage knows no bounds.

We cannot rely on the inherent rationality or "goodness" of the species because, as the face of our remorseless and hormonally-driven urge to acquire power and possessions, greed conquers all. Evil is *not* self-correcting but springs from our primitive primate urges to form dominance hierarchies and to acquire territory. There is no evidence that, once activated, these urges have any mechanism that terminates them on the basis that "enough is enough" or "let's leave some for the others." Biology doesn't think like that. In a process similar to biological habituation, the more people have, the more their sense of entitlement grows.

What has this to do with the political movement known as fascism? Strictly speaking, it doesn't have much as fascist economies routinely breach all the rules of an efficient market. In pure fascist doctrine, the state is all and workers must play their allocated part without demur. Unions are emasculated, strikes are forbidden, there is often conscription of labour and the centralised state makes major decisions as to wages, prices, availability of services and allocation of investment. That is a long way from the efficient market hypothesis. However, the wealthy don't complain as anti-labour laws and lucrative military contracts fatten their bank balances, which probably accounts for the egregious corruption so characteristic of fascist regimes. Thus, Polanyi's work has a lot to do with the principle being developed here, that, in human affairs, the drive to dominate is *both* universal *and* insatiable. The neoliberal or "efficient market" economy ("free market") actually causes the transfer of massive wealth to a small segment of the society at the price of the impoverishment of everybody else. It is no more than the mechanism of a dominance hierarchy applied to economic affairs, essentially applied fascism. Of course the wealthy like the idea of a market economy. There is no better way of making them wealthier and more powerful.

At its extreme, an efficient market would allocate no value to people who, by age or infirmity, are unable to provide labour, and would therefore let them starve. That should not come as a shock: there are plenty of highly influential people who regularly put forward this argument, albeit lightly disguised in economic jargon about efficiency, but the main way the wealthy get their way (as they mostly do) is by alarming the populace with the spurious claim that state provision of essential services is socialism, socialism is slavery, and you know the rest. To reprise Aneurin Bevan's prescient quote, noted in Chapter 2:

> The whole art of Conservative politics in the 20th century is being deployed to enable wealth to persuade poverty to use its political freedom to keep wealth in power.

The net effect of an efficient market economy is to concentrate wealth in ever-fewer hands, building ever-steeper dominance hierarchies to the unfettered delight of those at the top. Gradually, the working population must sink into the wage slavery they thought they were voting against. But this exposes yet another lie at the heart of the fascist/neoliberal state: that while people at the top of the pile are motivated to work by the noble urge to make money, workers at the bottom are driven by... what? Under normal circumstances of a neoliberal economy, workers are driven by fear of what will happen if they don't work, like losing their homes and starvation. Under abnormal circumstances, such as viral pandemics, massive bushfires, floods, wars, buildings collapsing, etc, workers are driven by altruism. They feel the urge to help sick people, to save entire communities from being burned to the ground or washed away or to help defend other people's homes and families, because that's what decent people do. That is, the profit motive which works so efficiently for the rich doesn't apply to the lumpenproletariat, the *untermenschen* who actually run the factories and the mines that make rich people richer.

If, during the pandemic, health workers had done what the rich routinely do (and pharmaceutical companies did), and raised the price of their labour when it was so desperately needed, including going on strike for higher pay, the entire neoliberal experiment would have immediately broken down. One after the other, or all at once, western economies would have collapsed in a heap of illness, death, debt and recriminations. Transport and energy markets the world over are now organised to raise prices when demand goes up, but workers aren't like that. The thought of striking would never have occurred to the heroic nurses and medical staff and orderlies and cooks and cleaners and ambulance drivers running the health services during the emergency. Police, firemen and other emergency workers did *not* demand danger money, they stifled their worries and kept working. They were exhausted, they were burdened, they were troubled and dispirited because the industrialists and financiers and politicians and bureaucrats who should have organised the protective equipment and the vaccines abjectly failed in their duty to the nation, but still the health and emergency staff kept going. And dying.[24]

You will never be told this but the whole of the neoliberal project relies totally on selfless devotion and loyalty, it only works when workers *don't* follow the neoliberal rulebook. Farmers don't get up at 4.00am in the depths of winter just because they like seeing the dawn reflected on frost, nor do they harvest their crops in 45C heat to get a sun tan, they do it because they are committed to a life they love. Mothers don't get up at 2.00am to feed their babies because they expect to make a profit, they do it because that's what motherhood means. But love and loyalty have no cash value in neoliberalism, so the wealthy pretend they don't exist. It's an easy pretence for them as the 1% are amoral, they have no devotion or loyalty themselves and they assume everybody else is the same. They profit from other people's devotion, as the CEOs of the drug companies and owners of private hospitals have profited mightily during the pandemic, but they don't pay for it. They assume workers are as psychopathic as they are themselves, and treat them accordingly.

This is also true of militarism. Ordinary people, as Göring said, have no interest in war, they don't profit by it. They have to be worked up to it by the two groups who will profit, power-hungry politicians working hand-in-glove with money-hungry financiers and industrialists. But again, politicians and financiers don't raise armies by offering recruits wages that balance the risk of loss of life or limb (not forgetting loss of sanity, which is probably worse), they rely on the very sense of social duty that Mrs Thatcher cruelly mocked when she denied the reality of society. Suddenly, when wars are planned, a society of patriots springs into existance, as it did when Thatcher needed national

---

[24] HM Queen Elizabeth II awarded the George Medal to the UK National Health Service for its selfless service during the pandemic. Her handwritten citation, published on July 5th 2021, stated inter alia: "Over more than seven decades, and especially in recent times, (NHS staff) have supported the people of our country with courage, compassion and dedication, demonstrating the highest standards of public service." Meantime, Prime Minister Boris Johnson's government bypassed normal procedures to award to their cronies contracts worth many hundreds of millions of pounds for essential goods such as PPE that were not delivered on time, if at all, or were substandard and unusable.

support to recover the Falkland Islands [25]. This has always been the case. In Victorian Britain, poverty was seen as a crime and destitute individuals were herded into workhouses that were deliberately made so bad that only the truly desperate would enter them. Once in, there was no escape, the taint of being raised in a workhouse could never be washed away. Until war broke out, that is, then suddenly all the criminally poor were herded into another institution, the military, because, as the posters shrieked, "Your country needs You." Until then, the country didn't want to know they existed. And until an emergency erupts and the wealthy remember that unused human resource which can be mobilised on the cheap with a few flags and drums, there is no such thing as society, unions need to be broken because there is no alternative, sentiment has no cash value in a rational economy, and so on. All because, as Thatcher kept shouting "There is no alternative." True, there is no alternative, until suddenly there is.

However, those wedded to economic rationalism and laws forget, or affect to forget, an important principle called the law of diminishing returns. That is, workers can be held down and squeezed, and tied in ever-tightening knots of mortgage, health and student debt but the return must decline. Eventually, there will come a point when the system breaks down, the workers refuse to play their appointed role in the great game of financial fraud that the international economy has become. You can fool some of the people all of the time, or all of the people some of the time, but not all of the people all of the time. And it is already starting to happen.

As for capitalism's destruction of the natural environment which Polanyi predicted, that is well under way. Left to their own devices, capitalists would simply bulldoze everything and sell it. Not for them the values that mean a mine can't be built in a World Heritage area, or whales must not be hunted to extinction, or concerns about matters with no truth value, such as global warming [26]. For example, it is now known that as early as 1977, the giant oil company, Exxon-Mobil, was warned by its own scientists that continued burning of fossil fuels

---

[25]   *She* needed to recover them, otherwise she would have looked a fool but the passengers on the Clapham omnibus would surely have handed them to the Argentines if they'd asked nicely.

[26]   In the strict sense, global warming is indeterminate as it hasn't happened yet. However, industrialists and their apologists argue that because it isn't true, therefore it is false, which is entirely a specious argument.

would have major, potentially devastating, long-term effects on the world climate. This didn't fit with Exxon's business plan so they suppressed the research and launched a well-funded program of climate-change denialism. All the companies involved in the so-called opioid epidemic in the US knew perfectly well that their products were dangerous and highly addictive, but they continued marketing them, boosting sales by concealing the facts of their products' dangerous side effects. Hundreds of thousands of working class people in the US have died, and millions of other lives ruined, because of this shining example of the neoliberal market economy.

There are innumerable examples. Every half-sensible person knows that many, if not most, matters on earth are priceless. They do not have, cannot have, a cash value, and that attempts to do so will result in destruction of our most treasured artefacts and natural assets. Nonetheless, economists and financiers continue to push the neoliberal project as though there is no alternative. But that's just propaganda, there is always an alternative, it just won't make the rich richer, that's all. The 1% sanctify the principle of working to get richer, but that scheme only works when the 99% don't follow that principle, when they work for other reasons such as duty or devotion. Eventually, workers must get sick of being held down, there is only so much entertainment that can distract them. A recent attempt to capitalise on the popularity of football to the advantage of the wealthy, the so-called Super League, was crushed by the fans. The iron law of economics, the law of diminishing returns, will not be denied. As Kenneth Boulding noted: Anybody who believes that exponential growth can go on forever in a finite world is either a madman or an economist.

Finally, a question for neoliberal economists: If you insist that all human activity must be driven by the profit motive, that schools and universities must teach only courses that will lead to productive jobs, meaning those valued by the neoliberals (which excludes humanities subjects such as philosophy, most history, politics, literature and other arts), so that we can build a beautiful new world where everybody has a well-paying job in finance or industry, what then? What will people do if nobody has studied music, literature, history, philosophy, or even softer sciences such as ecology (not necessary because the mine is going ahead anyway), conservation ("If Tasmanian devils have any value, they'll conserve themselves"), archeology and so on? We will have a society of miseducated technicians who will soon be bored rigid and will turn to drugs and alcohol and mischief-making. Of course, besides selling them the drugs and alcohol, neoliberalism has a remedy for people who get depressed or suffer major mental disorders: "Go ahead, hang yourself, you're a non-productive burden, a drain on other people's money anyway. And all you old and disabled people, sitting around eating and filling in time until you pop off, why don't you do our market economy a favour and jump out the window? As for you unionist trouble-makers, the burgeoning privatised prisons industry will be pleased to profit from your misery."

We have already seen what happens when politicians and bureaucrats make decisions on what basic viral research should be funded. All warnings on novel coronaviruses were ignored for about fifteen years, and then what happened? Even without counting the lives lost and ruined, the pandemic has cost trillions when the basic research would have cost no more than hundreds of millions, if that. Neoliberalism would not fund research on climate change ("Fear-mongering Luddites"); instead, all the money would be spent on building new, bigger, faster missiles to deliver new, more powerful neutron bombs that will kill every living thing in range but leave the buildings intact. Because that is exactly what neoliberalism dictates. It all flows from the innate need to crush everybody else and climb to the top of the pile.

As shocking as it may sound, there are some things in life that people must do without the expectation of reward, the activity is its own reward. If material acquisition, consumption and clawing one's way to the top of the hierarchy are the point of life, very soon, people will be asking "Why bother?" And then they may just turn to unpaid political activism.

So in one respect, Thatcher was right: if everything in society has a cash value determined by a small and wholly self-interested coterie of power-hungry technicians, and they determine that society's culture, traditions and value structures are worthless, then there is indeed no such thing as society. There's nothing left, because these are the features that make society worthwhile, they are the glue that holds humans together, that distinguish us from colonies of insects. Absent them, all that is left is an ant nest of mindless workers scurrying along their autistic paths to unmarked oblivion, held to their tasks not by anything positive, such as affection, loyalty, family ties and so on, but by terror. Ultimately, and just as Polanyi predicted, neoliberalism destroys the society on which it feasts. Thatcher's sneering slogan that there is no such thing as society was a self-fulfilling prediction, which is itself one of the cardinal features of irrationality.

5.5: Even the hoax is a hoax.

> The virus is a hoax, just a common cold.

> The virus is a deadly plot to kill old people/to inject us and turn us into zombies.

> Brexit will free us to race ahead.

> Nobody has ever been to the moon, the landings were staged in Hollywood.

> Saddam Hussein's weapons of mass destruction can reach London in 45 minutes.

> Russian interference let Trump win.

> The election was stolen.

> Communism/ Islam/ China is trying to destroy us (choose one or more or write your own).

The Tower of Babel had nothing on today's news, but Ghandi would have been ready:

> An error does not become truth by reason of multiplied propagation, nor does truth become error because nobody sees it. Truth stands, even if there be no public support. It is self-sustained.

To an outsider, one of the most striking features of right wing extremism is how nobody believes what they see, how easily and quickly people accept that hidden behind every facade is a machinery of evil, a conspiracy to destroy the nation/religion/football team. Nothing is random, there are no innocent errors and, above all, my nation/religion/football team can do no wrong. Since I support it ("My country right or wrong"), I too am never wrong. Conveniently, while nations and football teams are sometimes cheated out of winning, infallibility is written into the charter for religions. For them, if anything goes wrong, it has to be someone else's doing, but that only reflects what people wanted to believe anyway.

If we want to talk about conspiracies, about why people believe patent nonsense, we really have to start with the concept of belief, which takes us to the branch of philosophy known as epistemology. For convenience, we can start at the beginning:

5.1. Humans emit different sorts of sounds. Sounds arising in the larynx are known as vocalisations or vocal acts.

5.2. Some vocal acts carry no additional meaning beyond the sound itself (cries of joy, pain or annoyance, coughing, laughing, yodelling).

5.3. The remaining non-random vocal acts are known as linguistic acts, meaning they are generated according to a predetermined code, better known as language.

5.4. Linguistic acts carry information from the speaker to the audience. There are different kinds of linguistic acts, such as questions, exclamations, orders or assertions.

5.5. Assertions are linguistic acts whose informational content can be assigned a truth value.

5.6. Truth value is the state of being true, or false, or indeterminate (We won't start on theories of truth but will use the pragmatist view that truth is both the end of enquiry and the beginning of action).

5.7. A proposition is the informational content or the underlying meaning of an assertion. A proposition doesn't change just because the sentence structure or even the language changes.

5.8. A declarative sentence conveys a proposition (information, meaning) as a well-formed sentence within the grammar of the particular language. Declarative sentences have truth values. A declaration that asserts something about the past or present can be true, false or indeterminate. Apart from death and taxes, all assertions about the future are indeterminate.

5.9. A speaker's mental state toward the proposition in an assertion constitutes his propositional attitude.

5.10. Belief is a propositional attitude of truth (as in "I believe what I am saying is true").

5.11. Knowledge is justified true belief, where justification is independent and objective evidence of support for the belief (again, we take the pragmatic view). In the final analysis, a belief is what you are prepared to act on after you have eliminated your doubts.

5.12. False beliefs are possible but false knowledge is not. It is impossible to say "I believe X but I know it isn't true." (Qualify that: it is impossible to say it and expect to be taken seriously; we'll come back to this point).

There is an important precondition to all this: Beliefs do not exist in isolation. Each individual belief I hold is nested in, supported by, connected to, consistent with, and therefore, at least to my mind, *justified by,* a very large set of more basic or prior beliefs. Each of those supporting beliefs is further nested in qualifiers until we reach the most fundamental beliefs we have about ourselves and the nature of the universe, i.e. our ontological stance. The further down the line we go, the more tightly the beliefs are held. In practice, this means that older beliefs are held more strongly than newly-acquired information, effectively becoming part of the personality and therefore part of the basis of self-esteem. We actively defend our fundamental beliefs against refutation, most commonly by denying the validity of recent, contradictory material. That way, we can feel justified, meaning "It feels right, it feels comfortable, I feel vindicated." That is, for ordinary purposes, belief is ultimately a matter of personal comfort or emotion.

In practice, I believe or disbelieve a new item of information depending on whether it gels with my prior beliefs, with little regard for the factual evidence supporting it. If a new item of information grates with or contradicts my prior beliefs, I cannot immediately accept it is true, i.e. initially, my propositional attitude toward it is disbelief. The only way I can believe it is by changing my older beliefs, which is painful and/or humiliating in that I will lose status so, mostly, I find a way of not doing it. I would rather disregard new material than question my basic belief system. This is the basis of the well-documented notion of "confirmation bias." Somebody says something and, without the slightest effort, I dismiss it: "I don't believe it, he would never do that sort of thing." Faced with irrefutable evidence of something that contradicts our most basic beliefs, we are shocked and fight it as long as possible, but the usual mechanism of maintaining comfort (eliminating cognitive dissonance) is simply to deny the truth of the new information:

"Trump won, I know he won. They're lying, it's all fake news."

"There's no virus, it's just the government trying to infringe our rights."

"The virus is a Chinese conspiracy designed to weaken our nation."

A person who says that sort of thing is not delusional, just an idiot [27]. It is classic human folly. Faced with the choice of accepting information he doesn't like, that conflicts with his prior beliefs, he rejects it. For a sane person, what counts is why it is so important for his candidate to win, or why he needs to deny anything the government says, to the extent he deliberately warps reality. Partly, it's because reality is pliable, nothing more than what we all agree it is: "Reality is a shared delusion." We humans have always indulged our creativity by twisting reality into bold new shapes. For the rest, when reality contradicts our fundamental beliefs, we experience it as mental distress. Changing these beliefs is generally not considered an option as it involves saying "Looks like I've been wrong all these years," which is felt as a blow to the self-esteem, a loss of prestige and status. Far easier it is to modify our perceived reality by using any of the plethora of subterfuges available to the ordinarily creative person. For a masterclass in avoiding reality, just listen to the average politician.

Ideally, as part of every citizen's education, we would be taught the process of examining each belief in turn, allowing us to discard false or unproven beliefs. The classic exposition of this type of inner exploration was by the French polymath, Rene Descartes, who arrived at two rock solid convictions he could not further doubt. First, he started and ended with the conviction that God exists although, a few times, he even showed that doubts on this point were not contradictory. Second, he concluded that the only other thing he could trust was that he existed. If I can think, he said, if I can ask "Do I exist?" then, as a matter of incontrovertible fact, I can be sure I exist. *Cogito, ergo sum,* I think, therefore I am. I have to believe I exist, I cannot doubt it

---

[27]   Based on content alone, these types of assertions are often indistinguishable from delusions, but the decision on whether a belief is delusional does not rest on content alone.

otherwise I couldn't ask the question (although that sort of doubt is quite common in people developing psychotic states). Learning to examine one's deepest beliefs dispassionately is not comfortable and it certainly doesn't sit well with religions, governments and so on, so it never quite manages to get on the curriculum.

Why do we believe anything else? In order to survive, we have to, there really is no alternative. Inevitably, from the belief that I exist and desire to continue existing flows a further set of beliefs: I have to believe this water is safe to drink; that this bridge is strong; my money is secure in the bank; the surgeon knows what she is doing; my children are safe at school, and so on. Each of these will lead to further beliefs, on and on. The ideal is that each belief is nested in justified true beliefs but that's rare. In ordinary life, a lot of beliefs we hold are actually wrong, or stupid, or contradict each other but, as long as we don't question them too closely, they will all fit together without too much uncomfortable grating and jarring. The discrepancies will only start to show when we stray from our quotidian ruts, or what is now called "outside my comfort zone" [28].

Many important beliefs are acquired preverbally or even non-verbally, early in life when we don't really know what's going on. A lot will be implicit rather than explicit, so we don't actually know what they are but they still influence us directly. Thus, in daily life, people routinely act on very incomplete or even wrong information, and still believe (i.e. feel) they are right. And, of course, these days, everybody is enjoined to trust their feelings even though, nearly 400 years ago, Descartes showed that emotions can't be trusted.

Why doesn't a wrong belief self-correct? Because we don't like changing or even questioning our most fundamental beliefs, they are too closely tied to the set of rules that define us as personalities. A person raised in a society which held that all black people are inferior may be polite and friendly to everybody but still recoil when a black person brushes past. When told this, he may deny it because questioning his beliefs will automatically cause loss of status in the dominance hierarchy, either by demoting him ("I always believed I was a nice person but now it seems I'm just a bigot like everybody else") or

---

[28]   These days, people seem to believe they have a right to dwell forever inside their "comfort zones," meaning zone of ignorance, and nobody is allowed to say or do anything to upset them. Descartes would have fallen off his chair with laughter.

by promoting others. A classic example was Hitler's response to Jesse Owens winning at the 1936 Berlin Olympics. He walked out. He was humiliated and refused to accept that a black man could beat his superior Aryan runners. It is acceptable to react badly once but it must be used as a learning experience and not repeated. The definition of an idiot is a person who repeatedly acts on inconsistent beliefs while insisting he can't be wrong, that is, he defends his beliefs in the face of directly contradictory information (recall the aphorism which Einstein apparently *didn't* coin: Insanity is doing the same thing twice and expecting a different outcome).

The philosopher, Edmund Gettier, said he had found a gap between justified true belief and knowledge. There is a large literature on this point but it's not entirely convincing as one of his examples related to a future event, which is necessarily indeterminate. For ordinary purposes, we can say that a reasonably-minded and reasonably educated person, looking dispassionately at the relevant information, will assign the correct truth value to a proposition (true, false or indeterminate). Something is either true or it ain't, and if it ain't, it's either false or indeterminate. That's the end of the matter.

This isn't just a matter of dry philosophy, this is important, just as the outlandish claims listed at the top of this section are important. Currently, the great majority of people dying of the virus in Western countries have refused immunisation for reasons which are not just plain silly but are potentially suicidal and/or homicidal. Truth really is a matter of life or death. Why, then, has a former president of the US claimed hundreds of times that he didn't lose the 2020 election, that he actually won but it was stolen from him by a conspiracy, when he gives no evidence to support his claim, and all experts agree that all evidence says he lost and nothing says he won? Is he an idiot, is he lying, or is he mad?

I think we can dispense with Trump: he says anything that comes into his head if he thinks it will be to his advantage. He has no regard for the concept of truth as a value that exists independently of what he wants. If he accords truth any value at all, or even understands the concept, what he *wants* to be true and what *is* true are one and the same thing. The real question is why anybody would believe him to the extent of invading the nation's Capitol building to force an illegal change of government (aka *coup d'état*). This is part of the bigger question of why people believe nonsense. Why do people say they believe something when they have no evidence, or there is even evidence against it? The answer to that is: Fear. Fear of being proven wrong, of humiliation and exclusion, of not knowing, of randomness, of being chewed up and spat out by forces that don't give a damn about us. People are actually frightened to say "I don't know," the corollary being that by saying we know something, we gain a sense of power, even if it's only power over our own anxiety. Ignorance isn't bliss, it's sleepless nights.

We believe a new proposition when it sits comfortably with our prior beliefs. That is, we accept an idea if there is no cognitive dissonance, that jarring sense of something not being right. Henry Mencken again: "It is the nature of the human species to reject what is true but unpleasant and to embrace what is false but comforting." So: we are thrilled to believe the most outlandish stories about somebody we don't like but we dismiss as "the usual jealous gossip" the same story about somebody we do like. There is, for example, no story about English perfidy that the French will not believe—*Les anglais, ils sont capables de tout*—and, of course, vice versa, with a double serve of scorn.

We believe what we want to believe. What we want to believe is decided by what we already believe and what we want the belief to do. We believe anything that makes us feel comfortable and reassured, and dismiss by any ploy available anything that grates. At Pt 5.12 (above), I said: It is impossible to say "I believe X but I know it isn't true." There are plenty of people, especially in politics, who will say: "Yes, I know I told you yesterday that black is black but today, I'm telling you black is white so you'd better believe it." For them, truth is simply what allows them to win an argument, to dominate other people. Appearing to win is the most important thing in life, as in: "If saying black is white allows me to dominate these stupid people, then black is white, and I'm justified in saying this because everybody knows they're fools who need to be pulled into line." Thus, there is no account of Donald Trump's immoral and/or criminal behaviour that a right wing American will accept or, if accepting it, not dismiss it as either too trivial to consider, or not as bad as the other side, or excusable under the circumstances...

When, for example, Bill Clinton had an affair with a young female intern, everybody on the right wanted him run out of town; when women accused Trump of much worse, they were branded as lying bitches but, when he later boasted of sexually assaulting women, people (men and women) laughed and said "Oh boy, what a man. He's got my vote." If one of Mr Putin's opponents dies in suspicious circumstances, he is vilified as a murderous tyrant; when successive American presidents conduct long-term, systematic programs of murdering suspected "terrorists" by drones, killing nine civilians for each probable/possible "terrorist," that's fine, we're fighting The Good Fight. If ISIS in Syria kill a US citizen, that's grounds for an invasion; if the US kills its own citizens, they were criminals. The essential point is that our emotive response to new information is determined by our prior belief systems (aka prejudices). Belief is just an attitude to an item of information, and we adjust our attitude to new information so that it accords with our prior beliefs, i.e. the old information with which we are comfortable. We protect our core beliefs by valuing cognitive harmony over truth; we protect our cognitive harmony by adjusting truth. By this elementary technique, humans daily convince themselves of the most egregious rubbish but they are not thereby insane or psychotic.

The other side is fear of what might happen if we tell people "No, I don't believe what you say, that's just your opinion." This may mean social death or it may mean literal death, depending on the context, but it takes us straight back to our tribal yearnings. The person who laughs when the chief stubs his toe or who calls the shaman a fraud will be in trouble because the chief and shaman are determined to remain on top so you'd better not laugh at them. We don't want to be excluded or sent to the bottom of the hierarchy, and most of us aren't keen on being burned at the stake. We shape our beliefs to fit with our deeper need to be accepted as one of the tribe. Other times, we accept as true what we are told because it makes us feel better and stops all sorts of trouble. Then we get the chance to tell other people what they have to believe: "This is how it is, I got it on good authority so you'd better believe it." It gives us power over them, levering us up the hierarchy by pushing them down, which feels good in itself [29]. Later, admitting error becomes too painful so we find excuses not to budge, as astronomer Carl Sagan noted:

---

[29]   Remember that most people are not so concerned with how many people are above them in the hierarchy as how many people are below them. By focusing on dominating, we take the pain out of being dominated.

One of the saddest lessons of history is this: if we've been bamboozled long enough, we tend to reject any evidence of the bamboozle. We're no longer interested in finding out the truth. The bamboozle has captured us. It's simply too painful to acknowledge, even to ourselves, that we've been taken. Once you give a charlatan power over you, you almost never get it back ... Evidence that contradicts the ruling belief system is held to extraordinary standards, while evidence that entrenches it is uncritically accepted [6].

Philosopher Daniel Stoljar noted the same phenomenon in his analysis of the prevailing physicalist ontology:

The first thing to say when considering the truth of physicalism is that we live in an overwhelmingly physicalist or materialist intellectual culture. The result is that, as things currently stand, the standards of argumentation required to persuade someone of the truth of physicalism are much lower than the standards required to persuade someone of its negation. (The point here is a perfectly general one: if you already believe or want something to be true, you are likely to accept fairly low standards of argumentation for its truth.) [7].

You can, of course, believe what you like as long as you don't talk about it but the trend now is for people to spout what would once have got them locked up, *and* they expect their screwball ideas to be taken seriously. Bizarrely, people are offended if derisive laughter greets their claim that yes, mass vaccination is a plot to inject tracking devices into everybody so the government can turn them into mindless zombies or kill everybody. We have reached the point where nobody wants to hear humdrum facts, people expect to be thrilled every time they turn the TV or computer on. They want to believe the silliest nonsense around, and the crazier it is, the faster it spreads on social media [30].

This is not just your ordinarily silly people panicking in the suburbs. Sky News, a division of the Murdoch empire, has just been suspended from social media for a week for deliberately spreading false information about the pandemic. Does the editor regard as true what the experts say is false, meaning is he an idiot (well-meaning or otherwise); or is he lying; or is he mad? It's important, lives depend on

---

[30]   Five times faster, in fact.

it. George Carlin commented, "Tell people that there is an invisible man in the sky who created the universe, and the vast majority will believe you ... Tell them that the paint is wet and they have to touch it to be sure." As the Romans knew, *Mundus vult decipi, ergo decipiatur.* The world wants to be deceived, so go for it. People eagerly seek confirming material and actively adjust disconfirming until it matches their prejudices. We want to be proven right; being right is powerful, it feels good and, compared with all the ditherers, gives us a boost up the dominance hierarchy known as society (Sky News, of course, are only obeying free market doctrine to increase their sales).

So it's not quite so simple as saying people want to be deceived. First and foremost, we want to *feel* we're right but we don't come to the class with a blank slate. We carry a great deal of prior baggage. If feeling right means ignoring, manipulating or discounting facts to fit with our prior convictions, then a pleasant falsehood will almost always clobber a painful truth. Truth is the first casualty of war, including the minute-to-minute wars of daily life. Of course it is, people want to fight but first, they have to justify it to themselves. Justification means rearranging the facts until they support our position. We do this more or less unconsciously, just because it feels better. Learning not to do this is painful, so most people, including many scientists and politicians who ought to know better, don't bother.

There have been long and indecisive philosophical debates over what it means to say "self-deception," or whether we can in fact deceive ourselves. If we look at points 5.10 – 5.12 above, at what point does unjustified belief become justified? Mere belief is cheap, as Carlin said; what counts is solid evidence which, as every researcher knows, is hard to come by. People decide what they want to believe on the basis of what feels comfortable or confirmatory *of their fundamental beliefs*; they believe what they want to believe just because it makes them feel good, and they dismiss the rest. We scan the evidence and pick out the bits that suit us. We look at Purported Fact A, compare it with Purported Fact B, and make a choice. This is not difficult to understand, we do it all the time: "Should I believe what my tribe are saying, or should I believe that outsider? No, that's too scary, I'll stick with my tribe, it's safer." It's only a problem for philosophers and economists who like to believe that humans make rational decisions by dispassionately weighing the evidence (that opinion alone is enough to prove humans are irrational: Thank you, professor, now using just your model of human rationality, could you kindly explain warfare? Certainly, take your time).

Overwhelmingly, we make decisions very quickly, using information and impulses that we don't fully understand or don't even know, and we don't like to admit we could be wrong: "Is she the sort of woman who would cheat on her husband? Well, all women are so I'll believe she did." Afterward, we need to argue that we're right because being proven wrong bumps us back down the ladder again. Error invites scorn and scorn is painfully humiliating. The impulse to dominate is so powerful that even the notion of truth revolves around preserving our status in society.

Sigmund Freud said "All human behaviour is over-determined." What he meant was that the behaviour we show at any instant is the outcome of a myriad factors operating too fast for conscious awareness. Some factors are public, some are private, some we could know if we made the effort while lots, Freud said, we can't know, they are unconscious. Wilhelm Stekel, one of Freud's earliest associates who soon fell out with him, said that we choose not to know. Essentially, we glance at the facts and make a quick decision about what is going on behind the scenes, then we slam the book shut and refuse to reconsider the matter. Ordinary decisions are made according to whatever makes us feel better; truth may or may not get a look in. With a bit of effort, we could uncover the truth but mostly we don't want to. It's like a man who has an endless line of excuses as to why he doesn't add up his income and expenses: it would show he's broke. Somewhere, he knows it but if he doesn't examine his finances, he can carry on partying and fool people into believing he's a great bloke who made it by his own effort.

It is the case that people believe rubbish for a raft of personal (psychological) and public (social) reasons. All too often, it is because we want to believe bad about our enemies. If somebody says something that confirms our prejudices, we embrace it, cherish it, embellish it and pass it on but we don't look deeper just in case it isn't true—and we get angry when somebody else does. We don't want to believe our enemies are capable of doing good: "I can't stand him so don't try to tell me he's a nice person. He did? Well, I'm sure he had an ulterior motive." He is our enemy first, the evidence comes later. We make decisions very quickly, based in a host of largely unknown factors but … we're inconsistent. The reasons we use to justify decisions can change almost from minute to minute. The final decision depends on who's around, what's happening, dimly-remembered childhood events and so on. Different reasons bubble up, briefly they seem important then they fade away and the opposite reason takes its place.

And Yes, Virginia, that is not a model of human rationality. It is a model of human *ir*rationality, which warfare, greed, drugs and alcohol, corruption, crime, neglect, gambling, inequality, environmental destruction and so on show is the correct model of human thinking. We have the capacity to think rationally, but we rarely bother. For example, we have designed weapons systems that can lob a thermonuclear weapon on a city on the other side of the planet to a metre's accuracy. That is an example of applied rationality. We just haven't bothered to work out whether we ought to do this sort of thing: even the bomb's existence is unassailable proof of our ultimate irrationality. Closer to home, for months in 2021, the UK was convulsed with the story of Geronimo, a male alpaca with TB. The Agriculture Department said the unfortunate animal had to be destroyed, then the media got the story and there were near-riots over the "cruel government." Nobody seemed to recall that, each day in the UK, a million or more animals are killed (two million if fish are counted) as food for humans.

Why then does a person believe the virus is a hoax? It depends on who he is, where, when, at what stage of life, who's around, what he wants in life or what he doesn't want, what his mates believe and what his mother-in-law says he ought to believe, what he can afford, his childhood, on and on. People choose what they want to believe by manipulating and reweighting the evidence to suit their prejudices. The prejudices come first and determine what evidence they see, or how they weigh it. Early in his career, the great Lord Lister noticed this was true even of science:

> I remember at an early period of my own life, showing to a man of high reputation as a teacher some matters which I happened to have observed. And I was very much struck and grieved to find that, while all the facts lay equally clear before him, only those that squared with his previous theories seemed to affect his organs of vision.

Top of the list of prejudices are those we have dwelt on so far: the social imperative ("My mates are all saying the virus is harmless so

maybe I'd better keep quiet or they'll think I'm weak/ My hero says it's
a hoax and I don't want to think he could be wrong"), the dominance
imperative ("I know the truth, you're an idiot so keep quiet"/ "You
can't tell me what to think"/ "OK OK, whatever you say, stop yelling at
me"), the territorial imperative ("I know something you don't know"),
xenophobia ("If they're saying it, it must be a lie") and fear ("Omigod,
what if the injection's dangerous? Can we trust the government?").

Add to these a host of personal aims in the dominance game, such
as the crushing need to prove everybody else wrong, especially people
in authority, or to be seen as unique or smarter than everybody else or,
on the other side, the need to be seen as compliant and acquiescent
(fear of causing trouble or arguments), the need to be polite and
agreeable (fear of disapproval), laziness, on and on. We could call this
stochastic psychopathology: if we throw a couple of contrasting ideas
to a group of unselected citizens, they will sort themselves into groups
who believe and disbelieve, but each for a dozen different reasons. That
is, they will predictably form tribes based on what they believe, even
though the individual outcome is largely unpredictable (and may not
make sense, either).

It gets back to the question of why people believe anything. Answer:
We have to. I have to believe the floor will support me, that this food is
safe to eat, that my car's brakes are safe, that the injection is safer than
not having it, that the plumber, the cook and the pharmacist know
what they are doing, and so on. If I'm not sure about any of these
things, meaning I'm not prepared to act on it, I have to take steps to
improve the odds. That's all. Some people don't trust anybody in power
and believe every official statement is a lie, so they automatically
believe the opposite of what they're told, even if it's patent rubbish.
They don't want to be told what to do so that forces them to defend
themselves, which they do by aggression. Others are desperate to find
something, anything, that will justify their position so they aren't
forced to admit they were wrong. They clutch at straws to avoid the
intolerable humiliation of people laughing at them, marginalising them,
pushing them down the hierarchy. It all goes back to domination.
Others will believe anything they're told because uncertainty fills them
with fear and paralyses them.

The only question remaining is why nonsense is so prominent now.
In times past, people who had odd ideas kept them to themselves but
now they feel the need to broadcast it to the world. Thank social

media, but also thank the times of fear and uncertainty. What bothers me is that people never get the conspiracies right. There are indeed conspiracies, such as spurious weapons of mass destruction, massive financial fraud, manipulation of the stock and precious metals markets by options and futures traders, misrepresentation of psychiatric and opiate drugs, corruption and, above all, the fossil fuel industry's denial of global warming. Unfortunately, people would rather get angry over fantasized Russian interference in elections, or believe the Chinese released the virus to get even with the West or to kill off its old people or, implausibly, China is preparing to invade Australia. Who believes nonsense? Frightened people, angry or domineering people, insecure, troubled or poorly educated people, dramatic people, intelligent people with an insatiable urge to defeat the experts, people who want to make money... And who joins fascist groups? Frightened people, angry or domineering people, insecure, troubled or poorly educated people, dramatic people etc, looking for certainty in uncertain times. The man who says he knows, who promises he can lead the people to safety, is guaranteed a wide audience. The woman who says uncertainty is built into our perception will be booed off stage. Certainty feels better than uncertainty, even if it is wrong.

Fine, you say, that explains part of a fascist movement, the part that believes the rubbish they are served and follows the leader, but what about the leader? How do we explain the person who starts these crazy rumours? Is he an idiot, a madman or a liar?

5.6: Fools, fiends and follies.

Just in case there is a person in Patagonia who hasn't heard, there is a movement known as QAnon sweeping the US and spilling over its borders. Followers believe a person who calls himself Q, who they say is highly placed in the intelligence community, releases cryptic messages on the internet to reveal the secret plots at the heart of the US government. According to Mia Bloom and Sophia Moskalenko, authors of *Pastels and Pedophiles* [8], the phenomenon seems to have evolved from an online computer game but it has acquired a life of its own. Q-followers believe what most people would say is the craziest stuff, about cabals of high-placed paedophiles who kidnap children and torture them to gain a chemical called adrenochrome which has all sorts of wondrous properties. Donald Trump was supposed to have cleaned out the evil ones but they thwarted him, which accounts for why a lot of people refuse to believe he didn't lose the election, or that he will be returned to power on January 20th, no, in March, er, make that August 13th, oh that's right, it'll be after the 2022 midterm elections but if not, he'll surely win again in 2024. That is, like delusions, their beliefs are immune to refutation but, unlike delusions, that is a matter of choice, not necessity. They could say "Oh dear, looks like I'm wrong. Silly me," but they choose not to and try to bluff it out. Admitting error is humiliating as it would allow other people to mock them and look down on them, and they will do anything they can to avoid that.

Who started this? Nobody knows but the content is so bizarre that if he exists, Q is probably psychotic. So was the Rev. Jimmy Jones but nobody realised it. History is replete with psychotic cult leaders; all that counts is why people follow them. Again, the answer is stochastic psychopathology. People believe because they're frightened or they want to conform or they are themselves pretty mad or … on and on. It's also perfectly feasible that the Q phenomenon started as a joke. It certainly sounds like the sort of joke that clever undergraduates would start, just so they can laugh at all the gimps who fall for it. But then, as Bloom and Moskalenko describe, people like retired Gen. Michael Flynn moved in and started to make big money out of it. If it's a joke, it's well and truly out of control because Q-followers were prominent in the January 6th insurrection.

In trying to account for bizarre beliefs, we quickly get stuck in circular explanations. Very often, it reaches the point where all we can say is "Well, that's just how he is." Starting with madness, the idea of a delusional or crazy belief has been accepted in most cultures throughout most of human history. A delusion is defined as a fixed, false belief, out of context with the subject's intellectual, sociocultural and educational background. Mainstream psychiatric opinion is that delusions are the result of some unknown physical disturbance of the brain, most likely at the level of the chemicals that transmit information between nerve cells in the brain, or what is known as the "chemical imbalance" thesis. It says: "We don't know why your son believes the CIA is shining X-rays on his brain from a geostationary satellite but we don't have to know, it means nothing. Give him these tablets and come back in a month." The alternative is to say that his bizarre beliefs have an inner psychological significance, that they represent some deep-seated conflict but unless he is prepared to talk about it and accept the deeper meaning (which is rare), he won't change. There is, however, a big difference between a person who develops his own delusional beliefs and those who accept what he says. People take up crazy ideas either because they are attracted to them (the crazy ideas confirm what they already believe), or because they are driven to them through fear, as the least scary explanation for a disturbed personal life.

Moving on, are the originators of ridiculous or dangerous beliefs just loud-mouthed idiots who would change their minds if they did a bit more homework or understood more about the quantum theory or immunology they keep spouting about? Are they the sorts of clever but uneducated people who tell themselves they understand a complex text, pick out the bits that suit their prejudices and then build an elaborate theory based on this misinformation? This is how Adolf Hitler actually operated. Hitler had about ten years of basic schooling but he read voraciously, stuffing his head with writers such as the philosopher, Arthur Schopenhauer. Like most autodidacts (self-taught), young Adolf thought he understood (nobody understands Schopenhauer [31]) and used this to impress people and win arguments. It impressed him, too, but what he didn't learn in his self-directed education was the concept of self-criticism, of how to apply systematic doubt to one's most precious beliefs.

As is so common, Hitler read to have his opinions confirmed, not questioned. In Chapter 2 of *Mein Kampf*, he makes it quite clear that when he arrived in Vienna in his teenage years, he knew next to nothing about Jews and had no opinions one way or the other. After a few years of living hand to mouth in the slums, which would not have exposed him to the better classes of Viennese Jewry, he concluded they were the authors of his and Germany's misfortunes and could quote figures and arguments to support his case. Once he had worked all this out, he dismissed all information to the contrary as foreign propaganda: "I'm right, they're lying." The rest is history but it shows again (if we needed it) that ill-educated, self-righteous and intolerant people in positions of power are a menace.

---

[31]   Of his philosophical peers, Schopenhauer is reputed to have said: "I should like to see the man who could boast of a more miserable set of contemporaries than mine." His eager acolyte, the future Führer, would have confirmed the lugubrious master's opinion of humanity's intellectual capabilities.

Donald Trump repeatedly states he won the 2020 presidential election. Is he mad, is he lying or just an idiot? The answer is a cautious probably. Firstly, is he a fascist? On Sept 19th, 2022, Rep. Pramila Jayapal tweeted: "Donald Trump is a fascist. Period," but I would say he is not. He doesn't have the political awareness or determination to commit to anything other than promoting himself and feathering his own nest. Fascists, as mentioned, must submerge themselves in something very much bigger. To get to the top, they must first become a hard-working cog in a machine. Trump didn't accept that anything was bigger, more important or more interesting than himself. Despite vast sums of dark money and free advertising from the mainstream media, he gained less than half the vote but it was enough to get him installed in the White House where, as the puppet of his donors, he amused and distracted the crowds. Meanwhile, working behind the scenes, the sinister operatives from the Republican National Committee were busy dismantling the regulatory and welfare systems of the national government. Trump *used* fascist memes and symbols, only because they resonated with his own prejudices and earned lots of applause, but he had no commitment to them; he stopped, as the Americans say, "hating on" the Russians, conjuring up instead the illusion of an army of illegal immigrants trying to steal into the country as *ennemi du jour*. Same message ("The country is in mortal danger"), different enemy.

Did he believe any of this stuff? I don't think so, not in the normal sense of "believe." He spouted whatever bit of self-serving nonsense came into his head; if it got a cheer, he used it again but if it didn't, he forgot it to the point where, two days later, he would deny he ever said it. While a great deal of what he said was openly false and met the definition of lying, he wasn't lying in the normal, cold and deliberate sense of the word. He was just spouting foolish nonsense in the hope that somebody would believe him and he could make a profit. In other words, he was a charlatan, a thoroughly reprehensible human being whose election was symptomatic of the political crisis that afflicts the USA.

That's psychotics and fools, now we come to the liars, the people who deliberately set out to deceive the public. Philosopher Harry Frankfurt defines a lie thus:

> Telling a lie is an act with a sharp focus. It is designed to insert a particular falsehood at a specific point in a set or system of beliefs, in order to avoid the consequences of having that point

occupied by the truth. This requires a degree of craftsmanship...
[9]

This differs from what he calls bullshit, a statement, more art than craft, tossed out to induce a change in the *emotional* state of the audience so that some of them will believe something which may or may not be true. The bullshitter isn't concerned with the truth, only with the effect he has on the audience, and doesn't bother himself over sceptics or doubters. They are not his quarry, he wants only people who will shout their support for his ideas. After a lifetime of practice, Trump was a virtuoso bullshitter. On the other hand, in 2003, when then-president George W Bush and British PM Tony Blair announced that Iraq had stockpiled weapons of mass destruction (WMD) which, in Blair's notorious expression, could hit London in 45 minutes, they were lying. That is, when the UN Monitoring Commission told them that Saddam Hussein didnt have such weapons and had never supported Al-Qaeda, they didn't like the news. They wanted to avoid the consequences of the public knowing there were no such weapons because it would negate the grounds for their planned illegal invasion of Iraq. As a result, they removed the word "not" from the statement, telling the public instead that they intended "... to disarm Iraq of weapons of mass destruction, to end Saddam Hussein's support for terrorism, and to free the Iraqi people."

In a last-ditch attempt to forestall an invasion of his country, which he knew would devastate it, Saddam actually offered to go into exile but this was rejected by the "Coalition of the Willing" and the news suppressed. On January 31st 2003, Bush and Blair announced that Iraq's failure to disarm itself of the phantom nuclear, chemical, and biological weapons was "an immediate and intolerable threat to world peace." All of this, they knew, was false. As the subsequent invasion confirmed, they were fully aware there were no such weapons, so the invasion met the UN criteria for a war of aggression, the worst of crimes against humanity. Then, instead of admitting they were wrong, they changed the subject. So why do people lie? As this example shows, people lie because (a) humans have the capacity to lie and (b) they will do so if they know they can get away with it, or (c) it wins votes and/or (d) they can make money from it. That is, the deceiver uses his position to dominate the deceived.

There was a time when politicians would simply try to evade the truth; now they stare coldly (or earnestly) at the camera and utter bald falsehoods. Sorting the lies from the delusions from the bullshit falls upon the voters, many of whom are insufficiently educated, too frightened, not smart enough, too lazy, too confused or too prejudiced (or all of the above) to sort it out. Which, of course, suits fascists very well. The last thing they want is critical thinkers making a nuisance of themselves.

5.7: Conclusion: The kaleidoscope of fascism.

To summarise, at the core of fascism are a series of contradictions kept under the tightest control by the twin forces of ever-increasing enthusiasm for the cause and the secret police. Eventually, the pressures thus generated must escape control, leading to the inevitable failure of the fascist enterprise.

The heightened sexuality and sensuality of fascism emerges as an androphilia whose opposite side is misogyny. In the patriarchal fascist society, women are the counterpoint to male self-obsession and self-glorification. In the homeland, women are second-rate citizens—sexual receptacles, baby factories and drudges. In the conquered lands, they are victims, their fate sealed as physical and sexual slaves of lesser importance than males as they can't work as hard. In a true slave society, such as the US Confederate states, women's major role was to breed children, in which role the slave owners were more than willing to assist.

Dishonesty and fascism go hand in hand. The fascist refuses to entertain the notion that he may be wrong because wrong means humiliation, loss of status, demotion in the hierarchy. He twists the truth to suit his ends. If things don't work the way he wanted, he twists it again to blame somebody else. But the core of the fascist enterprise is a lie, the falsehood that one group of people is necessarily better than the others and is therefore entitled to a dominant position. Without this lie, fascism is impossible: we can't all be dominant, we can't all be winners. In fact, we can all be winners but only if we work together to lift the entire society. Look at the great cathedrals and temples of the world, the palaces and mighty forts dominating cities and landscapes, the huge battleships and armadas of aircraft built to awe and subdue their neighbours. These days, the cathedrals and palaces are full of gawking tourists, the battleships lie on the ocean floor or have been scrapped, the aircraft smashed to bits or stored in deserts ... If all that effort had been put into building houses and roads for the people, the societies would have roared ahead and quickly come to dominate their neighbours purely for economic and cultural reasons.

In the 1930s, Japan built the world's mightiest battleships, the gigantic *Yamato* class, but they were useless against aircraft carriers (which Japan already knew from sinking the *Prince of Wales* and *Renown* in early 1942). Disarmed, postwar Japan quickly became a major economic power from which all of its citizens benefited. While we see international relations in competitive terms, it is impossible for one nation or group to gain and hold power indefinitely. However, by foregoing the cut-throat competition that has been the norm since the dawn of time, all citizens benefit. Fascism doesn't broadcast this; instead, it spews out a constant stream of biased propaganda larded with falsehoods to convince its people that you're either on top or you're enslaved, if not dead. But that's a message people want to hear: people cheer at being told "We are the exceptional nation, we're the greatest, the richest, the most powerful in history." They don't want to hear that they're nearly broke, their social services and infrastructure are a mess; yes, we can develop a vaccine in record time, we just can't bring ourselves to give it free to all those black and brown and poor and drug-addicted and criminal and (shudder) foreign people...

For every person who thinks he can get ahead by pushing his way up the ladder, there is one who realises he can't make it by that path so he gets his sense of domination by making sure that nobody dominates him. This attitude is not compatible with a stable society but the sense of competition, of the need to dominate or be dominated, is so strong in us that we never question it. We don't think in terms of stability, we worship growth for growth sake even though there is a point where it is no longer necessary, and we have long since passed the point where even our present lifestyle is sustainable. However, the rich have also long since graduated from the race to survive; now they are in a race to outdo each other, even with rides into space, and the workers and unemployed can look after themselves. Since 1978, the average salary of an American CEO has risen 1,322% while that of the average worker has risen 18%. We are now back almost to medieval levels of inequality, where kings and bishops lived in vast palaces and dined on larks' tongues while the workers lived with their pigs in hovels and ate nettle soup. "Don't tread on me" can also say "I'm sick of being treated like an underdog," a warning which the plutocrats ignore at their peril.

It must not be forgotten, which it almost always is, that the French and Russian and Chinese and other revolutions occurred for a reason. It wasn't just that a bunch of blood-thirsty monsters got up one morning and decided it would be fun to chop the heads off an entire class of wonderful people, they were driven to it by desperation. The legitimate needs and ambitions of the great bulk of people were completely ignored by the self-indulgent elite who ran the societies entirely for their own benefit, so extremists took over. By definition, extremists are extreme, they are people who do not restrict themselves in pursuing their goals but who yearn to let loose their inner dogs of war, all they need is an excuse. Of course, they would argue that it became a case of fighting fire with fire: the only way to fight total domination is by building a vast political and military machine whose sole goal is total domination. Yes, they have a case. Also known as fascism.

Note:

In 1974, Friedrich Hayek was awarded the Nobel Memorial Prize in economics but even at the time, it was controversial (note that this award was not bequeathed by Alfred Nobel himself, but was established by the Swedish Riksbank in 1968). Although it is not an academic treatise, *Road to Serfdom* has had a major influence over the past 75 years and was read by many politicians eager to find justification for opposing social spending (in fact, it probably wasn't read by many because it is so badly written that most of them wouldn't get past the first few pages, or would just skim it to pick out the bits they like). Essentially, it is propaganda, a prolix and tedious phillipic against something called socialism, arguing that socialism destroys countries and leads to fascism. That would probably have been news to Hitler who loathed socialism because it was avowedly internationalist, which he despised, but it has convinced a lot of people in Britain and the US.

Socialism, insofar as Hayek defines it, is essentially Stalinist collectivism at its most brutal and, beyond the name, bears no relationship to, say, the British, Scandinavian or Australasian welfare states. However, his virulent hostility has been ingested by the entire right wing establishment, especially in the "Anglosphere," and is used to attack and eliminate any program they don't like (e.g unemployment benefits for the poor, which don't make the rich richer, unlike the equally socialist military budgets, which do).

Hayek was one of the originators of the so-called "trickle-down" theory of economics, that by further enriching the rich, they would invest their wealth to create industries that would employ the poor and improve their lot. This was the justification for the Thatcher-Reagan-Trump tax cuts for the wealthy. However, forty years on, we now know that the policy has failed unconditionally. Using data from 18 OECD countries since 1980, Hope and Limberg from the International Inequalities Institute at the London School of Economics, where Hayek taught for about 18 years, have shown that tax cuts for the rich actually make things worse:

> We find that major reforms reducing taxes on the rich lead to higher income inequality as measured by the top 1% share of pre-tax national income ... In contrast, such reforms do not have any significant effect on economic growth and unemployment [10].

That is, and just as Polanyi predicted, the entire neoliberal project has failed at the very point by which it was justified. This would not have surprised John Maynard Keynes, who criticised Hayek's book *Prices and Production* from 1931 as "...one of the most frightful muddles I have ever read ... an extraordinary example of how, starting with a mistake, a remorseless logician can end in Bedlam." And what will the neoliberals do with that study? Ignore it, of course, because otherwise they would have to admit they're wrong, which humans hate doing.

References:

1. Orwell G (1945) Notes on nationalism. *Polemic*. London, May 1945. Reprinted 1953 in *England Your England and Other Essays*.

2. Andersen K (2017) Fantasyland. How America Went Haywire: A 500-Year History New York: Random House.

3. Hayek FA von (1944). *The Road to Serfdom*. London: Routledge.

4. Polanyi K (1944). *The Great Transformation: The political and economic origins of our time*. Boston: Beacon Press. (See esp. Chap 6: The Self-Regulating Market and the Fictitious Commodities: Labor, Land, and Money).

5. Murray C, Fritjers P (2017) *Game Of Mates: How favours bleed the nation*. Brisbane: Publicious.

6. Sagan C (1997) *The Demon-Haunted World: Science as a Candle in the Dark*. London: Hodder/Headline.

7. Stoljar D (2010). *Physicalism*. Oxford: Routledge.

8. Bloom M, Moskalenko S (2021). *Pastels and Pedophiles. Inside the Mind of QAnon*. Stanford, CA: Redwood Pres.

9. Frankfurt H (1986). On Bullshit. *Raritan Quarterly Review* 6 (2): 81–100. (Fall 1986).

10. Hope D, Limberg J (Dec. 2020). *The Economic Consequences of Major Tax Cuts for the Rich*. III/LSE Working Paper No. 55.

Chapter 6: Fascism, illusion and reality.

> I consider the survival of [fascism] within democracy to be potentially more menacing than the survival of fascist tendencies against democracy.
>
> Theodor Adorno

6.1: Fascism's rise.

To summarise the central points of this work so far, fascism is not a political doctrine or program *sui generis*. Instead, it is a set of political memes and tactics that amplify certain universal human characteristics and can therefore be grafted on to any socio-political program, even a football team. On a national level, the starting point for fascism's rise is widespread fear, resentment and despair over the perceived decline and loss of status of the nation. A militant party takes advantage of a crisis, real or manufactured, to spread the message that the whole nation is in danger but can be saved by implementing their program, essentially putting the nation on a war footing. To this end, it uses a combination of propaganda and actual violence to achieve its goal of regimenting and militarising the whole of society, thus turning the nation into a weapon to destroy its internal and external enemies.

As it has no defining doctrine, fascism is never more than a loose cluster of social, mythical and political themes which can be applied to any group with a common purpose. It is the triumph of style over substance, emotion over knowledge, fantasy over reality. It appeals to people who are attracted by but don't look beyond the superficial excitement, politely known as "low information citizens." They are enthralled because the party offers simple answers to complex problems ("It's all a conspiracy by our enemies"), and equally simple solutions ("Destroy them") which flatter its target audience by making them feel valued for a change. Another important group it attracts are those who see prospects for self-advancement and self-enrichment which, due to lack of qualification, lack of contacts or bad behaviour, would not otherwise be open to them. These recruits, who tend to be somewhat smarter, better educated, quicker at understanding complex issues, and unburdened by scruples, lose no time in manipulating the movement to their personal advantage.

People join the rallies to be imbued with a sense of power they don't feel anywhere else. Fascism is immensely exciting for them as it licenses their most basic urges, rage, hatred and the lust for violent revenge, by wrapping them in a sacred cause. The price they have to pay is that they then cannot leave the movement through fear of feeling an outcast. However, very few will want to leave as, by swapping their previously drab lives for a role in a vast process of cleansing and rebirth of the nation or religion, etc, they feel part of something very much bigger, more powerful and more important. In fascist movements, rebirth or palingenesis is a violent event; the more violent, the more the weakness and treachery is burned out of the nation or religion until only true believers are left. Violence itself is seen as cleansing and sanctifying. This is the opposite of formal religions where spiritual rebirth is a silent, contemplative process; religious sects that practice loud and public "rebirth" will likely use other fascist tropes.

A recurring feature of fascism is that it is not an elite movement. It is constructed by social outsiders to appeal to social outsiders, particularly those on the lower rungs of the social ladder, to challenge the corrupt or incompetent elite. Leaders and followers often take an aggressive pride in their lack of sophistication but that leaves them open to being suborned and manipulated by wealthy, sophisticated political actors. Ordinary members of the movement are likely to be of limited education, opportunities, resources and achievement, which they resent and blame on others. They are traditionally conservative and resistant to change; deeply suspicious and resentful of differences and of outsiders; and enraged by what they see as betrayal by the traditional elite. They see violence as the solution to most problems and are intensely self-righteous in their belief that, unless they take matters into their own hands, matters will only get worse. Violence in serving the cause is justified, and violent actors quickly gain status in the hierarchy.

Fascism is not a unitary or static entity. It has appeared many times in human history in a variety of guises and settings. However, the central element is always the same: a small group of fanatically-motivated men take control of a collapsing nation, society or sect in order to rebuild it in their vision of a splendidly militarised but mythic past, vanquishing their enemies in order to build a glorious, regimented future in which they are the new elite. They believe that these goals are so important that they justify any means to that end, encouraging their followers to abandon traditional morality and hew to their self-serving notion of right conduct.

Fascist ideals are not brought into being by a single leader or party but are selected from an existing range because of their value in enhancing one of humanity's most basic impulses, the aggressive drive to build dominance hierarchies. These recurring motifs do not belong to left or right but can be used by opposing political parties, by religions and by social movements who see themselves in the role of an oppressed minority. Fascist elements are a non-specific call to battle directed at regrouping weakened, scattered and demoralised forces. The movement manipulates the clichéd political tactics it knows will motivate the populace, specifically, the drive to dominate coupled with its mirror image, fear of domination. Beyond taking power, fascism itself offers no further objective.

The fantasy of fascism is an end to national and personal degradation and humiliation, and rebirth as a powerful, sanctified and purified entity dominating its surroundings. The reality of fascism is that it is incapable of building a peaceful and creative polity. Ultimately, the violent forces it unleashes must turn on themselves or be destroyed by the enemies created by its own aggression.

6.2: Fascism's enablers.

It's a truism to say that anybody who, starting with next to nothing, wishes to get to the top of a field will have to be committed. This is true of musicians, artists, footballers, students, farmers, workers and, of course, politicians. The early days of any political party or social movement are ineffably boring. Only the truly devoted can put up with the endless meetings; standing on rainy street corners handing pamphlets to indifferent or contemptuous passers-by; the interminable ill-tempered debates over trivial points of policy; the bitterly personal squabbling and character assassination masquerading as policy discussions; the late nights and lost weekends spent rubbing shoulders with fools, cranks and bumpkins just to get their votes... To make it worse, half the members will be out of work and looking for an exciting new life but none will have any money.

This painful process quickly sorts the vaguely supportive from the brutally devout and ambitious; only fanatics can survive this type of apprenticeship. But even to the man who plans to reshape the world to his own design, the barriers will often seem insurmountable. What he needs, what an outsider never has (because that's what outsider means), is contacts with the rich and influential. So in order to advance his cause, he needs to find a way of meeting a few well-connected people in high places with money to spare and the nous to see that what he proposes is just what the country needs. Well, that's how the tyro sees it. What the insiders see is probably quite different but the harsh reality of politics is that regardless of the magnificence of your manifesto, nobody will hear of it unless somebody opens a door and surreptitiously ushers you into, if not the actual corridors of power, then certainly the basement. That is, for every Great Leader who makes it, there must be a well-connected visionary who sees in him a potential saviour of the nation and kickstarts his career. Either that or the insider is sufficiently Machiavellian to think he can control the forces the newcomer hopes to unleash. Without a political midwife, the upstart will join the hundreds or thousands of other leaders without a following and sink without a trace. There is no fascism without enablers.

The person or group who facilitates the embryonic fascist is characterised by two features. Firstly, for whatever reason, enablers are strongly sympathetic to the goals and tactics of the movement. Secondly, they must have direct access to and influence over the centres of power via connections and money, or be themselves a centre of power within the existing political structure. Traditionally, there were several sources of enablers. The first was the socio-political establishment, formerly the nobility but now the "power elites" of mostly inherited money and influence, otherwise known as capital. Second place would be a toss-up between the country's major religious organisations, meaning churches in Western countries or the equivalent hierarchies in Muslim, Hindu or Buddhist nations, and the military/police complex. Next place went to organised labour and last but certainly not least was the "fourth estate" of the press, now known as The Media.

Each of these five power centres can be strongly oriented toward fascism in its own right. Inevitably, inherited money comes with a strong sense of entitlement and privilege, balanced by an equally strong resentment of and hostility toward anybody who would challenge either the money or the privilege. Always, the handle of the silver spoon is embossed with a bunch of sticks and an axe head; the privileged child has to fight against the fascist tendencies spilled on his innocent head with his baptismal water. A quick glance at the leaders of post-war Britain, Australia, the US and others suggests most of them surrendered without a murmur. While the establishment are usually too corrupt, too lazy and too contemptuous of the hoi polloi to consider running a populist movement themselves, they have no hesitation financing a budding Führer if they think it will be to their advantage. Mostly, as the Trump tax cuts in the US showed, it is. Of course, when he is no longer useful to them or too toxic, they ditch him without a backward glance—unless he is smarter than they thought and turns the tables on them.

The *sine qua non* of fascism is a hierarchy. Any hierarchical organisation is halfway home and will have to take the greatest care it doesn't slide down the slope to the full-blown fascist state. Churches, of course, are traditionalist hierarchies incarnate. The very few, such as the Society of Friends or Quakers, that eschew a power structure and who don't immediately ingratiate themselves with the establishment rarely have much impact and are among the first to suffer when the blackshirts take over. Increasing secularism in the West makes it unlikely we will see a traditional clerical-fascist government again but the church's influence as behind-the-scenes enablers should not be underestimated, for example, in Poland today. However, frank clerical-fascist regimes are the norm in many Muslim countries. Saudi Arabia came into being after the collapse of the Ottoman Empire when Ibn Saud, the head of an insignificant Bedouin tribe, reached agreement with an obscure fundamentalist sect called Wahhabists and grabbed power. Ibn Saud got the temporal and later financial power, and the Wahhabists got the Arab soul. And they have never let go. Fueled by a deluge of unaccounted and unscrupulous money, an intolerant Wahhabism has been sown around the world. The malign influence of the mating of these two forces will be troubling the world for generations to come.

Similarly, without a hierarchy, there is no military establishment. The whole point of the military is to exert dominance, to spend lots of money, to make a big mess smashing perceived enemies, and to have a fun time doing it with a few rapes thrown in for laughs. As enablers, the military mindset is already halfway to fascism. For every person in uniform of a moderate political disposition, there will be a far-right extremist. An antifascist, on the other hand, won't survive basic training: the hierarchy will quickly detect his egalitarian attitudes and crush him. One of the striking features of the Trump insurrection at the Capitol was the numbers of current and former members of the military and police, feeling fully justified in doing something that, if done by a non-white person or a "leftie," would have provoked them to homicidal hysteria. All too often, we find generals whose ambitions greatly exceed their training and their common sense, leading them to believe they can do a better job of identifying the nation's enemies than the appointed politicians. Equally often, they believe the nation's enemies have infiltrated the existing political establishment and they feel called upon by history to act as saviours. In Pakistan, Turkey, Brazil and Argentina, fascist generals have a tradition of sweeping elected governments out of power only to make a complete mess of governing themselves. The Nazis were a little different as they kept the Wehrmacht quiet by promising them whatever they wanted but, in the early days, there was no doubt that Hitler's government was merely tolerated by the military who could have overthrown them in a trice.

Because the mass right wing is a tool of capital, it loathes organised labour. While a fascist party may ride to power on the backs of downtrodden workers, such as in the Soviet revolution, organised trade unions are among the first competing power structures to be neutralised. Regardless of their hue, fascist governments invariably dismantle existing trade unions, imprisoning or exiling the union leaders or dropping them out of aircraft, replacing them with docile worker organisations that will do their bidding. So even though they provided the serried legions that put the fascists in power, and despite being lauded as heroic builders of the revolution, workers soon find they are worse off than before. As fascist enablers, their day in the sun is all too brief.

Finally, there is what used to be called the Fourth Estate, the press. The term possibly originated with Edmund Burke in 1787 but was in wide use fifty years later when Thomas Carlyle wrote: "Burke said there were Three Estates in Parliament; but, in the Reporters' Gallery yonder, there sat a Fourth Estate more important far than they all." These days, informational media include print, radio, television and the infinite range of the internet. While their impact has increased exponentially, there is nothing about them that Carlyle would not recognise. Lacking a direct power base, so-called media barons exert their influence by manipulating politicians through control of their publicity. Any politician who makes an enemy of the owners of the media is likely to be unemployed before long; conversely, media enablers can turn a failed real estate dealer into a president.

Traditionally, all political movements had their own newspapers. Lenin had *Iskra*, Stalin had *Pravda*, the Nazis had the *Völkischer Beobachter* and *Der Stürmer*, or they could rely on sympathetic left- or right-leaning presses. As propaganda sheets, newspapers are influential so, today, we are seeing a slightly different phenomenon, when right wing governments close left wing papers or they are forcefully taken over by right wing magnates who then neuter them or even hand them to the government. This is the practice in Russia, Hungary, Hong Kong and various Latin American countries. Hence we see the rise of opposition blogs on the internet which are harder to control and not dependent on advertising.

In respect of hidden, lethal pressure, probably no media conglomerate in history has been as successful as the Murdoch empire. Despite its name, *Fox News* in the US has openly abandoned any pretence of balance, offering instead a 24/7 torrent of vitriolic right wing propaganda. It was the main vehicle for Trump's 2016 surprise victory, albeit over the Establishment's seriously-flawed candidate, and served as his eager mouthpiece throughout his term. But its success is not necessarily homegrown. Years before television and the internet, each and every item in the Fox repertoire had been anticipated by a prolix but unknown scribbler in Munich who later became one of history's more successful propagandists, Adolf Hitler.

In Chapter 6 of *Mein Kampf*, Hitler dwelt at length on the role of propaganda in building a political party for the salvation of the nation in its hour of need, i.e. a crucial plank in any fascist movement. In the 1939 translation by James Murphy, he says:

> The receptive powers of the masses are very restricted, and their understanding is feeble. On the other hand, they quickly forget. Such being the case, all effective propaganda must be

confined to a few bare essentials and those must be expressed as far as possible in stereotyped formulas. These slogans should be persistently repeated until the very last individual has come to grasp the idea that has been put forward ...

The aim of propaganda is not to try to pass judgment on conflicting rights, giving each its due, but exclusively to emphasize the right which we are asserting. Propaganda must not investigate the truth objectively...

The broad masses of the people are not made up of diplomats or professors of public jurisprudence nor simply of persons who are able to form reasoned judgment in given cases, but a vacillating crowd of human children who are constantly wavering between one idea and another. The great majority of a nation is so feminine in its character and outlook that its thought and conduct are ruled by sentiment rather than by sober reasoning [1].

Everything, he said, must therefore be directed at swaying sentiment, not reason. This, as readers can verify for themselves, is the very essence of the Murdoch/*Fox and Friends* formula, the central spell in the Murdoch magic, written years before Murdoch was born. There is, however, a major difference between the output of the Nazi Ministry of Propaganda under its very able minister, Joseph Goebells, and that of News Corp. (*sic*; at least the Nazis were honest) under the steely control of its main shareholder. In 1923-24, when he was writing his magnum opus, Hitler genuinely believed Germany was in great danger, that he and his then-tiny group had to mobilise the masses before the nation fell into a new dark age, dragging humanity after it. Whatever his other failings, nobody could accuse Hitler of insincerity: he wasn't in politics for the money [32].

Murdoch, on the other hand, doesn't believe the world is in danger. His ubiquitous media outlets consistently deny the looming dangers of climate change, of the Covid pandemic, nuclear war, the militarisation of society, excessive debt, environmental damage, parliamentary corruption ... In short, anything that alarms people of a leftist or even centrist bent will be pilloried by the well-paid chorus at News Corp. At the same time, Murdoch himself has never displayed any interest in

---

[32]   Much later, he earned royalties from sales of *Mein Kampf* and from having his silhouette on postage stamps.

parliamentary politics. Not for him the interminable hustings, the cut and thrust of open debate, the nail-biting wait for the outcome of the polls... One thing is clear, Murdoch would never risk failure. As he showed in his teeth-grindingly disingenuous performance before the British House of Commons enquiry into the *News of the World* phone hacking scandal in 2011, defeat would be intolerable. Also, he has accrued far more money and power by avoiding the back benches.

So what drives him? What is his goal? It seems beyond doubt that the exercise of brute power is a major factor, but money for himself and his many rich and powerful friends would be a close second. That the world is being driven headlong into a fascist whirlwind by such a person is cause for the greatest concern. The only comfort is the thought that, as is so often the case with media barons, his huge and malevolent propaganda machine is unlikely to long outlive him. Unfortunately, what comes later, the forces he has willingly unleashed, may well be worse.

6.3: Fascism's fall.

The prime illusion of fascism is the intoxicating vision of crushing and scattering one's enemies and standing triumphant over the ruins of their ambitions. The reality could not be more different. Of Mussolini's government, Luigi Barzini wrote:

> The regime had created an imaginary Spartan country, in which all men had to make believe they were heroic soldiers, all women Roman matrons, all children Balilla (a Genoa urchin who, in 1746, started a revolt against the Austrian occupation by throwing a stone). This was done by means of slogans, flags, stirring speeches from balconies, military music, mass meetings, parades, dashing uniforms, medals, hoaxes, and constant distortions of reality. The Italians woke up too late from their artificial dream, those still alive, that is, hungry, desperate, discredited, the object of derision, *cornuti e mazziati,* or "cuckolded and beaten up," governed as in the past by contemptuous foreigners in a country of smoking ruins and decaying corpses, in which most things detachable had been stolen and women raped (1983).

The same was true of post-war Germany, a shattered and divided nation with some 7.5million of its citizens dead, its supremely graceful cities incinerated, its world-beating science and industry destroyed, agriculture reverted to subsistence, and the culture and institutions of a brilliant nation destroyed in just twelve years of Nazi rule. Japan, with 5.25million deaths and its cities levelled by firebombing and nuclear attacks, paid a similar price for its foray into ultranationalism but the country that suffered the most was the USSR, with some 25million deaths. This tragedy followed the 20million deaths suffered during Stalin's tyranny, including nearly 4million during the Holodomor, Stalin's own Terror-Famine, in Ukraine in 1932-33. Of the many fascist dictatorships established in the 1920s and 30s, only Spain and Portugal survived past 1945. Actively supported by the US, these limped on until they finally fell apart in the 1970s, to nobody's regret. That is the inescapable reality of fascism.

For fascism, failure is inevitable, written in its political DNA. Its leaders have only the sketchiest vision of the future; mostly, they don't think much beyond whipping up the rabble in order to take power, build a police state and destroy their enemies. But what is the point of a police state? Its only point is to keep itself going, for which it needs a constant supply of enemies, both internal and external [33]. External enemies are easy to find, simply pick an argument with somebody and invade. After his US-sponsored war against Iran of 1980-88, Saddam Hussein's Iraq was nearly bankrupt; he decided they needed Kuwait's oil; somebody found a piece of paper which indicated Kuwait may once have been a province of Iraq, so they moved in. That was the beginning of the end for the Baathist regime. A war with another country will either end in defeat, as in the Axis in 1939-45, or must lead to more wars, which will eventually bankrupt the country, as in most empires to date. It would appear that the US is now deep in this phase.

Internal enemies are also not difficult to find, simply nominate a minority and encourage the rabble to vent their frustrations on them. It may be a religious minority, such as Shia Muslims in Saddam's Iraq, Jews in Czarist Russia and Germany, Hazaras in Afghanistan or B'hai in theocratic Iran; a political minority, such as communists in Nazi Germany, Indonesia or the US, or "capitalist roaders" in Maoist China; a racial group, such as people of African descent in the US, Jews in

---

[33]   c.f. Oscar Wilde: "The bureaucracy is expanding to meet the needs of an expanding bureaucracy." Similarly, the fascist police state expands to arrest citizens disillusioned by the ever-expanding fascist police state.

Nazi Germany, Tutsis in Ruanda, or Rohingya Muslims in Buddhist Myanmar (Burma); or they can be just "traitors" in general, as in Stalin's USSR, North Korea and practically everywhere else at different times. But there must come a time when the enemies are eliminated; does that signal a new era of peace for the population? Not at all. The war-like fervour must be maintained, there can be no relaxation of the military atmosphere or the ceaseless hunt for spies and traitors, otherwise the movement loses its entire reason to exist, to save the nation in its hour of need, and the leaders would have to get another job. Fascism exists to save the nation but the nation can never be saved or the fascist movement will wither and die. The battle must go on. And go on it will because when the groaning citizens call out "Enough is enough," they too must be rounded up and shot.

The late stages of the USSR indicate what happens when people lose interest in an eternal battle to rejuvenate the threatened nation. Corruption, alcoholism, crime, incompetence and apathy reigned during the "years of stagnation" until the Union finally fell apart. The same thing happened in Ceausescu's Rumania. One day, the people got sick of being told what to do by brutal, greedy and incompetent, self-appointed leaders, and simply refused to play their part in the perpetual revolution. In China, the ruling Communist Party appears to have taken note of this and has cranked up its sense of crisis but it can't last. Eventually, the state will run out of enemies [34] and must then either turn on itself, as in Stalin's Red Terror, or collapse.

Recent developments in the US seem to indicate that it is at the point of turning on itself, starting to consume itself but it is probably not quite there yet. What we see is a group of marginalised fanatics attempting to create a crisis so they can gain more recruits and take over government. Theirs is a two-pronged approach, both clearly evident under Trump. On the one hand there is a rapidly growing disenchantment with the mainstream policies of the alternating "Demopublican" capitalist governments, which are leading to ever-widening inequality, destruction of public institutions, permanent indebtedness of the working population, impoverishment and alienation of minorities, decline in health and education standards, breakdown of infrastructure, etc.. As a result, the wealthy grow ever-

---

[34] This assumes, of course, that the US will get over its antipathies toward socialism and all things Chinese and will get on with sorting out its own mess. For insecure fascist regimes, foreign threats are manna from heaven.

wealthier and, moreover, use their wealth to change government policies to hand them even more wealth.

On the other hand, we see the institutions of government being taken over by fanatical, ultra-right wing Christian nationalists who use the power given them by gerrymandered elections to hollow out the entire welfare state, even while increasing spending on the military-industrial-spying-police-carceral complex in the name of "national danger." Their policies are directly leading to the sense of despair in the alienated working classes, thus generating the sense of crisis that they then exploit. This is very similar to what happened in Nazi Germany, when the Prussian secret police, the Gestapo, were made the secret police of the whole country, and with the Nuremberg racial laws, etc. It must never be forgotten that, after 1923, the Nazis didn't break the national laws, mainly because they rewrote the laws to suit themselves. This is what we see in the US with, for example, the Patriots Act, the Authorisation for Use of Military Force (2001) and the resurrection of the 1917 Espionage Act to suppress whistle-blowers. Sophisticated fascists do not break the law. They simply change the laws to give them what they want while throwing their opponents into prison.

By any measure, the fascist form of government is a threat to world peace and the welfare of nations. But if that is so patently clear, why does it keep recurring? The answer lies in understanding the factors that bring it about.

6.4: To create fascism: Let the Left beware.

Fascism is the outcome of a concurrence of a range of themes in human life, some permanent and some recurrent; some innate, some situational, and some, human failings on a large scale. It has long suited the Allied nations who defeated the fascist nations in World War II to locate responsibility in the people who were subjected to fascism, ignoring the fact that most had no say. "It couldn't happen here," is their rallying cry. In particular, Western liberalism locates the fascist virus in the German psyche (whatever that is), which excuses them from guilt for their contribution to the bloodbath of the War and blinds them to the fascist stirrings in their own societies. For example, Winston Churchill's servile reaction to meeting Mussolini in Rome in 1927 shows how his notorious hatred of Bolshevism in particular and Russians in general led him to collude in Fascism's rise:

> What a man! I have lost my heart! ... If I were Italian, I am sure
> I would have been with you entirely from the beginning of your
> victorious struggle against the bestial appetites and passion of
> Leninism ... Your movement has rendered a service to the
> whole world. The greatest fear that ever tormented every
> Democratic or Socialist leader was that of being outbid or
> surpassed by some other leader more extreme than himself. It
> has been said that a continual movement to the Left, a kind of
> fatal landslide toward the abyss, has been the character of all
> revolutions. Italy has shown that there is a way of fighting the
> subversive forces ... She has provided the necessary antidote to
> the Russian poison. Hereafter no great nation will be
> unprovided with an ultimate means of protection against the
> cancerous growth of Bolshevism [2, p169].

In Mussolini, Churchill found a kindred anti-Bolshevik fanatic; in
turn, Mussolini found in Churchill a racist royalist imperialist, meaning
a fascist in all but name.

The innate impulse toward fascism is a universal constant in human
affairs, specifically the hormonally-based drive to dominate and
control. This is the direct cause of a very large part of the suffering we
see around the world. People of all nations, all ages, sexes, intellects,
everything, hate the idea of somebody beating them in a dispute. It
ranges from petty arguments over rubbish bins or barking dogs in
suburbia (which occasionally result in homicides), travels via "road
rage," to street battles between opposing parties and ultimately to
hostile nations standing eyeball to eyeball on a vast pile of nuclear
weapons. It is all about "I'm in charge, you have to do as I say"/ "No I
don't, nobody tells me what to do."

Most people, however, overlook this imperative in themselves and
attribute any friction to their enemies. In particular, Western governments fail to see that their foreign policies are almost entirely based in
an uncontrolled urge to force their will on other people who, needless
to say, are equally determined to resist. In fact, they do see it but they
are always able to justify it to themselves as unpleasant but necessary.
Western nations have always believed that their wishes or ambitions
are legitimate, whereas anybody who opposes them or who has
ambitions of their own, is necessarily acting with evil intent. There is
always an excuse for why it is necessary to bend your neighbour to
your will.

Situational factors which contribute to the rise of fascism include a widespread sense that the government is failing its citizens, that the country has been humiliated, that external and internal enemies are at work to destroy the nation, that the situation is deterioriating and only urgent, desperate action can avert calamity. The gravity of the matter calls for a suspension of traditional morality and law, a complete change of personnel at the level of government, and the mobilisation of the popular will to confront the enemies. As part of this process, society is regimented and militarised with draconian punishments for anybody who fails in his duty.

On the individual level, because of the national emergency, people who would normally not get anywhere near the corridors of power are able to take control of the government. These include narcissistic personalities who take advantage of the classic fascist theme of self-glorification; psychopathic personalities who take advantage of its aggression or profits (usually both); and paranoid personalities eager to see the nation's troubles as the result of conspiracies. When these features coincide, the result is a dynamic, charismatic, power-hungry and ruthless clique which electrifies the masses. Unfortunately, as history shows so clearly, the people who suffer most will be those ordinary, and ordinarily responsible, people who wanted only that their country would get back to normal, with food in the shops, hospitals that can be trusted and trains that run on time.

What is the risk of a nation making a swerve to the hard right in order to implement a fascist program? In order to demonstrate the central point that the origins of fascism lie in all of us, we can look at some case examples. The first is my country, Australia, which, per capita, is the wealthiest nation on earth and should thus be fairly resistant to the urgings of the "rabid right." In its splendid isolation, Australia is one of very few net energy and food exporters on earth. The well-educated population enjoys a generous welfare state with high standards of health and education; clean and well-planned cities routinely voted the most liveable in the world; astounding natural resources in a breath-taking setting; there is every imaginable recreational facility from wondrous beaches to safe snow fields; immediate access to every source of news and information on earth, on and on. Really, Australia's got it made. Discreetly located out of sight, on the far side of the globe from all the major belligerents, one would have thought that Australians would have the sense to keep quiet, keep their hands to themselves and get on with making their fortunes. Not so.

Australia never misses an opportunity to throw itself into other people's wars, wasting lives and vast sums of money, earning no good will and amassing pointless hostility in the process. Politically, successive Australian governments have tied themselves to the American war machine, carrying on the pre-war (that's World War II) tradition of tying themselves to the British war machine—before it fell apart. In order to do this, they maintain a steady drumbeat of alarming stories of how the country is at risk of invasion by one or other Asian power, stories collectively known as the Yellow Peril. Initially, it was Japan, followed by Communist China ("the Reds"), which produced the Orange Peril. After a brief and implausible flirtation with the idea of Islamists storming through the suburbs, they are now banging the Chinese theme again, warning quite literally of "the drum beats of war" [35]. Overlooked in the entirely artificial panic is the question of whether China has the slightest concern about threats from this country, or covets anything we have that they aren't already buying at a discount.

Motivating the *faux* panic is a recurrent theme of politicians fomenting fears of foreigners for their personal advantage. Unfortunately, there is also a sector of the electorate who are innately scared of and hostile to The Other, particularly Oriental Others, and are therefore receptive to this paranoid message. If we look at the list of features developed in Chap. 2.4, it is clear that, at present, Australia is at low risk of a sharp move to the right of politics. One of the most protective factors is a deep-seated mistrust, if not outright contempt, of politicians coupled with what is called the "tall poppy syndrome," the strong tendency to attack anybody who tries to stand out from the crowd ("cut them down to size"). Various attempts over the past twenty-five years to build a hard right political machine (currently known as Pauline Hanson's One Nation Party, which shows how ineffective it is) have amounted to very little but the tendency is certainly alive. Actively fostered by the Murdoch press, ranting right wing commentators on radio and TV have a large and potentially flammable audience.

---

[35] https://abcnews.go.com/International/wireStory/australia-security-official-warns-staff-drums-war-77331057

A major factor restricting fascist penetration of Australia's body politic is the relative absence of an organised, politicised tradition of charismatic Christianity. As seen in the recent census, Australia is one of the least religious countries in the world, a trend which is apparently accelerating. This has to be seen as a protective factor. The recent prime minister is the first member of a pentecostal church to reach high political office. However, his dire performance during two emergencies, the vast bushfires of the southern summer of 2019-2020, and the Covid-19 pandemic, coupled with his persistent dishonesty, have pointedly underlined the difference between claiming the high moral ground, and actually proving the claim by good works. Compounding their failure to make a mark, the charismatic and pentecostal churches are struggling to recruit or retain the younger generation, so their influence is likely to diminish with time. Again, the traditional Australian contempt for authority serves as a protective factor against inroads by fascist parties but history shows that underestimating their termite-like patience is dangerous.

The next country to consider is not small, not peripheral and not irreligious. India is physically very big, blessed with human capital, soon to be the world's biggest population, and quite possibly the most religious. country in the world. For most of its independent history, India was governed by the avowedly secular Congress Party but their inability to control their corruption has opened the path to the champions of Hindutva or Hinduness, the Bharatya Janata Party (BJP) and their various social and political support groups, especially the Rashtriya Swayamsevak Sangh (RSS). There will long be debates over the fluid notion of Hindutva but three elements predominate: the concept of a single nation over a defined geographic area, west of the Indus River between the Himalayas and the Indian Ocean; a single ethnic population; and a single culture, essentially Hinduism. As it stands, that's not a particular danger to anybody, except the Hindu religion is inherently hierarchical with, it must not be forgotten, deep racist influences. With those added elements, Hindutva and the political parties that support the doctrine show significant features of fascism. In fact, many people would say the RSS crossed that line when it was formed in 1925.

Taking the points listed in Chap. 2.2, we can assess where India stands on "the road to fascism."

(1) *Hyper-nationalism*: The BJP government under PM Narendra Modi makes full use of the nationalist "drum" to build enthusiastic support. It reminds voters of India's vast history and achievements and never misses an opportunity to mention the humiliations under Moghul and British rule, nor its natural dominance in South Asia and the Indian Ocean littoral regions.

(2) *Exclusive control of government*: The BJP has crushed the opposition parties and governs in its own right nationally and in numerous states, many of which are far larger than most European nations.

(3) *Populist program* of *radical national and social renewal*: The declared purpose of the BJP and its allied organisations is to rebuild India to a national-racial-religious program so that it can take its rightful place on the international stage.

(4) *Eradicating the internal and external enemies*: Islam. Where would the BJP be without the omnipresent threat of Islam, in the form of nuclear-armed Pakistan next door trying to wrest control of (Muslim-majority) Kashmir from its rightful owners (India) and the world's largest Muslim population trying to convert Hindus at home and eat their sacred cows? In fact, Pakistan has nuclear weapons because India got them first; Kashmir has been under a brutal military occupation for decades; and religious freedom is guaranteed under India's constitution. Mr Modi was declared persona non grata in the West for his role in the widespread slaughter of Muslims in his home state of Gujarat when he was Chief Minister in 2002.

(5) *Existential crisis of sociopolitical decline*. India's history has been one long crisis, greatly magnified by its humiliating defeats by China in 1962 and the Chinese economic miracle.

(6) Appeals to *frightened and disempowered* common people. The BJP is very much a mass movement, whereas Congress was very much the party of the established elite.

(7) People feel *betrayed by the traditional elite*. The corruption of India's elite is legendary.

(8) The new populist government is *ultimately captured* by established capital. Modi has very close relations with India's vast stores of capital, especially the industrialists Gautam Adani, the richest man in Asia and reputedly second richest in the world, having gained $70billion in the first nine months of 2022, and the runner-up, Mukesh Ambani.

(9) Fascism is *regressively conservative*. The entire BJP program is socially conservative.

(10) It is *anti-elitist, anti-intellectual* and *anti-modernist*. These are not big points with the BJP which values education, sometimes even for women.

(11) *Authoritarian, rigidly hierarchical* and *ultracompetitive*. India itself is authoritarian, rigidly hierarchical and ultracompetitive.

(12) *Flamboyantly and aggressively militarist*. While the RSS is organised along paramilitary lines, this is not a major feature of the current Indian government. Mr Modi only ever appears in traditional garb; he has no military service or rank.

(13) *Mythical, historical or religious themes*. Whatever the BJP loses in militarism, it gains in mythical, historical and religious themes. This is endless.

(14) *Aggressively masculine, patriarchal/misogynist*. Traditional Indian society is strongly paternalistic; in practice, women have fewer rights, e.g. rape is common but most women will not report it as they are likely to be raped in the police station.

(15) *Extreme reaction to intense political insecurity*. This is a little difficult to assess as India has been in a state of chaotic semi-paralysis since independence, lurching from one crisis to the next, borne down by its oppressive bureaucracy and religious orthodoxy.

(16) *Free of traditional morality*. The BJP has abandoned many restraints of the previous governments, e.g. eliminating Kashmir's autonomous status, and its citizenship law, which granted members of Hindu and Buddhist religions, among

others, preferential status in immigration but effectively blocked Muslims.

(17) *Heroic and self-sacrificing commoners.* Not a common feature, possibly because the BJP has little control over India's fractious media.

(18) *Incorporating and promoting the dispossessed.* Modi makes a great deal of his supposedly humble origins but the Dalits ("Untouchables") still have an uphill battle to advance themselves.

(19) *Politicises and militarises daily life.* Not to the same extent as China or other communist countries but anybody who wants to get ahead needs to be very aware that making enemies in the BJP is a sure way to kill a career.

(20) A ceaseless turmoil of *threats* (from the internal and external enemies), *self-glorification* and *promises*. The joint and several threats from Islam and from China never sleep.

(21) *Brutal amorality in which the public are invited to participate.* What is called communal violence, i.e. between Hindu and Muslim, has always been a problem in India, from Partition to the present. Congress governments tried to minimise it with very limited success (e.g. see the widespread anti-Sikh riots following the assassination of Indira Ghandi in 1984) but the BJP, RSS and similar organisations have actively inflamed relations, leading the demolition of the Babri Masjid (mosque) in Ayodhya in 1992, and the Gurarat riots in 2002.

(22) *Justifying and institutionalising their most violent urges.* Partition in 1947 resulted in mass slaughter; mob violence has never really stopped but it is tolerated and covertly encouraged rather than formally institutionalised.

Led by Narendra Modi and the BJP and its supports, India is heading in a bad direction, away from a tolerant, secular plurality, toward a nationalist-racist-religious revival. It isn't clear why India bears Pakistan such ferocious hostility; what is clear is that their three wars and endless militarism are only destabilising the region and keeping their populations poor.

And now to ... Russia. Oh dear, Russia. Queen Victoria loathed Russians, including her relatives, the Czars. Churchill quite liked rich, aristocratic Russians but he regarded the Bolsheviks as the very spawn of the devil. Americans loathed and wanted to destroy the godless USSR but we now know it was actually Russians they hated. In the twentieth century, Russia/USSR was invaded five times in under thirty years. After their victory in the Great Patriotic War (World War II elsewhere), they declared: "Enough is enough. Nobody will ever be allowed to threaten us again." So what did the West, led by the US, do? They surrounded the Slavic heartland with weapons of mass destruction set ready to fire (called "containment") and complained when the Soviets responded in kind. And now, following Putin's calamitous invasion of Ukraine, it seems American (and British, and French, and German and everybody else's) capitalists may finally achieve their most passionately-held dream, the collapse and disintegration of the largest and richest country on earth, leading to the ultimate feeding frenzy. We, the unconsulted voters, can only wait and see what emerges from the looming catastrophe.

Meantime, starting with Yeltsin and accelerating under Putin, Russia has degenerated into a kleptocracy, a government of thieves, appointed by thieves and run for the benefit of thieves. As mentioned in Chap. 2.3, the country has been stripped of vast, almost inconceivable sums of money by the very people entrusted with its management. According to Alexei Navalny, Putin's arch-foe now in prison after several attempts at murdering him, Putin has built a billion-dollar palace on the Black Sea coast but he doesn't live there. This raises the interesting question: We know that fascists can be thieves but can thieves be fascists? By that I mean, can a person who is in it for what he can get also be committed politically to an ideal? The answer is Probably not. As I said earlier, fascists have to serve an apprenticeship standing on street corners in the rain, handing pamphlets to people hurrying home from work and most thieves aren't interested in such hard work. Putin was always a thief, seriously corrupt from the very beginning of his career fifty years ago. All his friends and associates are the same. They run the country, if that is the correct expression, to enrich themselves and he keeps them under control by the simple threat of cutting off their money, throwing them into prison or arranging a quiet but painful death. But Russia shows all the features of a proto-fascist state, so isn't that a contradiction? No, it isn't. Yes, they are politically conservative ultranationalists, and they believe the country is under threat but no, they don't believe most of it. This is window-dressing, to get the people onside while they continue looting the country. Where it will end, who knows but it doesn't augur well.

(1) *Hyper-nationalism*: Russians have always been proud of their country but their leaders will play on this as it suits them, and Putin\ does. Does he believe the nationalist talk? Probably, but only in the sense that he doesn't want anybody telling Russia what to do. But who does?

(2) *Exclusive control of government*: The Putin clique has absolute power of life and death and opponents need to be very careful. But he does actually win elections, mainly by beating the nationalist drum.

(3) *Populist program* of *radical national and social renewal*: He promises Russians they will regain their former status as a superpower.

(4) *Eradicating the internal and external enemies*: Dealing with the internal enemies is quite easy. Those that can't be bought off are either scared off or bumped off. The external enemies are a little more resistant. The US economy needs enemies, and Russia is the eternal standby, the enemy you have when all other enemies have let you down.

(5) *Existential crisis of sociopolitical decline.* After the dissolution of the USSR and the US-engineered financial collapse under the incompetent and fearsomely corrupt drunkard, Boris Yeltsin, Russia was minutes away from being a failed state, with all that that implies.

(6) Appeals to *frightened and disempowered* common people. Russian people have had a lot to be frightened about over the past few hundred years.

(7) People feel *betrayed by the traditional elite.* If there is a single enduring theme in Russian history beside the limitless suffering of the common people, it is the corruption, incompetence and selfishness of the elite which, of course,causes the common suffering and continues unchanged to the present.

(8) The new populist government is *ultimately captured* by established capital. There has been a slight change to the script in that the new populist government captured the stolen capital and has hidden it offshore. Nobody knows how much money has been stolen from Russia. In 2016, US lawyer and target of Putin's wrath, Bill Browder, claimed that Putin alone had about $200billion stashed in foreign countries. Others toss around figures like $2trillion in total stolen but the answer is "a very large sum of money that could have transformed the country."

(9) Fascism is *regressively conservative.* The most conservative branch of the Orthodox Church has been actively promoted and, with it, hostility to divorce, abortion, homosexuality, drugs etc, all of which are widespread in Russia.

(10) (10) It is *anti-elitist, anti-intellectual* and *anti-modernist.* The Putin clique is openly resentful of high achievers of any sort except financial, and they will be taken down.

(11) *Authoritarian, rigidly hierarchical* and *ultracompetitive.* As an ex-KGB colonel, Putin has reinstated the secret police (FSB) and operates a barely-concealed police state in which opponents are bankrupted, driven overseas, beaten up, imprisoned or murdered, or all of the above. That's competitive.

(12) *Flamboyantly and aggressively militarist.* Due to its victory over the Nazis in the Great Patriotic War, the military has an almost mystical status in Russia, on display each year during the Victory Parade in May.

(13) *Mythical, historical or religious themes.* Endless, as they can draw on Russia's sublime contributions to music, literature, mathematics and science.

(14) *Aggressively masculine, patriarchal/misogynist.* This is perhaps not so coarse as in Hitler's Germany or Mao's China but there are very few women in high levels of government or business in Russia.

(15) *Extreme reaction to intense political insecurity.* When Putin took power, the Russian people were pleading for stable government.

(16) *Free of traditional morality.* Putin himself appears to be devoid of what is called a "moral compass." There is strong evidence to indicate that his group engineered the Moscow bombings that killed hundreds of people and led to his being appointed president.

(17) *Heroic and self-sacrificing commoners.* This does not appear to be a major theme, perhaps because after nearly a century of Soviet Heroes, people were a bit tired of it.

(18) *Incorporating and promoting the dispossessed.* It is said that 80% of senior government officials and political appointees to major companies are former members of the KGB, FSB, military or police. They are all outsiders, not from the elite, mostly with the narrow education and even narrower points of view that come from growing up in the security system.

(19) *Politicises and militarises daily life.* Not to the extent under the former communist governments but Russian citizens all know they have to watch what they say and do and who they associate with.

(20) A ceaseless turmoil of *threats* (from the internal and external enemies), *self-glorification* and *promises*. Russia is subject to a ceaseless blizzard of threats. What Americans saw and again see as "containment" is, to the Russian people, an overt existential threat. Almost certainly, we will never know the full story behind the Russian invasion of Ukraine, just as we will never see the truth about the Western invasions of North Korea, Vietnam, Iraq and so many other countries but, to the Russians, having a hostile protofascist state on their doorstep was intolerable.

(21) *Brutal amorality in which the public are invited to partici-pate.* While it has not reached the point of SA stormtroopers rushing through the streets smashing communist, socialist, Jewish and other establishments, the brutality of Russia's military in Chechnya, Dagestan, Georgia and now Ukraine is consistent.

> (22) *Justifying and institutionalising their most violent urges.*
> Again, it hasn't reached the stage of declaring entire national
> groupings as "enemies of the state," partly because the
> Russian Federation contains so many national groupings, but
> a record of dishonesty and violence is no impediment to
> rapid advancement in Russia today.

The next country to consider is one that, for historical reasons, might, at first glance, be relatively resistant to the fascist virus, but my thesis is that no nation and no group is immune. As fascism stems from the universal human drive to dominate, it is unfettered by race, history, religion or even by sex. Women may not be the stormtroopers marching down the streets, but they lovingly wash and iron the uniforms and sew on the badges, they stand on the curb, cheering and weeping ecstatically, throwing flowers and kisses. Even if not its beneficiaries, even if ultimately they suffer grievously, women are fascism's domestic enablers.

Can an overtly religious nation or movement be fascist in practice? Indubitably, the answer is it can, as fascism is a set of practices, attitudes and beliefs, not a single doctrine. Fascism is about the accumulation and exercise of power, and all governments and all religions are about power. So if we take the twenty-one features of fascism listed in Chap. 2.4, replacing the word 'nation' with 'religion,' it is clear that a theocracy or religious movement can correctly be classed as fascist. This is true of Iran, which is a classic clericalist-fascist state, but also of Saudi Arabia, which is actually more repressive, more violent and more destructive in terms of exporting its fanatical ideology (Wahhabism) than Iran, although mainstream media in the West work diligently to ensure nobody knows it.

Also in the Middle East, Israel finally came into being as a socialist haven for European Jews who had survived the fascist Holocaust [3]. Since the Yom Kippur War in October 1973, when the nation's survival seemed at risk, the general political climate in Israel has swung far to the right. The moderately socialist Labour Party governing in 1973 has been reduced to a rump, and right wing Likud governments since have depended on the fickle support of far-right and extremist religious parties, which have made the most of their influence. Outside the Knesset, however, there is steadily-growing support for the most uncompromising interpretations of the country's *raison d'être*. For example, the American-born, ordained Orthodox rabbi and convicted terrorist, Meir Kahane, openly espoused a fanatical version of historical Jewish claims, arguing that all Arab inhabitants of what was Palestine should be forcibly expelled in order to establish an exclusive Jewish theocratic state. In the US, he was co-founder of the Jewish Defence League which has been classed by the FBI as a right wing terrorist group. In Israel, he founded the political party, Kach, which he briefly represented in the Knesset. Before being banned as racist by the Israeli government, his party, embracing what is loosely known as Kahanism, met all criteria for fascism. Kahane was assassinated in 1990 but his legacy lingers, in Israel, within elements of the Bennett/Lapid government which took office in June 2021, and outside the country. This is especially true of the US, whose implausibly influential Zionist lobbies, both Jewish and pentecostal Christian, effortlessly raise enormous sums of money to subsidise the illegal "settler" movement in occupied Palestinian and Syrian territories, gleefully rewarding their ever-greater excesses.

There is evidence of the growing influence of the most uncompromising, ultra-Orthodox views in Israeli politics, as well as signs of social intolerance in the way, for example, repatriated Ethiopian Jews have been treated. For a moderate or left wing Israeli, the biggest problem lies in the central role of Jewish religious history in the nation's affairs. Even after an absence of 2,000 years, the modern nation was established to gain control over traditional Biblical lands. Mainstream Israeli political opinion does not recognise prior indigenous claims in the way, for example, Canada, New Zealand and Australia recognise Aboriginal land rights. These are warning signs which the country ignores at its peril. The important point about fascism is that, as Karl Popper warned, tolerance of the intolerant has its limits. There is no point waiting, as moderate Italians and Germans did in the 1930s, until the fascist party is in power before objecting to its intolerant policies. That's too late. Dachau, the first German concentration camp for political prisoners, was established just seven weeks after Hitler was appointed Reichskanzler. The time to act is well before the uniformed fascist delegates and their troopers storm into parliament and arrest the opposition.

If a genuinely fascist movement were to arise in Israel, what form would it take? We can use the checklist from Chap. 2.4 to build a picture.

(1) *Hyper-nationalism*: Jewish religious tradition casts themselves in the role of a divinely-appointed Chosen People. Nazi policy, as Hitler made clear in *Mein Kampf*, saw the Aryan race as the "Super Men" by virtue of its Darwinian suitability, but appealing to God for justification is the end of the line. Israel's is the ultimate racist hyper-nationalism.

(2) *Exclusive control of government*: Jewish religious parties see left wing parties as little better than traitors, and will not deal with them. Their goal is total control of the government.

(3) *Populist program* of *radical national and social renewal*: The whole Zionist movement was such a program. It was designed to remove Jews from the unwholesome influence of mixed communities to establish their own, exclusive community built according to traditional and religious principles. It is not widely known that, at the time it was first promulgated, Zionism was widely dismissed and despised by mainstream European Jewish thinkers and politicians.

(4) *Eradicating the internal and external enemies*: An Israeli fascist party would have a veritable banquet of enemies to choose from. Internally, there are the remaining Arab Israelis whom Kahane at least wanted forcefully expelled. These apart, Israel is surrounded by hundreds of millions of people who feel their kind have suffered a grievous wrong. It seems unlikely Israeli fascists would declare war on Christianity, partly because there are too many Christians who would relish such an opportunity, and partly because they get so much support, political and financial, from Christian Zionists. Imagine Israel openly declaring the US the "Great Satan," even if that is what a lot of them think. However, minor anti-Christian sentiment at a local level is quite possible, e.g. if a Christian wanted to move into one of the exclusivelyJewish settlements in the Occupied Territories. Finally, there is the question of non-Zionist Jews, left wing and/or secular, often derided as "self-hating Jews." Through-out history, fascist parties have spent their first few years in power ridding themselves of their internal enemies, and Jewish tradition could be taken as supportive of such a move. For example, when Moses came down from the mountain

with the Ten Commandments, he found his brother Aaron had organised a golden calf for the people to worship. Enraged, Moses ordered the tribe of Levi to slaughter the sinners, "… and there fell of the people that day about three thousand Men" [36]. For literalists, that is an immensely powerful authorisation.

(5) *Existential crisis of sociopolitical decline.* Zionism itself is a reaction to a perceived existential crisis for the Jewish people.

(6) Appeals to *frightened and disempowered* common people. As the writer and activist, Miko Peled, makes clear [4], Israelis live a beleaguered life, widely believing they are surrounded by hostile hordes whose only ambition is the total destruction of Israel and all its people.

(7) People feel *betrayed by the traditional elite.* Ultra-Orthodox Israelis believe successive secular governments have compromised their duty, allowing the dilution of the faith and the people, failing to implement religious laws and, above all, failing to secure the ancient Biblical lands.

(8) The new populist government is *ultimately captured* by established capital. Israel's enviable standard of living is underwritten by regular injections of US and other foreign aid, as well as a steady flow of donations from overseas Jews and Zionist Christians. There is no question that the steady drift away from the country's original socialist objectives is heavily influenced by the political attitudes of the donors such as, for example, the late Sheldon Adelson, who sponsored a free daily newspaper pushing a hard rightist line. Tales of corruption among senior government members abound, with the recently-deposed prime minister, Benjamin Netanyahu, facing numerous charges.

(9) Fascism is *regressively conservative.* Orthodox Judaism is quite likely the equal-most regressively conservative body in the world. There is constant pressure on the Israeli

---

[36] Exodus 32: 26-28. We are told Aaron escaped that fate through pleading with his brother that he had been pressured by the people. It isn't clear if he saw the irony of Moses ordering mass slaughter of his tribesmen while holding a tablet saying "Thou shalt not kill" but he apparently knew enough to keep quiet.

government to enact traditional law. A fascist party would certainly make that a central plank in its policies.

(10) It is *anti-elitist, anti-intellectual* and *anti-modernist*. Orthodox Jews study traditional writings, almost to the exclusion of the modern world. As an aside, under current law, religious students are not required to undertake military service but if the country became a religious autocracy, who would defend it? Undoubtedly, an authority could be found, say in Exodus, justifying compelling every male to take up arms and every woman to serve the men.

(11) *Authoritarian, rigidly hierarchical* and *ultracompetitive*. All orthodox religions are authoritarian, that's what orthodox means. An Israeli fascist movement would certainly be rigidly patriarchal, and competition with non-Jews would flow from those factors.

(12) *Flamboyantly and aggressively militarist*. Israel is heavily militarised while the military itself occupies a sanctified role in the country (see [4] for lengthy description).

(13) *Mythical, historical or religious themes*. Yes, correct. Without end. Just as the clerics have done in Iran, an Israeli fascist party would immediately move to establish itself as the guardian of the totality of the nation's traditions, of its history, its culture, language, religion, its laws, finances and policies, etc. In fact, with just a different holy text and a change of name, the model of the Iranian clerical dictatorship would fit perfectly into the Israeli context.

(14) *Aggressively masculine, patriarchal/misogynist*. Most likely this would happen as an intensification of traditional concepts. While patriarchy/male dominance isn't central to fascism, it certainly increases its appeal among men who enjoy being dominant.

(15) *Extreme reaction to intense political insecurity*. Israel's existence has been one long existential crisis. Their wars are fought, not "over there" but "right here." As a measure of the proximity of the perceived military threat, during the regular bombardments of Gaza, Israeli citizens are known to take chairs to sit on nearby hills to watch the explosions.

(16) *Free of traditional morality.* There is scope for ambiguity here, as "traditional" to an Israeli Jew means Mosaic, while the traditions normally implied in the term are seen as Western, and therefore decadent. Application of, say, Levitican laws would certainly be traditional and, as divine laws, truly moral, but also a direct denial of modern concepts of morality, e.g. stoning people to death for homosexuality or cursing their parents etc.

(17) *Heroic and self-sacrificing commoners.* This is a prominent narrative in the ethos of modern Israeli life.

(18) *Incorporating and promoting the dispossessed.* The Law of Return is specifically directed at drawing in and resettling Jews from all over the world without qualification. That would be a major part of any fascist movement and could easily lend itself to ethnic cleansing of the remnant Arab population within Greater Israel.

(19) *Politicises and militarises daily life.* The country is already on a more or less permanent war footing. It would be expected that the military would be given even greater prominence, as well as establishing religious police along the lines of Iran and Saudi Arabia. A fascist Israel would be a religious fascist state, with all that that implies about minimising or even eradicating secular influences among the citizens. Given the ineffable complexity of traditional Talmudic law, not to mention the fissiparous inclinations of many of Abraham's children, religious police and courts would certainly be kept busy.

(20) A ceaseless turmoil of *threats* (from the internal and external enemies), *self-glorification* and *promises.* The threats are a permanent fixture of Israeli life. One would expect a party for the Chosen People would be strong on self-glorification, while promises of heaven on earth from building the new temple would be central to the appeal of such a party.

(21) *Brutal amorality in which the public are invited to partici-pate.* The settler movement in Israel has repeatedly been deemed illegal in international law but settlers would

comprise the storm troops of any fascist party. They are not renowned for their lenient attitude toward those Arabs who feel they have prior claims on the land.

(22) *Justifying and institutionalising their most violent urges.* Almost certainly, a fascist party would adopt policies leading to ethnic cleansing in the historic territories claimed, or would at least be very hard-pressed to restrain its member-ship from such actions. Ethnic cleansing is justifiably regarded as a crime against humanity but, given the program on which the overtly racist Meir Kahane was elected to the Knesset, there is certainly support for it in the Israeli community. Israeli attacks on Palestinians and on Gaza have contributed to the country being labelled an apartheid state.

This indicates that Israel is at considerable risk of seeing a slide toward the fascist end of the political spectrum, with potentially catastrophic consequences for the entire Middle East. This should not be a surprise. Friedrich Hayek [5, p189-90] was quite explicit: by his anti-Semitism, Hitler expelled or exterminated "... many (Jewish) people who in every respect are confirmed totalitarians of the German type." Many of those who left Germany ended up in Israel where they were active in the protofascist Irgun and Stern Gang. However, an Israeli from any part of the political spectrum may protest: "That's not fair. As a matter of demonstrated fact, we *are* facing an existential threat." Agreed, there is considerable local hostility toward Israel but that's not the point. Fascist tendencies come from within individuals who choose to give them political expression, and fascists always use the current sociopolitical exigencies to justify the violence they want to unleash. If they can't find any, they will make them up because they are enraged long before they have any actual evidence.

Violence is a human attribute. There is no fascist movement until a group of like-minded people agree to form one and, as outlined above, the situation in Israel today is such that an extremist group could easily take control to push a frankly fascist political agenda. For example, possible triggers could include events such as a violent reaction against pandemic lockdowns interfering with religious expression; or perhaps increasing unemployment due to climate change, resulting in pressure on the government to annex Palestinian land for Israeli farmers or restrict water to Arab villages; a sudden drop in national income caused by a reduction in the flow of overseas funds; a resurgence of

Arab nationalism as a reaction against their current, distressed state ... the possibilities are more or less endless. It is also true that, rather than responding with the obvious thrust to the right, successive Israeli governments could have managed the perceived threat differently, negotiating suitable compromises but fascists are never interested in compromise. For them, it's our way or no way.

Given its institutional structure, Israel may look to be fairly secure from the ultrarightist wing but politically, it is in a much more tenuous state than, say, Australia. Fascism by the back door is a real danger, the "boiling frog" analogy. Remember that restrictive laws only ever ratchet up, they are never dismantled. No politician wants to be accused of being "weak" in the face of threats.

6.5. To end fascism.

There is nothing we can do about reshaping personalities, and nothing we should do. Whatever steps governments take to limit access to power by specific individuals will fail and will probably make matters worse. Moreover, any attempts at "selective repression" would feed the paranoid element in the community, giving them endless free publicity.

We could do a great deal about situational factors such as economic collapse, international aggression, famine, disease and other natural disasters, but the record is not encouraging. Donor states make decisions on helping other countries based not on their needs but on what is good for the aid donor. The pandemic alone provides long lists of examples of so-called security ambitions trumping humanitarian needs. A potential solution lies in the model of the transnational European Union, meaning shifting power away from individual nations toward relatively neutral and inert bureaucracies. However, the EU has recently undergone the trauma of the UK leaving, motivated almost entirely by the primeval wish to "take back control." Handing control over one's life to others is directly counter to the second most powerful innate drive in human affairs, the hierarchical drive. The fact that the concept of society itself imposes on all of us the demand that we cede a degree of self-control is lost in the storms of outrage provoked by the suggestion.

This is particularly true in the US, where merely mentioning the term "world government" provokes apoplexy. Of course, Americans are more than happy with the idea that the US should function as a self-appointed "world policeman," responsible to nobody other than itself, or that the dollar is already functioning as a world currency. This places the US at the "top of the pile," and it is the thought of being demoted, even to equal first with China, that triggers the blind frenzy which is so typical of people who feel threatened at the most primitive level. As it has existed since 1945, the American attitude of "our way or no way" is not compatible with a peaceful world.

The major factor encouraging the rise of fascist governments around the world is the principle of "our sons-of-bitches," espoused so firmly by the US and UK (see Churchill's quotes, above; while Mussolini led the only fascist government in Western Europe [37], he was seen as "our naughty son-of-a-bitch"). Neutral or left of centre governments are routinely destabilised, if not invaded, with the intention of installing right wing governments which are seen as more pliable allies than the governments illegally removed. The clearest example of this was deposing Iran's elected, leftist-nationalist Mossadegh government in 1953 in favour of the fascist monarchist regime of Shah Reza Pahlavi. In turn, this was overthrown by popular revolution in 1979, leading to the current clericalist-fascist government which, due to its fear of a recurrence of 1953, retains a firm grip on power. Using the same plan, the US-engineered coup against Patrice Lumumba in Congo in 1961 brought to power the truly abominable Joseph Mobutu Sese Seko, a worthy successor to Belgium's monstrous King Leopold II. The same thing happened to Chile's Salvador Allende, resulting in many thousands of deaths under the openly fascist Pinochet regime, to Sukarno in Indonesia in 1965 (up to 2million deaths) and in a dozen other countries.

There have been scores, if not hundreds, of similar attempts against small countries but the major problem in studying them is the storm of self-serving propaganda surrounding activities by Western government, making it difficult to discern the truth. Fortunately, and however badly they mistreat their citizens, small fascist countries are generally little more than a nuisance to their neighbours. Some recent exceptions include Saudi Arabia attacking Yemen because they didn't like the Shiite-dominated government, and Eritrea attacking Tigray province of Ethiopia because they thought they could get away with it, both of which have resulted in humanitarian disasters.

---

[37]   Apart from imperial Britain, which didn't consider itself part of Europe anyway.

When it comes to large countries, Western Europe and Japan were sufficiently burned by World War II to remain roughly within a centrist path in government but the urge to fascism in both has simply gone underground. The problem lies with the three great powers, the USA, the USSR/Russia, and China. Each of these now meets the criteria defining fascist states. Each of them also meets criteria for being a paranoid state, meaning official government policy states that the country is surrounded by malicious actors; must regiment itself and be militarily prepared to defend itself against all possible hostile events; and is justified in taking pre-emptive action against presumed hostile actors.

Following 1945, the USSR had five very good reasons to suppose it was surrounded by enemies, meaning two invasions by Germany in 25 years, one by Poland, one by Japan, recurrent border clashes with China and ingressions by Western troops hoping to support the Kerensky Provisional Government. However, instead of being granted a period of peace after VE Day, to rebuild its shattered country, the USSR government was declared the major threat to world peace by the US government. It was then subjected to long-term policies of military confrontation and containment, which eventually bankrupted the Soviet regime and contributed substantially to its collapse. Unfortunately, the new Russian Federal government took Western advice and tried to swap to a capitalist economy overnight, which caused further collapse, out of which emerged the oligarchs and the kleptocratic and increasingly fascist Putin government. Russia certainly feels under threat because of NATO encroachment and the efforts of the US and UK governments to install a hard right wing, anti-Russian government in Ukraine, which Russia has declared it would never tolerate.

As a major power, the Russian government is entitled to the same international consideration as all other powers, namely, the sense that its borders are secure and it will never be threatened again. For 75 years since World War II, Soviet and subsequently Russian foreign policy has rested almost entirely on one principle: Nobody is allowed to threaten us. Which, of course, is exactly what the West has done for 75 years. Repeated attempts by the Western powers to destabilise Ukraine have backfired, with the reincorporation of Crimea in the Russian Federation, the establishment of the semi-autonomous Donbass region and now the invasion. However, Western governments never take failure as cause to desist; failure is read as "Try again, try harder." The unremitting sense of external threat within Russia, which underwrites the oppressive and immeasurably corrupt Putin/KGB regime [5], is diligently cultivated by the Western powers and contributes to Putin's longevity, just as US/UK animosity perpetuated the former Soviet government long after its citizens had tired of it. Similarly, long-term US hostility to the legitimate revolutionary regime in Cuba has been an abject failure, serving only to cement the Castro government in power. It is based in pique and as a sop to the Cuban "exiles," most of whom are senile or dead, to maintain the Republican vote in Florida.

In an obviously prepared question at his first press conference, January 29th 1981, former US President Ronald Reagan was asked:

> **Reporter:** Mr. President, what do you see as the long-range intentions of the Soviet Union? Do you think, for instance, the Kremlin is bent on world domination that might lead to a continuation of the cold war, or do you think that under other circumstances detente is possible?

> **Mr Reagan:** Well, so far detente's been a one-way street that the Soviet Union has used to pursue its own aims. I don't have to think of an answer as to what I think their intentions are; they have repeated it. I know of no leader of the Soviet Union since the revolution, and including the present leadership, that has not more than once repeated in the various Communist congresses they hold their determination that their goal must be the promotion of world revolution and a one-world Socialist or Communist state, whichever word you want to use. Now, as long as they do that and as long as they, at the same time, have openly and publicly declared that the only morality they recognize is what will further their cause, meaning they reserve unto themselves the right to commit any crime, to lie, to cheat, in order to attain that, and that is moral, not immoral, and we operate on a different set of standards, I think when you do business with them, even at a detente, you keep that in mind.

In *Mein Kampf*, Hitler said of what he regarded as the Jewish-controlled press that they understood how the Big Lie was more likely to be successful than a small lie. In modern times, the emphasis has moved to the half-lie, a carefully crafted version of the truth that misleads by artfully omitting crucial facts and shifting emphasis amid clouds of irrelevancies. The significant omission in Reagan's little speech is that orthodox Marxist doctrine says that while capitalists remain in the world, they will never stop trying to overthrow socialist governments, so there can only be peace for socialism when all governments are socialist. That is not what Reagan said. As for lying, cheating, murdering and invading, it was Reagan's government that ordered the mining of Nicaragua's ports and sold missiles to Iran via Israel to finance the fascist Contras fighting the Sandinista government, then tried to conceal their crimes.

Throughout its existence, the People's Republic of China has been in a similar position, constantly surrounded and threatened by the US and its associated forces (including Australia). More recently, the usual US rhetoric about falling behind in the race to dominate the world has intensified as it realises that China is not going away but is in fact drawing level, or even ahead. The thought it may have to share top position in the world has terrified the US. The so-called trade war engineered by the far right wing of the Trump administration failed, although the equally so-called Wuhan virus or "kung flu," in Trump's dire attempt at a witticism, has been grist to the propaganda mills in Washington. All this has achieved so far is to encourage China to regiment its people further, stifle dissent, expand its military forces and develop new weapons to counter what they see as the existential threat from the US. That is, because of the perception of threat, the People's Republic of China is rapidly reshaping its ostensibly socialist government in the form of a despotic fascist autocracy.

All this is by way of saying that the quickest way to force a country to move toward the fascist end of the political spectrum is by threatening it. An external threat gives extremists their best chance to scare the populace into abandoning their traditional parties and falling behind the fascist banners. Since 1945, the major source of threats in the world, and often the only source, has been the US Government. The US believes it has the right, probably God-given but certainly reinforced by unequalled might, to interfere in any nation's affairs, anywhere, at any time, for any reason and entirely without criticism or recriminations. Two quotes will illustrate this. On July 3rd 1988, the missile cruiser *USS Vincennes* shot down an Iranian civilian airliner overflying the Persian Gulf, killing all 290 people on board (including 66 children). When questioned about this at a press conference, then Vice President George H Bush replied:

> I will never apologize for the United States — I don't care what
> the facts are ... I'm not an apologize-for-America kind of guy.

A similar attitude was on display by the current President, Joe
Biden, when he was giving a speech to support presidential candidate
Hillary Clinton, August 16th 2016:

> It's never, never, never, ever been a good bet to bet against the
> United States of America. We never bow. We never bend. We
> never kneel. We never yield. We own the finish line. That's who
> we are. We are America.

This is, of course, the same USA that waxes indignant if it feels some
other country has not followed the "rules-based international order," as
established and routinely breached by the USA.

The most important single move toward preventing the emergence
of fascist governments would be for nations to stop threatening each
other. At this stage, there seems very little ground for optimism that the
US ever could, ever would restrain itself from its compulsion to
assemble the world into a single dominance hierarchy, with itself at the
top. That is, the entire foreign policy of successive US governments
since 1945 has been impelled by the same innate impulse that drives
teenage boys squabbling in the schoolyard.

This points to a final question: After four years of the Trump
administration, and armed with the information provided by Julian
Assange's Wikileaks, and by Edward Snowden and other whistleblow-
ers, we now know that lying and self-delusion are deeply entrenched in
US politics; that overt liars and the wildly paranoid have no trouble
allying themselves in order to crush their perceived enemies; that a
great many people are prepared or even eager to fall into line with the
madness in order to advance themselves; and that fanatical Christian
heretics are determined to enact their apocalyptic fantasies behind the
cover of US military power, so does this not say that the integrity of the
US Government is no longer credible? That the narrative of being the
Exceptional Nation, the Shining City on the Hill, has run its course and
we need a new understanding of world affairs? I believe so.

With this in mind, what guarantees do we have that some or all the
major themes of US politics since the Spanish-American war are *not*
precisely of the same nature as Trump's lies, meaning deliberate, self-
serving falsehoods? This is not a trivial or rhetorical question: it now
seems there is a high risk, approaching certainty, that a very large part

of post-war world politics has been controlled by seriously corrupt, fascist fantasists in Washington trying to impose their vision of a dominance hierarchy on the world. Unfortunately, the US is so enthralled by its perception of itself as the most powerful nation in history that it has built this idea into the national psyche. It has no reverse gear, no means of admitting defeat, as when it was finally forced to withdraw from Afghanistan. It firmly believes it must be in control at all times, wasting resources on foolish, empty gestures of supremacy, but who are they designed to impress? Mostly the American electorate, which is narcissism on a national scale.

The central problem for anybody thinking of building a dominance hierarchy is this: How do we get off this thing? People have the idea that a hierarchy is an inert structure, perhaps along the lines of the pyramids resting timelessly in the sands of Egypt but it isn't. A hierarchy is a dynamic and inherently unstable structure, its lower elements constantly fighting for the means to survive or to force their way to the top and the top trying to force competitors down. Once a hierarchy is established, be it in the school yard or internationally, the only move from the dominant position is down, which we humans desperately don't want.

Because it has no content, fascism must end in collapse. It is like a pyrotechnics display, brilliantly lighting the night sky and thrilling its onlookers but, when morning comes, all that is left is smelly smoke from some broken and burned out fireworks. Fascism has no alternative outcome, but there is an alternative form of government, one based not in the idea of universal dominance but in equality and mutual respect.

6.6: Conclusion: Fascism, the unstable pyramid.

To summarise, the entire fascist enterprise consists of a program to give untrammeled political expression to the most basic human impulses. These are the drive to dominate everybody and everything in sight, and to divert all resources to satisfying one's own wishes. However, human wishes always vastly exceed human needs, and now exceed the earth's resources.

Fascism is an exercise in legitimising primitive drives to self-aggrandisement, self-indulgence and self-glorification. These drives, of course, are ultimately self-defeating as we can't all have as much of anything as we want, and the people at the bottom of the pile will soon tire of having their legitimate needs ignored. For example, there just aren't three women for every man, and the women will eventually object to being treated as cattle. Fascism is doomed by its own inherent contradictions but across the globe, fascist ambitions are increasingly embedded in the political process, an unsustainable state of affairs.

References:

1. Hitler A (1925) *Mein Kampf*. Tr. J Murphy 1939. Publisher not stated.

2. Langworth R (2011) *Churchill, by Himself. The Definitive Collection of Quotations*. London: Public Affairs.

3. Meir G (1975) *My Life*. London: Littlehampton Books.

4. Peled M (2016) *The General's Son: Journey of an Israeli in Palestine*. New York: Just World Books.

5. Belton, C (2020). *Putin's People: How the KGB Took Back Russia and Then Took on the West*. London: Farrer, Strauss and Giroux.

6. Hayek FA von (1944). *The Road to Serfdom*. London: Routledge.

Chapter 7: Defanging fascism.

Looking at the world as a whole, the drift for many decades has been not towards anarchy but towards the reimposition of slavery. We may be heading not for general breakdown but for an epoch as horribly stable as the slave empires of antiquity.

George Orwell
In Front of Your Nose. Collected Essays, 1945-50

There is no escape for anyone when civilization is headed to destruction.

Ludwig von Mises, 1938.

7.1: Fascism as a political cycle.

If we learn nothing else from history, be sure that fascism will never be eradicated. Leftist German playwright Bertolt Brecht realised this even before Hitler's murderous Nazi regime had reached its peak:

> Don't yet rejoice in its defeat, you men.
> For though the world has stood and beat the bastard,
> The bitch that bore him is in heat again (*The Resistible Rise of Arturo Ui*, 1941)

Writing on humanity's state at the end of the War to Make the World Safe for Democracy, George Orwell also saw no cause for optimism. He found no practical difference between the evils of fascism, which had just been defeated at such terrible cost, and Stalin's monstrous regime drawing Eurasia into its maw. His view was that while the totalitarian danger may have been averted, it had not been eliminated as it survived intact in Western colonialism and its business partner, monopoly capitalism:

> Freedom of the press, if it means anything at all, means the freedom to criticise and oppose. .. In our age, the idea of intellectual liberty is under attack from two directions. On the one side are its theoretical enemies, the apologists of totalitarianism and on the other, its immediate, practical enemies, monopoly (capitalism) and bureaucracy (Essay: *The Prevention of Literature*, 1946).

Orwell died in January 1950, aged just forty-six, but his major fictional works, *Animal Farm* and *1984,* painted a chilling picture of the sociopolitical trends he saw already in place. By 1950, the world had congealed into two gigantic and antagonistic blocs, locked in what each of them saw as an existential battle. In the West, essentially meaning in the US as Europe was devastated, it was seen as a battle for supremacy while the Communist powers, the USSR and the People's Republic of China, barely six months old at the time Orwell died, saw themselves forced into a struggle for survival against the implacably hostile capitalist nations.

In 1946, still reeling from the horrors of World War II, people asked how humanity could descend to such depravity. But nothing has changed. Commenting on Agent Orange Day (Aug. 10th 2021), author Robert Koehler posed what he termed *The Question from Hell*:

> How is it possible to make such a decision—to place short-term military strategy ahead of moral restraint and compassion for civilians? And this leads to a second, larger question: Why are military and political leaders so unwilling or unable to envision the long-term consequences of their decisions, that is to say, the consequences that utterly transcend the significance of the war they're trying to win? Why are they so indifferent? Why are they so . . . stupid? (*Common Dreams*, Aug. 12th 2021).

We can answer these questions. It isn't necessary to argue that the perpetrators of major war crimes lack some vital sensibility that renders them different from ordinary people such that, in a critical sense, they are not-quite-human. Instead, wars are provoked and led by unremarkable people, and fought by ordinary people doing what they see as their duty. Consider this: in their obituary of the late Gen. Colin Powell, former Chairman of the US Joint Chiefs of Staff and former Secretary of State, *The Economist* said that he served two tours of duty in Vietnam and earned a number of medals, but he stated he had no idea why he was there 38. This is surreal to the point of insanity. Powell was obviously intelligent but he is saying he travelled to a foreign country in an army that shot its citizens, bombed its bridges and railroads, its ports and factories, burned its crops and villages and poisoned its forests, and we are expected to believe he didn't know why he was doing these things? In fact, we do know why he was doing it: regardless of the avalanche of propaganda emanating from Washington, any pricklings of his conscience were stilled because humans are thrilled by the prospect of killing and destroying.

So when somebody said "It is your duty to go over there and blow away a heap of gooks," he was keen to do just that. He didn't ask why, he didn't need to know why. He did his "duty" without considering the morality because duty and the innate drive to dominate were one and the same thing; morality, and any anxiety it may provoke, were trumped by duty. In the course of doing their duty, ordinary people will often do bad things but not because they are different from other citizens. Turning aside from the recent past, the raw material of the next war lies within each of us, quite literally in our DNA, driving us to join dominance hierarchies on our own territory after having crushed our neighbours. Socialisation, dominance, territoriality and fear of strangers: these are the four great innate imperatives that mark us and they have nothing to do with freedom, justice, democracy or the True Religion. Our blood lust was built into us long before those concepts were dreamed up. We saw this in the debacle of the Trumpian "insurrection" in Washington DC on January 6th, 2021.

While US intelligence and policing agencies had long maintained that right wing terrorism was the product of alienated "lone wolf" operators, such as the massive Oklahoma City bombing in April, 1995, extensive research by sociologists since the January 6th attack has shown a completely different profile [1]. Trump's self-appointed shock troops were more likely to be married, employed or self-employed, better educated and more law-abiding than the Timothy McVeighs and Terry Nichols. The most prominent finding was that, of those charged, their address decided their involvement, not, for example, their political party, religion, etc. Insurrectionists were more likely to come from counties where the racial balance was changing, from white majority to white minority. It was the loss of perceived status that tipped

---

38   *The Economist*, October 23rd, 2021, p82.

conventional and mostly law-abiding people into joining the affray. Facts had very little to do with it. It was their perception that they were losing their treasured position at the top of the national hierarchy to people whom, they firmly believed, didn't hold the same values (patriarchy, fanatical patriotism, revivalist Christianity, guns, etc) that led them to their act of high treason, an attempted coup. Their sense that they are losing the race has not won them any sympathy in the courts. Rather, they have been condemned as privileged people with an exaggerated sense of entitlement. Spoiled brats, in other words, but brats with guns.

We see the same thing happening in the US with regard to its relationship with China. After 75 years as the richest, most powerful nation in history, a self-proclaimed bastion of democracy, the Shining City on the Hill, Land of the Free, holder of the reserve currency, maker and breaker of nations, etc., the US now finds itself face to face with the idea of sharing the top position on the podium with another country. And not just another country, but non-European, non-Christian, speaking a different language, eating different food and, *quel horreur*, socialist. That is, everything that the US holds dear is in danger of being shown as non-essential in the only race that counts, power. Rather than welcoming another country to share the burden of being World Number One, the US as a whole is reacting like the combatants who stormed the Capitol: "Give us what we want or we'll take it." There is no rational basis to American hostility. China is not going to attack the US, has no interest in bankrupting it, doesn't want its colonies or possessions and has better food anyway. The US is reacting wholly on an emotional basis, driven by the sense of impending loss of perceived status to act aggressively toward its former friend and ally. This reaction has been known throughout history, as described by the notion of the Thucydides Trap. However, for the whole country to behave on an international scale like the privileged and over-entitled Trump brats is something else again.

So can we try to eradicate fascism? Yes, but it won't work. We can swipe one head off the hydra but hardly has one generation recovered from the effort than another head has grown, with the added risk that the victor in any battle against fascism may have adopted its tactics to win, or will be so thrilled by its victory that it will appoint itself as unelected world policeman. We can, however, minimise the risk of fascism, not least by being aware of its tendency to arise in troubled times. Driven by capitalism's recurrent crises, fascism is a cyclical phenomenon and to contain it, we need to look at causes.

Ultimately, everything that humans do comes from the fact that we are, at base, human. People have opinions; as long as people exist, there will be people with differences of opinions. While once it was possible to disagree strongly with our neighbours and get by with just the odd bout of angry spear-waving, those days are long gone. Today, we have to get along. If we wish to survive, this time, there genuinely is no alternative to living in peace but our politicians are still locked in a mindset from the long-distant past. Our entire social structure is based in our innate, unreasoning pursuit of dominance but politicians are so deeplAs the old line goes, I could tell you a joke about trickle-down economics but 99% of you won't get it.y enmeshed in that system that they can't see it. To them, and to so many other influential groups, wanting to be top dog is the only game in town, that's what life *is*.

In order to survive, we need to reconfigure our apprehension of power as a zero-sum game, as a matter of vanquishing adversaries – essentially, of us good people wiping out all those bad people who oppose us, and feeling justified in the slaughter. Unfortunately, we are heading in the wrong direction, away from internationalism and egalitarianism toward parochialism and institutionalised inequality. Today, practically every country shows the same phenomenon, what I have politely called a "drift to the right," but which is really a mindless stampede.

It is most unlikely that there is a government today occupying the same place on the political spectrum as its predecessors in, say, 1952. Look at the UK which, starting in 1946, constructed the most far-reaching, effective and economical welfare state known. After the hard-right Thatcher government did its best to smash the social accord on which welfarism was built, the current (Johnson) government wanders aimlessly, decking itself in meretricious nationalist tropes and feeding contracts to its donors but actually having no policy other than holding power. In the US, Eisenhower's Republican administration was actually somewhat to the left of the current Biden Democratic cabinet. Israel we have mentioned, Russia, China, India, Brazil, Egypt, Pakistan, Turkey, Japan, Hungary, Australia ... it's the same everywhere we look. World-wide, left wing or centrist parties are weakened, sidelined or in such ideological disarray that they have no prospect of gaining power or even slowing the headlong *Ansturm zum Rechts*, the rush to the right.

What we are living through is yet another slow corporate grab for power wherein, freed of morality by their neoliberal charter, the wealthy have convinced the rest of the electorate to vote for governments openly in thrall to their wealth. It is no less than a covert *coup d'état*, a transfer of power from the electors to the wealthy. Dulled by recurrent crises precipitated by international capital, ordinary people have fallen for the fiendishly-clever ploy of believing that culture wars are more important than health or education services; that their interests are best served by smashing a lot of desperately poor foreigners whose "shit-hole" countries none of them could find on a map; that government spending is socialism and socialism is slavery; and that only *laissez faire* capitalism can lift living standards through its patented "trickle down economics" [39]. Not a word of this is true, of course, but it has been staggeringly successful in enriching the already rich at the cost of further impoverishing the poor, despite the fact that increasing inequality always leads to political instability. Partly, instability panics the wealthy to demand more privileges, particularly in the outrage they experience if and when working class people insist on a bigger share of the national pie, and partly it leads the "have-nots" to believe that the system is weighted against them and there is no hope, they may as well rebel as they have nothing to lose. But, as the tumbrils of history show, a hopeless working class is a dangerous class.

Today, the world is awash with debt. In the two years after the pandemic started, poverty and un- or underemployment have reversed their post-war trends and are increasing. In the same time period, America's 725 billionaires increased their wealth by an astounding $2trillion (i.e. on top of their previous wealth). Meanwhile, governments have adopted policies that protect and enrich the corporate world at the expense of the poor. This means that when the next major financial crisis strikes, and the omens are threatening, then the risk of most of the world falling under overt fascist control is dangerously high. If that happens, then the risks to the biosphere explode out of control, either by climate change or by widespread war, including nuclear war. So it becomes a question of how we manage our innate drives rather than either pretending they don't exist—or blaming the other side. How we manage them depends on what we believe, how we

---

[39]   As has been said before, I could tell you a joke about trickle-down economics but 99% of you wouldn't get it.

see things, which reduces to a question of how we weight different observations in order to come to a decision as to what we will do.

7.2: The fascist appeal.

We are all endowed with the same set of primitive drives characteristic of higher primates; each of us has a unique personality; and each has a set of values ranging from inviolable to fleeting. It is the interaction of these three features, innate drives, personality and values, in the particular environment that produces the observable outcome called behaviour. In practice, this says that, somewhere in the head, each of us has sets of standing instructions. We see or hear something and, almost immediately, we use those instructions to reach a decision to act. This is very fast, of the order milliseconds, and we are not normally aware of these processes, only their outcome. However, we don't question them, we own them. If somebody tries to take something of mine, I am immediately annoyed. I don't question this response but if anybody else does, I get annoyed at them, too: "It's mine. He shouldn't have touched it so don't tell me what to do." Politically, these intense and immediate reactions can be manipulated with ease, which is hardly novel but it seems to be a lesson each generation insists on learning anew.

This work shows how certain human characteristics are readily manipulated to produce the political movement we call fascism. The first three chapters define the central theme, that fascism has no program of its own, meaning it is not a formal sociopolitical movement in its own right. Instead, it consists of a long list of fundamental or primitive social and psychological factors, not one of which is exclusive to fascism, which can be applied to strengthen and amplify any social or political message. Each of these factors reduces to either a psychological or personality attribute, or a social factor driven by human biology, all operating at different levels of intensity in different people at different times.

The roots of fascism lie deep in the very roots of the individuals who comprise human society, meaning all of us. It is not a disease or an alien force that takes over a peaceful society and turns it into a raging monster. It is innate, simply the normal forces of human society taken to extreme, which is why it is arises so often, in so many forms, in so many places, ages, races and religions. Fascism is nothing more than the impulses which make us human promoted as ends in themselves and amplified to extreme. And that's why it is so hard to recognise: those impulses are *normal*. The essential appeal of fascism is that it feels good, it feels natural. We always like the direction it is heading so there doesn't seem much reason to oppose it. Until there is, but then it's too late.

It's probably fair to say that originally, all major religions and ethical systems arose to counter these universal urges. However, religion's pacific message opposes our very nature and the urges eventually prove too strong. Fascism can even take over religions and pervert their message, as in the modern heresies of prosperity gospel, Wahhabism and other fundamentalist sects. Heresiarchs quickly realise that in a species that delights in domination and vengeance, preaching frugality, abstention, egalitarianism and forgiveness is a poor trade so, and to their immense profit, they give their ecstatic audiences what they want to hear.

The personality types most commonly associated with fascism are the narcissistic, psychopathic, obsessional and the paranoid. The founders of a fascist movement are highly likely to be both psycho-pathic and paranoid. Apart from the rather theatrical Mussolini, which led people to underestimate him, most fascist leaders are coldly organised, profoundly suspicious and brutally determined. They tolerate people rather than warm to them but are sufficiently attune to their needs to know intuitively how to excite them. And this is why fascist leaders rarely come from the elite: they know how to excite the common herd because they are commoners themselves, they are at one with the prejudices of the working class and can talk directly to them. However, in broadcasting their message, the leaders rely on the self-glorifying theatre of narcissism to arouse the masses.

People get excited at football matches, and organisers are perfectly aware of the importance of staging to get their fans roaring. They provide bands, marching girls, flags and banners to build up the tension before the players appear, but the spectators themselves aren't the reason the show is taking place, they are there to watch the action on the pitch. A fascist rally is different: the players in the arena are also the spectators, they are excited by themselves. New members of the movement become players in the greatest drama of all, national salvation, they are watching themselves perform. Imagine how exciting it would have been for a group of factory workers from Hamburg to travel to Nuremberg for the 1934 Nazi party rally. They put on their uniforms, everybody comes to the station to see them off, they travel further from home than they imagined they ever would, they parade through flag-festooned streets of that fabled city, past cheering throngs and out to the parade ground, where the message was hammered home: You are powerful, you are the picture of perfect manhood, your family, your town, the whole world is watching because you are the future. And, when the young men looked at each other, they had to agree, yes, they were thrilling examples of manhood. Fascism's visceral message of sensual self-regard is inspirational and irresistible.

Without the shameless self-promotion, without the narcissistic theatre, fascism is just a bunch of boorish malcontents yelling on street corners. Politics may be Hollywood for misfits but it becomes serious when the populace are desperate because of threats, either real or Mencken's imagined "hobgoblins." In those times, people want to hear that their leaders understand what is happening to them, offering simple explanations for their fear and misery. Better still, they want simple solutions that excite what the churches vainly tell them is their baser nature. Narcissism provides the technology to cloak fascism's brutal message of dominance in terms that all humans love to hear.

Chapter 3 outlines the biology of dominance, the biology of survival, not of morality. Morality is acquired, not innate: there is no morality in molecules. Molecules are the same regardless of their location, be it a dog's brain or a human brain. Morality is designed by humans to restrain innate impulses but fascism is about letting them loose. It glorifies greed, savagery and rapacity, more or less the normal human attitude to the natural world. Fossil fuel companies don't see that what they are doing is wrong, making money always feels good/justified/ proper because it is part of the domination complex: "God gave us dominion over the world..." Perhaps, but while dominion gives power, it doesn't confer the right to destroy. Fascism only becomes psychopathology when, under the influence of personality disorder, the normal wellsprings of human life are released from moral control and urged to dangerous extremes. Starting from many different points on the political spectrum, the various combinations of biological, psychological and social factors produce the characteristic movements lumped together as fascist. Fascism just is tribalism writ large.

7.3: Fascism as religion and vice versa.

If we had to name the central mechanism of fascism, we could say it manipulates the most destructive elements in human life for political purposes. Very pointedly, fascist movements appeal to those characteristics that ethical systems, religious and otherwise, are directed at restraining. Thus, practically all fascist programs are heavily oriented toward male interests, pursuits and abilities. They exaggerate and amplify masculinity as the ideal, the very peak of human achievement, sometimes assigning women a part-time role as sanctified mothers but really recasting them as second-rate humans. This appeals to men, licensing what they would like to believe anyway and relieving them of any traces of guilt for pushing themselves ahead. It approves the male urge to dominate women, to feel superior to them in the attributes that count, namely, physical strength and aggression, bold determination and detachment from the effects of their behaviour on others. That is, fascism brings out the inner psychopath. Men are thrilled to be told they are engaged in a vast program to save their tribe from being overwhelmed by hostile forces, a battle in which no quarter will be offered and, due to the majesty of its cause, none need be given. Fascist men eagerly reclass their chosen enemies as inferior humans, even sub-human, thereby smothering any hints of empathy or sympathy for them, which leads directly to the horrendous crimes so typical of human society.

As a political movement, fascism's inevitable fate is that it must eventually collapse. It can collapse either from the vast corruption that results when an entitled political elite feel they are beyond the constraints of normal morality, by being crushed by the enemies it has provoked, or just by exhausting itself through bread, circuses, wars and suspicion. As nobody is ever allowed to say "That's enough, we can live with a few enemies," eventually it must turn on itself. Enemies are satanic in intent and power; anybody who tries to say otherwise is himself an enemy. Fascists can never stop looking for enemies because enemies are everywhere, they never sleep. If they can't be seen, it shows how diabolically clever they are so everybody must keep searching until they're found. Moreover, endlessly searching for enemies keeps the troops on their toes, watching each other as only the supreme leader can be trusted.

Just as plants need water, so fascism needs enemies, they are its cause and its justification. For the fascist church in the Medieval era, the enemy was Satan and his legions of demonic assistants. Following the publication of the *Malleus Maleficarum* in 1486, nobody was allowed to say that witches didn't exist. It meant that for the next 200 years, even the smallest, most shit-hole village in the country was under ceaseless threat of attack. Everybody was either a footsoldier in Christ's holy crusade or a Satanist in disguise, and Satan's disciples had to be hunted down and killed. That period overlapped with the wars let loose by Western Christianity's great schism into Catholic and Protestant camps, which did nothing to reduce fears of the unseen enemy. Eventually, Catholics and Protestants alike assumed the full trappings of clericalist-fascism.

Peace, comfort and prosperity are the enemies of institutional religions. So-called revivals are not mild-mannered pleas to return to the original message of the religion's founder ("Love thine enemy, care for the poor, turn the other cheek") but violent calls to arms in a war against mass indifference. Modern heresies such as prosperity gospel and the outer reaches of charismatic, evangelical and pentecostal movements are frankly fascist in form and content just because nothing else is so successful in pulling in the punters. Earnest entreaties to lead moderate, sober lives having failed, they have quickly moved to exploit the same technology as their brethren in the fascist political fringe. Christian in name only, their cherry-picked texts and self-serving venality would horrify the historic figure whose name they bear. The ultra-right wing Christian vote was a major factor in the election of Donald Trump to the US Presidency, and in the insurrection he fomented in Washington DC. This trend is also the case with extremist Muslim movements such as Wahhabism and Salafism (however they are defined) and their many political faces, including Al-Qaeda and ISIS. Even passive Buddhism is not immune. In Sri Lanka and in Myanmar, at least, Buddhist priests and politicians have been instrumental in organising pogroms against Hindu Tamils in the former, and Muslims in the latter. In Japan, of course, fascist politics and Shintoism had long been incestuously intertwined and, as many people would argue, in the form of the Yasukuni Shrine, still are.

And so to the modern era, when human society was split between perpetually-warring communist and capitalist camps. In the US, hatred of The Other has been more or less a defining characteristic of the country. Initially, it was hatred of the native population, then of the enslaved black population, and finally of anything socialist. "Anti-Red" fervour has been a constant since about 1848 when European immigrants fleeing civil unrest first imported the concepts but it always has been wholly artificial, whipped up by the wealthy who stood to lose most if socialism won. This continued, more or less violently, until the post-War era when anticommunism became an article of faith. In fact, communism was never a threat to the US. On the basis that the increasingly wealthy working population would never have supported fascism unless frightened, communism was reimagined as an excuse to wrench the country even further to the right, to entrench a bi-party, militarised, corporatist regime as the new normal. Even though the USSR collapsed in 1989, America's protean enemies never slept. First crusade was against the American-armed rabble known as Islamists but, after trillions of dollars of treasure and a million deaths, the US blinked first. Meanwhile, Washington has decided that, after all, its real enemies are Russia and China, pushing these traditionally prickly neighbours into an informal alliance, and so the cycle is renewed.

Around the world, right wing politicians in countries such as Australia, Britain, Hungary, Poland, Brazil, Saudi Arabia, Pakistan and Ukraine are actively encouraged by the American national security state, including money, training and endless political interference. The incessant fear-mongering has resulted in governments paralysed by their own fantasied preoccupations, to the extent of being unable/ unwilling to deal with real threats such as the pandemic, natural catastrophes such as floods and massive bushfires and, above all, global warming. Due to human short-sightedness, the risk is that, guided by their wealthy puppetmasters, our venal politicians will scream that what we need is more consumption, more capitalism, more repression, more militarism ... more fascism. I believe that this outcome is much more likely than the chance of our political class coming to their collective senses.

Why then are people so fascinated with the idea of getting to the top? In simple terms, we can't help ourselves. In practically every field of human activity – religion, sport, finance and industry, education, military, professions—we eagerly form dominance hierarchies which soon take control of the field. However, nature isn't fair in that people who get to the top are rewarded handsomely for their good luck, while those who don't make it are penalised. People at the top feel great and are eager to press on, to get more of whatever is going. Not only do they go through life feeling they deserve their good fortune, but they also know that the poor have brought their misfortunes upon themselves. On the other hand, those at the bottom of the pile feel terrible. They are likely to give up, to walk away from the struggle to get ahead because they feel everything is stacked against them. But one day, they realise they have nothing more to lose, and their fear and resentment boils over in violent revolution. This single point, of the rich always wanting more, is probably the major factor producing the instability that characterises human society.

The social reasons people move to the right wing can be rectified but we aren't doing anything about them. The great majority of people have limited goals in life. They just want a quiet and pleasant time, a reasonably interesting job and somewhere secure to raise a family. But the way we have set up the world, that doesn't happen. In Czarist Russia, the nobility led lives of breath-taking indulgence on the backs of the cruelly-exploited serfs on their vast, hereditary estates. Serfs were slaves in everything but name but, like the black slaves in the US, life didn't get much better following emancipation. They could stay on as peasant tenants, forever in debt and unable to get ahead, or move to the cities to work in the "dark Satanic mills" of laissez faire capitalism. Either way in either country, life for the landless worker was "poor, nasty, brutish, and short," not because of anarchy but because of "stable slave empires." Russia started out with a socialist revolution but, battered by civil war and international opprobrium, by 1925 it had turned sour. The only way for the revolution to survive was to adopt the methods of the right wing opposition, which Stalin was more than pleased to do. In no time, the revolution that started as liberation for the proletariat had turned into another brutally repressive dictatorship in which human life meant less than nothing.

Fascism and Marxism offer themselves as alternative solutions to the brutal capitalist state but they are merely opposite sides of the same repressive coin. In each case, there is union of party and state, so that military becomes an integral part of both, and thus of each family. This is still the case over much of the world. Driven by the blind urge to dominate, those at the top see no reason to restrain their appetites while those at the bottom are deprived of the political power to effect any real change. This is necessarily a recipe for endless trouble. For people at the bottom, life must get worse, their political options must narrow. Initially, workers are reluctant to do anything that could make them lose the little they have but one day, a politician starts to work on their fear and resentment, and a fascist movement is born. But at base, it all reduces to questions of the many faces of domination.

Politicians, religious leaders, generals and others deliberately whip up a climate of threat and insecurity to frighten and enrage their followers in equal measure. The leaders crave the power to dominate everybody, that's all they want but they will dress their lust in high-sounding words ("… to free the Iraqi people") when what they are telling their financial backers is "Let's hammer those brown bastards who've got our oil under their sand." However, the overwhelming majority of voters aren't sufficiently moved by the power games politicians play, or by plutocrats' misplaced oil, as Hermann Göring sneered at his trial. They have to be alarmed by Mencken's hobgoblins, appealing to their prejudices and fears, which was certainly Trump's only talent: "Caravans of rapists and drug dealers are heading for our border right now… Women are raped at levels that have never been seen before … we're going to send in the military to stop them."

As every politician knows, whipping up people using the dominance subterfuge is easy. The extremist Christian right wing uses it all the time. According to the Rev. Gary Frazier, leader of the Texas-based Discovery Ministries Inc, Islam is a "satanic religion," and they're coming for you, along with the usual battalions of homosexuals and lesbians, abortionists, drug dealers, vampires, sodomisers of children and animals and so on. These godless monsters, the preachers shriek, are coming to destroy our Christian way of life, we have to fight them over there or we'll be fighting them here. In their Manichean world of snow-white Us and pitch-black Them, there is no place for or even concept of coexistence. You're either triumphantly on top, or you're crushed underfoot and your children sold into sexual slavery. Religious fanatics do not understand that people with different points of view on the other side of the world are not much interested in what we do as long as they're left to live as they want to live. Fanatics believe that The Other wants to attack us but that is what Freud called a projection of their own wish. Fanatical Christian preachers want to destroy all other religions because that's what fanatical preachers do, that's what fanatic means. Puritanism, as Mencken said, is the haunting fear that someone, somewhere, may be happy. Fanatical religion is the haunting fear that someone, somewhere, may be happy with another religion and, even though their flock don't actually care, the thought of not being in total control drives the preachers mad. Eventually, their aggressive posturing provokes the hostility that the preachers then use to justify their own endless rage, which has nothing to do with other religions and everything to do with not being in total control. Personality disorder, in other words.

Politically, we see the same picture. One nation decides it's going to be top dog and all others must tug their forelocks and fall grinning into line, under threat of being invaded. Of course, the self-appointed guardian of world peace doesn't announce: "We're the indispensable nation, so all you inferior people must sit where you're told and think what you're told to think. While you're at it, you can give up your stupid clothes and wear ours, stop listening to your godawful music and listen to ours, speak our language because we won't be learning yours, eat our food, drink our soda and pay our prices for medications for the diabetes you'll get. You must buy our weapons and rush to fight who we tell you to fight and don't ask questions. And you must give up your satanic religions and worship only our gods, the Avenging Saviour of Revelations and his cousin Mammon, he of the Prosperity Gospel." Unsurprisingly, a lot of people don't like that message so they respond in kind. In turn, their reaction is not based on a careful analysis of the pros and cons of one political system vs. another, it is based on the instinctive human reaction to strike back at the perceived threat of domination.

Since the turn of the century, the drift to the right has turned into a race to the bottom. When people move to extremist groups, they are saying: "Things are no good, out of control, and I'll follow anybody who promises to take a firm stand to give me a good life." This is being manipulated by cynical insiders who understand that ordinary people are more easily moved to action by threats of outsiders invading our territory than they are by nebulous threats of global warming. For themselves, the rich don't care about the threat of global warming. They know they'll be able to move to their ski lodges on higher, cooler ground and the devil take the hindmost. Only one thing worries them, the thought of the street mob confiscating their fortune; nothing else bothers them.

The attitude that there could be a Master Race, or Chosen People, or Indispensable Nation, or world policeman or whatever, necessarily places all the other people on the planet in an inferior status, and they don't like it. It is *ipso facto* not compatible with a peaceful world. Any country, especially one with only 5% of the world's population, that insists it alone has the right to be Number One is setting up conditions that the other 95% will not accept. Inevitably, this will lead to trouble on both sides. As a matter of physiology, humans never willingly accept servility. Somebody will revolt against servility but, to make it worse, the self-appointed Superior Nation will panic when they see a competitor coming up through the ranks. Alphas never give up without a fight. For an alpha, every fight is a fight to the bitter end because not being Number One is worse than death. If the upstart loses the fight, well, there's always tomorrow but for the alpha, defeat is the end of the line. The thought of losing their treasured status as "The One and Only Indispensable Nation" strikes such a blow to the national self-esteem that the country would sooner pull the whole temple down than cede an inch to the upstart, even if the upstart is five times bigger.

The stampede to the right is now looking like the sort of infectious excitement that was seen on the *Titanic* when they saw their first iceberg.

7.4: Conclusion: "This machine kills fascists."

In about 1943, the leftist American country and blues singer, Woody Guthrie, painted this message on his guitar. Unfortunately, fascism has proven more resilient than he imagined. The reason is very simple: defeating fascism is not just a matter of defeating a group of people, or even wiping them out, because a new generation will bring another crop. Fascism is the political expression of some of the most powerful primeval urges that shaped humans, allowing us to survive and proliferate. These are the universal needs to socialise, to form dominance hierarchies, xenophobia and territoriality. The problem is that these are so deep-seated in our self-perception, so powerful and so immensely satisfying that we don't realise how destructive they are when they act in concert.

In 1943, the psychoanalyst Wilhelm Reich wrote:

> In its pure form, fascism is the sum total of all irrational reactions of the average human character [40].

He saw fascism as human *pathology*, universal and not specific to any nationality. My case differs in that fascism should be seen as one possible outcome of the sum of *normal* human drives, those which

---

[40]   Preface, (August 1942), to the Third Edition of *The Mass Psychology of Fascism* (1933), p. xiii.

largely define us, but exaggerated by circumstances and channelled by unscrupulous politicians. The problem is that fascism has an enormous innate attraction. It is the wicked delight of authorised violence in the pursuit of biologically-driven domination; it is the delirium of wanton destruction licensed by suspension of the ancient moralities painstakingly assembled to constrain our aggression. Fascism will arise whenever people feel things are going badly and want to lash out, meaning whenever our politicians fail us.

Because of the unswerving mediocrity, venality and mendacity of our current crop of politicians, bankers, industrialists and militarists, we live in seriously troubled times. As noted above, we are in the midst of a slow corporate *coup d'état*. We can either give in and let them set up 1984 or resist, but the coming war is no longer between left and right, white against black or Christians against all the rest – those are the lies foisted on us by the wealthy in furthering their ambitions. No, the coming war is a matter of reason vs unreason. When there weren't many humans around, we could get away with believing in good and bad skin colour or good and bad religions, all that juvenile stuff, but now the constellations of power have changed; survival of the planet depends on moderation, and moderation is not a natural state of *Homo sapiens*. We are extremist by nature as extremism is so much more exciting than being calmly reasonable. We would much rather shout and wave our fists at our enemies than bother ourselves with seeing things from their point of view. That's why people go to football matches on Saturday rather than read about it in the Sunday papers, for the ecstasy, not for the knowledge. In short, we need a revolution in our thinking but, as Mao said, a revolution is not a dinner party. Nobody should expect the entrenched elite, with their over-developed sense of privilege, to quietly defer to a new reality of egalitarianism. Karl Rove, a senior adviser in the GW Bush administration and notorious hawk, made this absolutely clear:

> We're an empire now, and when we act, we create our own reality. And while you're studying that reality— judiciously, as you will—we'll act again, creating other new realities, which you can study too, and that's how things will sort out. We're history's actors... and you, all of you, will be left to just study what we do.

Consider the funeral parade of the late Queen Elizabeth: of about 3,000 people marching, I counted only four who were not dressed in splendid military uniforms, and two of those were forced to wear civilian suits as they were in disgrace. Understand this: to signal the Establishment's displeasure, they had to dress in civilian suits. That shows how much we regard militarism as absolutely central to our existence: anybody dressed in a morning suit ranks below the military. This is the heart of the problem: militarism is about domination, and domination is at once the most exciting, the most pointless and the most destructive game in town. I submit that until we regard war with the same intuitive abhorrence as we now regard bestiality, incest and paedophilia, then the chances of the world surviving in anything like its present form are dramatically reduced, if not entirely negated.

One final question: What would happen if all the world were crushed under the heel of fascist governments. Answer: Reread Orwell's *1984*. That is exactly what he was talking about. Because fascism is built on the most destabilising of all human drives, the need to dominate, it is, as Orwell understood, impossible for fascist regimes to live in peace. They must have enemies, they have to struggle, because they cannot let the people slip into feeling comfortable in their lives. When the fire of revolution burns down, fascism dies.

But Orwell's dystopia is already happening. In the US, Republican-controlled states are setting up the machinery that would allow them to take power, permanently, by disenfranchising large sections of the community, removing checks and balances, gerrymandering, allowing unlimited corporate money to run the show, and so on. In Russia, the Putin regime has set up a modern version of the Czarist state, complete with repressed workers controlled by secret police to safeguard the privileged elite while they loot the nation. China is increasingly repressive, but only for the purpose of maintaining the CCP in power. Scattered around the world are dozens of dictatorships, a dozen or more failed states and many putative democracies are caving in to electoral authoritarianism. This is the danger: creeping fascism.

In a later commentary on his epochal novel, *Brave New World*, British author Aldous Huxley accurately saw the problems:

> By means of ever more effective methods of mind-manip-
> ulation, the democracies will change their nature; the quaint
> old forms— elections, parliaments, Supreme Courts and all the
> rest—will remain. The underlying substance will be a new kind

of non-violent totalitarianism. All the traditional names, all the hallowed slogans will remain exactly what they were in the good old days. Democracy and freedom will be the theme of every broadcast and editorial—but democracy and freedom in a strictly Pickwickian sense. Meanwhile the ruling oligarchy and its highly trained elite of soldiers, policemen, thought-manufacturers and mind-manipulators will quietly run the show as they see fit [2, p25].

But, in a warning which could have been crafted for today's world, he added:

A society, most of whose members spend a great part of their time, not on the spot, not here and now and in the calculable future, but somewhere else, in the irrelevant other worlds of sport and soap opera, of mythology and metaphysical fantasy, will find it hard to resist the encroachments of those who would manipulate and control it.

For myself, I believe that as bad as things are, they are on track to get very much worse. Driven by their paymasters, our criminally short-sighted politicians are allowing global warming to spiral out of control. When that happens, many people will see fascism as attractive but only as a reaction to the disasters engulfing their lives. To prevent catastrophe, massive social change is no longer an idyllic option. Some people would say there's nothing we can do, the problem is too big, too deep-seated. In fact, there are many areas open to intervention but they all start at one point: making the general public aware of the pressures that lead to the rise of fascist movements, of how fascists work, of what drives them *and* knowing the inevitable outcome of fascism.

Above all, everybody needs to know that fascism is not The Other. Fascism is us. The only machine that kills fascists is a mirror.

References:

1. Gellman B (2021). Trump's Next Coup has Already Begun. The Atlantic. Dec. 6th 2021. At:

   https://www.theatlantic.com/magazine/archive/2022/01/january-6-insurrection-trump-coup-2024-election/620843/

2. Huxley A (1958) *Brave New World Revisited*. New York: Harper Bros.

About the Author

Niall McLaren is an Australian psychiatrist, author and critic. He was born and educated in rural Western Australia, graduating in medicine at the University of WA in Perth in 1970. He completed his postgraduate training in psychiatry in 1977 and subsequently worked in prisons and then in the Veterans' Hospital, with a year's break working in the far southern region of Thailand. From 1983-87, he studied philosophy in order to undertake a PhD jointly in psychiatry and philosophy of science. In 1987, he left Perth city to travel to the remote Kimberley Region of Western Australia as the region's first psychiatrist.

As a psychiatrist with no staff, no hospital beds, no clinic and not even an office, nearly 2000km from the nearest psychiatrist, he was the world's most isolated psychiatrist. While there, he continued studying and writing and began publishing work highly critical of mainstream psychiatry. After six years in the bush, he moved to Darwin, the capital of Australia's Northern Territory, first as chief psychiatrist for the Top End, then in private practice, where he was closely involved with the large military population. He has since moved to Brisbane, in Queensland, and is emphatic that there will be no more moves.

His work is highly original and he does not admit to any intellectual debt to psychiatrists, living or dead. When he graduated in psychiatry, he was aware that the field was not what it claimed to be. It was clear that psychiatrists routinely made major claims on the nature of mind and of mental disorder that were not justified in the literature and, he intuited, could never be justified. This led him to the philosophy of science which established that psychiatry lacked a formal model of mental disorder. In turn, this problem arose just because it had no model of mind. As a result, modern psychiatry lacks a basis in any known concept of science. It is, in fact, at best a protoscience and, at worst, crude and highly misleading pseudoscience.

Almost invariably, his work provokes bitter antagonism from mainstream psychiatrists. Over the past forty years, orthodox psychiatry has committed itself totally to the reductionist biological approach to mental disorder, with no possible alternatives. Despite massive increases in expenditure on mental health, there is absolutely no evidence to support the oft-repeated claims that psychiatry is making great advances and people are better off than they have ever been. Every figure indicates that as psychiatry extends its reach, the mental health of the population declines. McLaren argues that this is just because psychiatry is not a science.

Because it lacks a formal model of its field of study, mental disorder, psychiatry is perpetually at the mercy of social and political fads and fashions. He maintains that biological psychiatry is nothing more than a passing fad and must eventually go the way of psychoanalysis, behaviourism and possession theory. In the meantime, it is doing an immeasurable amount of damage.

He recently published the results of a lifetime of work on a model of mind for psychiatry, the biocognitive model, which leads directly to a model of mental disorder. This is the first time in the history of psychiatry that such a model has been available. The present work, *Narcisso-Fascism*, was designed as a test of the biocognitive model by applying it to a completely unrelated field. What emerges is an entirely novel understanding of the politics of extremism which confirms what has often been said, "The fascist is within me," but also offers a means of controlling the phenomenon. Given the present state of world politics, this is definitely needed.

Index

In Anxiety--The Inside Story, the author takes a critical look at modern psychiatry's twin notions that all mental disorders are biological in nature, but anxiety is hardly worth worrying about. By the simple process of taking a careful, detailed history, Niall McLaren shows that anxiety is far more common and far more destructive than mainstream psychiatry realizes. Detailed case histories chart how anxiety arises as a psychological disorder and how it reinforces itself to the point where it destroys lives. McLaren concludes that anxiety is a major factor in most mental disorders, especially depression and bipolar disorder. This book will change your understanding of mental disorders.

ANXIETY
THE INSIDE STORY
HOW BIOLOGICAL PSYCHIATRY GOT IT WRONG
NIALL McLAREN, M.D.

Niall (Jock) McLaren writes as he speaks and he pulls no punches. I love this. People should listen to what he has to say about the academic corruption of his specialty, psychiatry. Read this book. The man is unique. And funny, as well.
-- Prof. Peter Gotzsche, Director, Nordic Cochrane Centre, Copenhagen

Debilitating anxieties are frequently misdiagnosed as "depression" by GPs and specialists alike. In this wonderfully accessible account of anxiety, Dr. McLaren demonstrates with great clarity--and very movingly--how a case history approach can help patients confront and overcome their psychological demons. He provides compelling evidence that instead of drugging people, listening to them attentively and analytically has to be the beginning of the healing process.
-- Dr. Allan Patience, University of Melbourne

"Niall McLaren presents a compelling case that psychiatric care in Australia and beyond needs to be completely rethought."
-- Robert Whitaker, author of *Mad in America* and *Psychiatry Under the Influence*

From Future Psychiatry Press
Learn more at www.NiallMcLaren.com

During their careers, many students become aware that, lurking in the background, there are complex and conceptually difficult questions that, all too often, their teachers either can't answer, or can't even understand. These are traditionally the questions addressed by philosophy, and this little primer is the result of another student's journey over many years. Niall McLaren MD has spent over three decades banging his head against the Really Difficult questions behind psychiatry, and offers his a personal view of how these questions should be approached. Very deliberately, he simplifies the convoluted language and reasoning that set philosophers apart, making it accessible to students of scientific fields in particular.

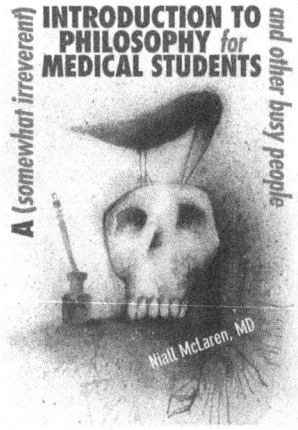

In this book, you will gain a background in the following fields:

- Religion and the origins of philosophy
- Mentalism, antimentalism and behaviorism
- Epistemology, as the study of knowledge itself
- Philosophy and the nature of science
- Philosophy and the nature of ethics

Included is a glossary explaining some of the many -isms that can be so daunting to non-philosophers because philosophers too have their jargon but it is not meant to intimidate. True, it can be complex, but the issues involved are complex. The goal of this book is to show that, with clear thinking, the complexities need not be overwhelming.

This is one of the very few books I have every intention of reading several times in rapid succession. It is such a bounty of iconoclastic observations emanating from an in-depth acquaintance with psychiatry and a love of philosophy that no single reading can do it justice: it just keeps giving." ---Sam Vaknin, PhD, author of "Malignant Self-love: Narcissism Revisited"

From Future Psychiatry Press
Learn more at www.NiallMcLaren.com

www.ingramcontent.com/pod-product-compliance
Lightning Source LLC
Chambersburg PA
CBHW061733270326
41928CB00011B/2213